WESTMAR COLLEGE

P9-DFD-583

History of American Life

PAUL LAUNE

A HISTORY OF AMERICAN LIFE

IN

TWELVE VOLUMES

ARTHUR M. SCHLESINGER
DIXON RYAN FOX

Editors

CARL BECKER

Consulting Editor

Business Seeks Aid from the Nation

A HISTORY OF AMERICAN LIFE
Volume IX

THE NATIONALIZING OF BUSINESS
1878-1898

BY
IDA M. TARBELL

THE MACMILLAN COMPANY

Fifteenth Printing, 1969

Printed in the United States of America

The change that is being wrought in all our methods of industry and trade and commerce, by the discoveries and inventions of our century, is wholly without parallel in history, and staggers the imagination of the boldest believer in progress. Steam, electricity and the other astonishing factors that are now for the first time introduced into the service of man, are revolutionizing the world of business.

> R. H. NEWTON, *Social Studies* (N. Y., 1886), 167.

The power of groups of men organized by incorporation as joint-stock companies, or of small knots of rich men acting in combination, has developed with unexpected strength in unexpected ways, overshadowing individuals and even communities, and showing that the very freedom which men sought to secure by law when they were threatened with the violence of potentates may, under the shelter of the law, ripen into a new form of tyranny.

> JAMES BRYCE, *The American Commonwealth* (London, 1888), II, 407-408.

One of the prime features of the existing situation is the increasing organization of workmen on one side, and a corresponding development of organization among the employers of labor on the other. . . . Such excesses as every fair-minded man has deplored in this country within the last twenty years are the almost inevitable result of a consciousness of power far in excess of the consciousness of responsibility . . . .

> N. P. GILMAN, *Socialism and the American Spirit* (Boston, 1893), 253.

CONTENTS

CONTENTS

ILLUSTRATIONS

(By the Editors)

ix

EDITORS' FOREWORD

PROBABLY no years have witnessed such vast strides in American business and finance as those covered by this volume. In 1878 a lusty young capitalism stood on the threshold of an era of unparalleled opportunity. As the country in the ensuing years rapidly filled in its unoccupied spaces, matchless natural resources were disclosed on every hand. The old spirit of the frontier, having swept across the continent to the rim of the Pacific, now turned back upon its course, infecting the new industrialism with a crude individualism and nerving its leaders to fabulous feats of economic exploitation. The enthronement of the machine was the outward sign of what, at bottom, was a revolution. By 1898 the first age of conquest was completed. The new masters of American destiny had established their dominion and were firmly intrenched in the changed business order which their boundless energy had contrived.

It may fairly be said that no other book on the subject offers so clear a picture of the sweep of American economic development—its freshness, its vitality, its lack of moral scruple—as Miss Tarbell's. But she is not content to treat this transformation as an impersonal process, with the human factors submerged in a spate of dreary statistics. Nearly every page bears the imprint of the personalities of the men who gave form and direction to the seismic economic forces that were remaking society. Many a graphic pen portrait restores to historical memory the names of persons who, had they employed their talents in politics, would long since have received their just dues at the hands of posterity. No reader of Miss Tarbell's volume is likely to forget the important rôle played in this age by such neglected figures as Norvin Green, Theodore N. Vail, Charles A. Coffin, Elihu Thomson, Frederick H. Newell and a host of others.

The foremost authority on the earliest and greatest of the industrial trusts and the author of a revealing book on the relations of pressure groups to tariff making, Miss Tarbell has long been a student of American business practices. She approaches the economic scene of the eighties and nineties with a maturity of judgment and breadth of vision which betray the spirit of the interpreter rather than that of the advocate. Not satisfied with a portrayal of surface developments, she searches into the motives that stirred men to the production of wealth, assessing their actions in terms of the then prevalent standards in the world of trade as well as in the light of a more advanced code of ethics.

Nor do the confusion and strife of the era blind her to the deeper trends. To many students the America of this age has appeared hardly more than a welter of crude explosive forces, a raw unlovely society in which a feverish acquisitive spirit testified to the rising power of urban capitalism. Miss Tarbell amply shows how the traditional American economy was wrenched into new and multifarious shapes, but underlying them all she perceives a unifying pattern: a tendency in every department of economic endeavor to organize on a nation-wide basis. Industry, transportation, communication, agriculture, labor—all responded to this centralizing urge, forming an interlocking, interdependent structure which betokened a significant new stage in American development. With the nationalizing of business the problem of government regulation became a national problem and caused Congress to embark on its first experiments in curbing corporate enterprise. The building of a continent-wide economy thus serves as the author's central theme, as the title of the book indicates. Confining herself to a recital of material growth, she leaves to a companion volume the story of the repercussions of the new urban industrialism on all aspects of social and cultural life.[1]

The consolidating process in business met with many resistances, notably on the part of the wage-earners and the farmers. Their efforts to safeguard their interests in an age of violent transition constitute an important part of the author's narrative and provide the volume with some of its most dramatic moments. Readers will not soon forget Miss Tarbell's account of the Haymarket riot, or of the turbulent advance of Kelly's "army" across the plains, or of the fiery apostleship of the "Boy Orator of the Platte" at the Democratic convention of 1896. Attention is given also to the radical philosophies that challenged the basic assumptions of the new capitalistic order: socialism, anarchism, the single tax and Bellamy's system of "Nationalism." Along with these are recounted the efforts of employers to promote industrial harmony through such means as profit sharing, model factory towns and the negotiation of trade agreements.

Not the least value of the book is the mirror it holds up to the troubled present. No reader can fail to feel the contemporaneity of many of the problems with which this earlier generation struggled. The maldistribution of wealth, the paradox of poverty amidst plenty, the fluctuations of the business cycle, the tug of war between capital and labor, the unequal position of the farmer in the national economy, the danger to a democratic society of vast economic power vested in irresponsible hands—

[1] A. M. Schlesinger, *The Rise of the City* (*A History of American Life*, X).

such were the deeper issues that vexed the eighties and nineties. In their efforts at solution, in their failures as well as their successes, wise men of our own day may find signposts for the future.

A. M. S.
D. R. F.

THE NATIONALIZING
OF BUSINESS
1878–1898

THE NATIONALIZING
OF BUSINESS

CHAPTER I

THE ECONOMIC OUTLOOK IN 1878

BY 1878 the American people were feeling the full impact of the new forces which had been remaking their economic life since the Civil War. Within the memory. of living man a strangely different America had taken form: an America which Lincoln would hardly have recognized and of which indeed he could scarcely have approved. To the generation which now came upon the scene fell the problem of mastering and guiding these mighty forces. The leaders of society, however, were not of one mind as to how this should be accomplished. Some saw only beneficence in a reign of untrammeled individualism with the real prizes going to the few. The major task, as they viewed it, was to press forward economic expansion at an ever swifter pace and without too nice a regard for human costs. Others were appalled at the passing of the older America with its assurance of generous opportunities for the common folk. They bent their energies to curbing concentrated capital and extending the benefits of the nation's wealth to the masses of the people.

This conflict of opinion had its unacknowledged philosophic basis in the challenge which socialism was throwing at the inherited frontier interpretations of individualism. In the twenty years ahead the conflict was

1

to assume many forms and to engage a variety of contending hosts: those who sought special privileges "for
the good of business" and those who opposed all forms
of privilege as contrary to a realization of the democratic dream; those who fought governmental regulation as an interference with business and those who
deemed it necessary for a healthful economic life; the
protected manufacturers and the unprotected farmers;
organized capital and organized labor.   Nor was the
outcome conclusive so far as the central issue was concerned.   The conflict, nevertheless, had a profound effect
upon American economic life.   In all fields of endeavor
it forced organization on a nation-wide scale and left
the country consolidated in vast economic units.   Whatever this might portend for the future, the generation
accomplished the Herculean task of forging a national
economic order.

The wealth over which the contest was waged had
grown in the twenty years before 1878 from a little
over sixteen billion dollars to nearly forty-four billion.[1]
This increase had come in spite of two major calamities:
a civil war which in 1865 had left prostrate eleven states
of the Union; and a depression, beginning with the
Panic of 1873, from which the nation was only just
beginning to recover.[2]   The primary sources of this
rapid accumulation of wealth lay in the opening of great
areas of grain-growing land in the region west and
northwest of the Mississippi and in the discovery of vast
mineral deposits—gold, silver, copper, iron and coal.
To these world-old wealth producers had been added a
new substance, rock-oil or petroleum, unknown to the
census of 1860 but which in the year ending May 31,

[1] J. G. Blaine, *Twenty Years of Congress* (Norwich, Conn., 1884-
1886), I, 617.
[2] See Allan Nevins, *The Emergence of Modern America* (*A History of
American Life*, VIII), chaps. i, xi, xiii-xiv.

1880, yielded manufactured products valued at $43,-705,218.[1]   Quite as significant for the country's economic future was the demonstration that in electricity the world had a new and exhaustless source of light and power awaiting harness.   Already it had been applied to the telegraph so effectively that rapid communication between the Atlantic and Pacific coasts and between the United States and Europe was accepted as a matter of course, and in the mid-seventies its uses in telephonic communication were beginning to be explored.[2]   The nation's natural dowry was of such great extent that it was generally believed that only the first step in its development had been taken.

The addition to American economic life of these new resources served as a tremendous challenge to the scientist, the engineer and the inventor.   Instruction in science and technology had increased until in 1880 there were nearly four hundred and fifty colleges and schools offering courses in chemistry and physics, in metallurgy, mining and mechanical and electrical engineering.   They were, for the most part, poorly endowed, the equipment generally homemade and the libraries small.[3]   Yet out of the scientific departments of high schools and freshwater colleges were to come some of the great inventors and engineers of the next twenty years, the men who were to unfold and make practical further possibilities of ore and oil and electricity.   Though their initial impulse and primary instruction came from the schools, their future development was to come largely from self-directed and independent efforts.

The geographic distribution of the nation's wealth reflected the varied economic growth of the country.   The five wealthiest states in the Union in 1860 were still the

---

[1] U. S. Compendium of the Tenth Census (1880), pt. ii, 1253.
[2] Nevins, Emergence of Modern America, 86, 88-89.
[3] Blaine, Twenty Years of Congress, I, 642.

five wealthiest states in 1878. In order of their ranking they were New York, Pennsylvania, Ohio, Illinois and Massachusetts. The proportion of increase in each case approximately matched the national increase. Although the South had lost the place it had held in 1860, its recovery, despite its devastating economic and political experiences, was assured. If Virginia had lost to Iowa her position as the sixth richest state, Virginia was re-establishing herself. And the majority of the Southern states were following her example.[1]

It was in the states west of the Mississippi that the effect of the augmented national wealth was most striking. Kansas, credited with less than $32,000,000 in 1860, now boasted $760,000,000. Nebraska's record was even greater in proportion. Colorado, not even noticed among wealth producers in the census of 1860, now was worth $240,000,000. California had an increase of six hundred per cent. And each of these states and neighboring territories believed, and believed rightly, that hardly a scratch had been made on the surface of its resources.[2]

Population had shifted with wealth—men and families following rumors of new wheat and corn lands, new mines, new industries. The fifty million people in the land stirred restlessly under the bombardment of announcements of discoveries of natural resources, novel inventions, new manufacturing and engineering undertakings. They made a mighty caravan moving westward and northwestward, to the cities and to the great open spaces, in whatever direction fresh sources of wealth beckoned. In the shifting masses of men and women there were two predominating types. Some went on a chance, hoping to "strike it rich," sell and move on to a new speculation. Others sought an oppor-

[1] Nevins, *Emergence of Modern America*, 1-30, 349-364.
[2] Blaine, *Twenty Years of Congress*, I, 616-618.

tunity to establish themselves permanently on farms, in businesses, trades or professions.

The extent of the natural wealth and of the opportunities for business expansion opened the way for consolidations of brains, privilege and money which operated with the largest latitude. In no other manner could the swift development which the ambition and the temperament of the nation demanded be insured. The brains for these consolidations came most frequently from the bottom rank, from men who saw more clearly than their fellows what could be done to meet the impatient demands of communities and nation. These men had not only personal ambition for wealth and power but also a genius for management on a large scale. They based their operations usually on exclusive privileges which competitors in the same field were unable to get. It had long been the practice of the government to make grants of one kind or another to encourage private economic undertakings. To this end tariff protection had been given to industrialists; large concessions of land with the mineral resources which might underlie them had been granted to builders of railroads; perpetual franchises and rights of way to builders of utilities. When the government conferred such privileges, the individuals so favored felt it their right to demand from those with whom they did business discriminatory treatment. Thus the big shipper demanded, and usually received, special rates on the railroads and privileged accommodations in cars, on docks and in markets.

It was not difficult for men armed with these advantages to draw the money they needed from the country by organizing stock companies and marketing their securities. In an earlier time individual savings had gone into the business or into land or farm mortgages near home, but now such forms of investment were giving way rapidly to the buying of stocks in railroads and telegraphs, in mining and industrial promotion. Money, in other words, no longer "stayed at home": it was becoming as mobile as men, nationalizing itself. When the census of 1880 tabulated the location of property owned by inhabitants of different states, it found that citizens of New York had $1,300,000,000 invested outside of the state; residents of Pennsylvania $450,000,-000. Half of the property of Nevada was owned in other states.[1]

The phenomenon of absentee landlordism was becoming more and more frequent. The resident manager of a mine or railroad or telegraph company did not necessarily represent local interests. He took orders from the great financial centers—New York, Chicago or even London—and these looked rather to returns on capital than to benefiting the locality. The character of management depended on whether its purpose was speculation or operation. That is, the great organizations which served the communities of the country were of the same two predominating types as the people who settled the communities.

Whatever the motives behind an enterprise, its management regarded it as a private business; and the larger it grew, the greater its wealth and power, the more solidly the owners resisted any attempt of the government to regulate its affairs. Thoughtful people recognized that the law had not kept up with the consolidation of finance and industry, and as the period opened there was a movement to reëstablish the authority of law in the field of business. To shape such tendencies the great corporations were annexing lawyers to their staffs. Where once the lawyer's chief interest outside of his profession had been office holding, now he extended his activities to embrace the strategy of Big Business. The drive behind the demand for regulation came chiefly

[1] Blaine, *Twenty Years of Congress,* I, 618.

from two of the essential factors in producing the nation's wealth: the farmer and the laborer. Alarmed by the growing concentration of wealth, they claimed that an equilibrium was necessary between agriculture and industry, between employer and employee, if there was to be a proper national economy.

Increasingly the beneficiaries of consolidation found themselves on the defensive. Few of them, however, were articulate when it came to a philosophic or even an economic defense of their position. The readiest and the most persuasive was one of the greatest of them: Andrew Carnegie. Carnegie belonged to that section of the population called by the census taker "foreign-born white males," of whom there were in the United States in 1880 over three and a half million.[1] Scotch by birth, he had come to the United States at the age of seventeen, settling in Pittsburgh with his family in 1852. Beginning as a bobbin boy at $1.50 a week, he was eleven years later the assistant of Thomas Scott, superintendent of the western division of the Pennsylvania Railroad, at a salary of $2400 a year. More significant were the investments he had made by this time, which were netting him an income of $47,860.[2] His first venture had been ten shares of Adams Express stock which in 1863 paid him $1440; his most successful, an investment in the Columbia Oil Company, from which in 1863 he had received $17,868.

He had already begun, however, to invest his savings in iron making, and in iron-bridge building, the importance of which he had learned while handling men and freight for the army. Carnegie steadily increased his iron holdings, but took no interest in steel until 1872 when he saw a Bessemer converter in blast and awoke to

[1] *U. S. Compendium of the Tenth Census*, pt. i, 625.
[2] B. J. Hendrick, *The Life of Andrew Carnegie* (Garden City, 1932), I, 120-124.

the fact that, as he said, "The day of iron has passed."
He at once set about building a steel mill at Braddock's
Field on the Monongahela River, calling it the Edgar
Thomson Steel Works. Profits soon became phenom-
enal. In 1877 the company earned forty-two per cent,
paid partly in stock, partly in cash; and this was, as
Carnegie himself believed, only the beginning. By 1880
the steel works netted the group $1,625,000; the fur-
naces and iron mills, $446,600—a total of $2,071,600.[1]

His own astonishing success plus the brilliant showing of the census of 1880 led Carnegie to give the world
his considered views of the economic and social progress
of the United States. To him it was an attestation of
triumphant democracy, and that title he gave to his
analysis of the country's achievements. "The old nations of the earth creep on at a snail's pace;" he wrote,
"the Republic thunders past with the rush of the express." [2] As a graphic foreword to the volume he
printed a table prepared by Edward Atkinson, a statistical authority, demonstrating America's vast superiority
in acreage over any and all countries of Europe. He
exulted at the growing number of occupations, the multiplication of schools, churches and libraries, the fact
that while the United Kingdom had thirty-three paupers
to every thousand persons, Italy forty-eight and Prussia
fifty, the United States had but five, of whom more than
a third were foreigners.[3]

Carnegie waxed most eloquent, however, in chron-
icling the country's industrial triumphs. There was no
contesting the comparisons he drew between the United
States and European nations. It was a splendid story
of material progress which he unfolded, and in his mind

[1] H. N. Casson, *The Romance of Steel* (N. Y., 1907), 91; J. H.
Bridge, *The Inside History of the Carnegie Steel Company* (N. Y.,
1903), chap. vi.
[2] Andrew Carnegie, *Triumphant Democracy* (N. Y., 1886), 1.
[3] Carnegie, *Triumphant Democracy*, 168-169.

it came from the superiority of democracy over monarchical forms of government. "Never will the British artisan rival the American until from his system are expelled the remains of serfdom and into his veins is instilled the pure blood of exalted manhood." [1] The consolidation of capital in the hands of a few strong men was, he claimed, the price society had to pay for cheap comforts and luxuries. These could only come through competition, and the competition to be effective must be carried on by giants, not pygmies. The results were not only beneficial for the race but essential to its progress. Business on a grand scale required special talent for organization and management, and that talent was rare. He pointed out that business leaders were more concerned about securing the right men for high executive posts than in securing new capital. If the right men were obtained, they soon created capital; otherwise capital soon took wings. [2]

This was the philosophy which guided the efforts of the great captains of industry and finance. Though challenged with increasing frequency and vigor, it continued to be the dominant philosophy throughout the score of years. Some of these men were unscrupulous and corrupt, but most of them were sincere and, according to their lights, upright and patriotic. They regarded themselves as pioneers in a new stage of America's growth, carrying forward more effectively the old work of developing the country's natural resources, finding fresh avenues of power and achievement and enlarging the theater of the nation's activities.

[1] Carnegie, *Triumphant Democracy*, 238.
[2] Andrew Carnegie, "Wealth," *N. Am. Rev.*, CXLVIII (1889), 653-664.

CHAPTER II

PEOPLING THE NATION

THE wealth over which the people of the United States were struggling in 1878 had been drawn from a magnificent estate of over three million square miles, not counting Alaska. Fully a third of this area still belonged to the federal government. The rest was in the hands of the states, corporations or individuals. Of this residue the farmers owned nearly half, approximately five hundred and thirty-seven million acres. The most densely inhabited section was that known as the North Atlantic division, embracing New England, New York, New Jersey and Pennsylvania. Here a land surface of 162,000 square miles accommodated fourteen and a half million people. The most sparsely settled was the Western division made up of eleven states and territories. There on a land surface of 1,176,000 square miles was scattered a population of a million and three quarters, about one to the square mile.[1] Outside of the Western division there was more unsettled land per man in Dakota Territory than elsewhere in the country. The center of population lay in Kentucky, eight miles southwest of Cincinnati; in twenty years it had moved a hundred and two miles. To attain its ambition of rapid development, the nation must push this center farther westward, in other words, fill in its waste places with people.

The national government led in the drive for settlers. The one million square miles it owned was what was left of an immense public domain originating in the

[1] Bureau of the Census, *Abstract of the Twelfth Census* (1900), 32.

eighteenth century in gifts by the states made on condition that these lands be held and used for "the common benefit of the United States." How best to secure that benefit? The government had adopted the policy of distributing the land on easy terms and in small parcels to actual settlers,[1] but by 1878 it was apparent, as President Cleveland was to tell the country a few years later, that

> Laws which were intended for the "common benefit" have been perverted so that large quantities of land are resting in single ownerships. . . . It is not for the "common benefit of the United States" that a large area of the public lands should be acquired, directly or through fraud, in the hands of a single individual. . . . A rapidly increasing population creates a growing demand for homes, and the accumulation of wealth inspires an eager competition to obtain the public land for speculative purposes.

And Cleveland added this prophetic word: "In the future this collision of interest will be more marked than in the past . . . ."[2]

The states went along with the federal government in its effort to entice settlers to the unoccupied lands. As each had come into the Union, Congress had bestowed upon it as a dower a part of the public domain within its boundary, to be used "for the common benefit." Where large tracts still remained in the states' possession, strenuous efforts were made to bring in settlers. Official immigration bureaus were set up for this purpose.[3] Mis-

[1] C. R. Fish, *The Rise of the Common Man* (*A History of American Life*, VI), 126-131; A. C. Cole, *The Irrepressible Conflict* (same series, VII), 115-119; Allan Nevins, *The Emergence of Modern America* (same series, VIII), 118-121.

[2] Message of December 9, 1885, J. D. Richardson, comp., *A Compilation of the Messages and Papers of the Presidents* (Wash., 1896-1899), VIII, 359.

[3] A. M. Schlesinger, *The Rise of the City* (*A History of American Life*, X), 15-16, 28 n., 55-56.

souri, for example, established a bureau charged with the duty of preparing maps, articles and pamphlets concerning the resources of the state, its undeveloped farm lands, its minerals and timber, its railroads and its waters.[1] Even some of the Eastern states were concerned with the problem. In their case it was not, as in Missouri, "land which has never been brought under cultivation." It was a growing anxiety about an increasing exodus from disadvantaged farming districts.[2]

The railroads, particularly those west of the Mississippi, were among the most active of the land boosters. Their future prosperity depended on peopling the country and developing its resources. "Each mile of railroad constructed in a new country is a kind of centrifugal pump furnishing for exportation hundreds of tons of the products of such country."[3] The drive for settlers was conducted largely through, or in coöperation with, the steamship companies and land companies. At one time the Inman Steamship Company had thirty-five hundred agents in Europe and as many more in this country, selling tickets to be sent to friends and relatives of immigrants already settled in the United States.[4]

In 1880 there were about 6,700,000 foreign-born in the nation. Because of the depression following the Panic of 1873 the annual number of newcomers during the decade 1870-1880 had averaged but 280,000. In the single year 1878 only 138,500 had come, the smallest number since 1862. But with the turn to better times the tide began rapidly to mount again. The year 1882 saw 789,000 arrivals, nearly three times the aver-

[1] *Appletons' Annual Cyclopædia*, n.s., IV (1879), 641-642.

[2] Schlesinger, *Rise of the City*, 67-72.

[3] M. F. Bernard in *Journal des Économistes*, quoted by D. A. Wells, *Recent Economic Changes* (N. Y., 1889), 176.

[4] Richmond Mayo-Smith, *Emigration and Immigration* (N. Y., 1890), 46, 186. See also Schlesinger, *Rise of the City*, 26-28, and J. B. Hedges, *Henry Villard and the Railways of the Northwest* (New Haven, 1930), chap. vi.

age annual increment of the seventies and the greatest influx yet recorded in a single year. Of this number three out of every five were adults between fifteen and forty years of age, excellent brawn for the task of developing America's natural wealth.[1]

It is little wonder that Andrew Carnegie exclaimed in amazed approval at this addition to the nation's labor force. "These adults," he said,

> were surely worth $1,500 (£300) each—for in former days an efficient slave sold for this sum—making a money value of $710,000,000 (£142,000,000), to which may be safely added $1,000 (£200) each, or $315,000,000 (£63,000,000) for the remaining forty per cent. of the host. Further, it is estimated that every immigrant brings in cash an average of $125 (£25). The cash value of immigrants upon this basis for the year 1882 exceeded $1,125,000,000 (£225,000,000).

In a final word he calculated that the average yearly augmentation of the country's wealth from immigrants "is now more than twice as great as the total product of all the silver and gold mines in the world."[2] The decade 1880-1890 brought nearly 3,000,000 foreigners to American shores.

Western Europe made the largest contribution to the incoming flood, over two thirds of the total during the 1880's. The country from which America drew most heavily in the early years of the decade was Germany. Nearly a third of all immigrants from 1880 to 1884 were Germans. Another third was recruited from the British Isles, Sweden and Norway. The remaining third consisted of "new immigrants," those from southern and eastern Europe, notably from Italy, Austria, Rus-

[1] Mayo-Smith, *Emigration and Immigration*, 28, 51.
[2] Andrew Carnegie, *Triumphant Democracy* (N. Y., 1886), 34-35.

sia and Hungary. The banner immigration year 1882—when more came than in any year until 1903—witnessed the climax of the movement from western Europe and the advent of noticeable numbers from the southern and eastern nations. This shift in the sources of immigration became steadily more marked. From 1885 to 1889 western Europe furnished 1,500,000 newcomers; from 1895 to 1899 it sent but 495,000. From the southern and eastern countries, on the other hand, came 493,000 in the former period and 747,000 in the latter. The reasons for this change were many: the overcrowded conditions in southern and eastern Europe, anti-Semitic persecutions in Russia, the establishment of new steamship connections between Mediterranean ports and the United States, and the unexampled opportunities for employment in America. At the same time, the industrial advance of western Europe made it less worth while for the people there to try their luck in a new land.[1]

However much a Carnegie might rejoice at the boundless extent of the influx, others were beginning to question the traditional national policy of welcoming all comers without discrimination or restriction. Organized labor was particularly alarmed because of the competition for jobs by immigrant workers used to a lower standard of living. As a result Congress began, somewhat haltingly, to apply tests of fitness to arriving aliens.[2] The first act of this kind, that of 1882, excluded lunatics, convicted criminals and persons likely to become public charges. Three years later a law was passed which prohibited employers from importing foreign workers under previous contract. This practice had contributed to the rapid increase of immigration from

[1] H. P. Fairchild, *Immigration* (N. Y., 1913), chap. vii.
[2] Fairchild, *Immigration*, chap. vi; R. L. Garis, *Immigration Restriction* (N. Y., 1927), 87-102.

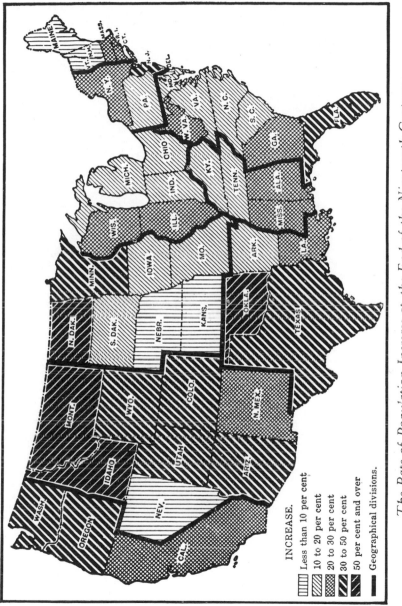

INCREASE.

Less than 10 per cent

10 to 20 per cent

20 to 30 per cent

30 to 50 per cent

50 per cent and over

Geographical divisions.

The Rate of Population Increase at the End of the Nineteenth Century

southern and eastern Europe.   Subsequent statutes stiff-
ened the administration of these provisions and added
new restraints.   As a special act of discrimination against
immigrants of the new type, Congress in 1897 passed a
bill for excluding aliens between the ages of fourteen
and sixty who could not read and write English or some
other language.   Two days before his official retirement
President Cleveland vetoed the measure on the ground
that literacy was a test of youthful opportunity, not of
mental capacity.[1]   Enactment of this law had to await
a later time.[2]

Meanwhile an immigration problem of a special kind
had arisen on the Pacific Coast.   Though Chinese
coolies had earlier been welcomed in California and their
right of free migration had been recognized by the Burlingame treaty of 1868, the hard times of the 1870's
had excited increasing opposition to them on the part of
white laborers.[3]   The Workingmen's party, headed by
Denis Kearney, an Irishman who owned a draying business, stood at the forefront of the agitation.   In Sunday
afternoon meetings on sand lots near the San Francisco
city hall, Kearney delivered fiery harangues against Ori-
ental cheap labor, always closing his address with the
exhortation, "The Chinese must go!"   So effective was
the propaganda that a new state constitution in 1879
forbade corporations to hire Chinese, prohibited their
employment on public works and directed the legislature
to impose conditions on their residence.[4]

Though the agitation in its more violent form spent
its force with the adoption of the constitution, organ-

[1] Richardson, comp., *Messages and Papers*, IX, 757-761.
[2] See P. W. Slosson, *The Great Crusade and After* (*A History of American Life*, XII), 299.
[3] Nevins, *Emergence of Modern America*, 150-152, 375-376.
[4] James Bryce, *The American Commonwealth* (London, 1888), II, 386, 394; Mary R. Coolidge, *Chinese Immigration* (N. Y., 1909), chap. viii.

ized labor kept alive the issue.   In the eyes of labor leaders the question had a national bearing because of the employment of the Asiatics as strike breakers in some parts of the East.   As the presidential election of 1880 approached, old-party leaders in Congress saw in the issue an opportunity to capture the electoral vote of California.   As a result, the Democratic House and the Republican Senate in 1879 joined in passing a bill revoking the Burlingame treaty and restricting Chinese immigration.[1]   Though President Hayes approved of the purpose, he could not approve of the method which Congress had chosen.   He therefore vetoed the measure and sent a mission to China to sound out the Manchu government as to an alteration of the treaty of 1868.

The outcome was the treaty of 1880 which permitted the United States to "regulate, limit, or suspend," but "not absolutely prohibit," future coolie immigration.[2] Under its terms Congress two years later adopted the first Chinese exclusion law, to remain in effect for ten years.[3]   Subsequent acts renewed the suspension from time to time, and in 1902 Congress made the prohibition indefinite.[4]   Although difficulties of enforcement were experienced, the shrill fears of the "yellow peril" were effectively silenced.

Meantime the dispersion of European immigrants through the country had been proceeding apace.   While many of them settled in the industrial centers, others went into the new agricultural regions.   There they were joined by countless numbers of disillusioned Eastern farmers, victims of the long depression of the seven-

[1] E. P. Oberholtzer, *A History of the United States since the Civil War* (N. Y., 1917, in progress), IV, 283-288.

[2] W. M. Malloy, comp., *Treaties, Conventions, International Pacts . . . between the United States of America and Other Powers* (Wash., 1910), I, 237-239.

[3] Oberholtzer, *History of United States*, IV, 298-305.

[4] *U. S. Statutes at Large*, XXXII, pt. i, 176.

ties. These native folk came from the Western Reserve of Ohio, from middle and western New York, from New England, Pennsylvania and elsewhere. Not always did they travel long distances: Missouri men sought the Red River of Minnesota; Kansans went to Colorado at the news of irrigation; people from North Carolina, South Carolina and Georgia moved over into Florida.

Sometimes it was rocks that had caused their migration: "You pick 'em up one spring and the next there they are agin." Sometimes it was the lure of lands that did not need clearing: "Nary a tree to grub out and I reckon a body could plow a furrer a mile long and not strike a rock as big as a hen's egg." [1] Sometimes it was incorrigible optimism and love of change and adventure. More frequently, however, it was the saddening conviction that they would never get on where they were. The explanations for their failure they found outside themselves: the "times," the banks, the trusts, the tariff. They would begin over. They did, and often with the same results.

To assist the ready movement of this mass of settlers four transcontinental railways were soon in operation and a fifth was under construction. The first of these, the Union Pacific, had been opened in 1869. [2] In 1881 the Atchison, Topeka and Santa Fé joined the Southern Pacific at Deming, New Mexico, forming a second somewhat irregular route. Two years later it straightened itself out by running its line due west from Santa Fé to California, while the Southern Pacific reached eastward to New Orleans. This gave two roads, roughly three hundred miles apart, south of the midcontinental route. [3]

[1] Pick Overturf's opinion of the Red River Valley. Ramsey Benson, *Hill Country* (N. Y., 1928), 3.

[2] See Nevins, *Emergence of Modern America*, 53-56.

[3] W. Z. Ripley, ed., *Railway Problems* (Boston, 1907), 417; L. H. Haney, *A Congressional History of Railways in the United States, 1850-1887* (Univ. of Wis., *Bull.*, no. 342), chap. ix.

Another through line, lying north of the Union Pacific, was the Northern Pacific, opened, as we shall see, in 1883. The Great Northern, paralleling the Canadian border, was still in process of building under the direction of James J. Hill.

The ambition of each man at the head of one of these transcontinental arteries was to control as large a block of adjacent territory as he could reach before a rival entered. If a rival did come to challenge this ambition, the usual procedure was to force him out of business or into the combination. The fact that a railroad had made a place for itself in a certain district did not protect it from attack. It was not so much along the tracks that the warfare was commonly carried on as in the field of finance. By 1878 railroad financing was largely in the hands of the men who had set out to develop transportation empires of which they would be the rulers. Four such domains were fairly well defined west of the Mississippi. The center of the first and oldest was San Francisco, the metropolis of the West Coast. In and out of it flowed the wealth of the mines and timberlands of the Coast. The men who controlled the roads centering in San Francisco governed these vast resources. They were Leland Stanford, Collis P. Huntington, Charles Crocker and Mark Hopkins.[1] They were the builders of the Central and Southern Pacific lines which before the close of the century were to pass into the hands of one of the ablest railroad consolidators and operators the country has ever seen, E. H. Harriman.

Three cities of the Southwest and Far West, St. Louis, Kansas City and Denver, were the feeding points of a second immense railroad kingdom. Its satrap, Jay Gould, had come into the Western country after a long

[1] Gustavus Myers, *History of the Great American Fortunes* (Chicago, 1909-1910), III, 124.

and successful career of plundering the Erie.[1] By 1880,
having gained control of the Union Pacific, he undertook a grandiose scheme of consolidation which eventually was to embrace what was called the Gould group:
the Missouri Pacific, the Texas and Pacific, the St. Louis
and Southwestern, the International and Great Northern, the Denver and Rio Grande, the Missouri, Kansas
and Texas, the Rio Grande, Western and the Wabash—
a trackage of over sixteen thousand miles.[2] Throughout the eighties Gould was working steadily toward the
realization of his ambitions. His business methods and
his financial maneuvers were such as to make him both
the most feared and the most hated man in the Southwest.

In the far Northwest the young state of Oregon and
its adjacent territory, forming a third smaller but
extremely promising transportation empire, had been
staked out by Henry Villard. He had gone to the Coast
in the seventies to represent a group of German clients
who held bonds in certain small lines from which they
were getting no interest and no reports. In the course
of his examination of the properties he was greatly impressed by the fertility of the Columbia Valley and its
tributaries, the endless stretches of timber, the possible
mineral wealth. He dreamed of a transportation system
which would be a "benevolent monopoly," by means
of which he might direct settlers in producing what he
alone would carry. He did not rest until he had collected all the small water and rail transportation companies of the region into what was called the Oregon
Railway and Navigation Company.

In spite of the fact that he was neither a railroad man
nor a financier, Villard had no trouble in getting money

---

[1] See Nevins, *Emergence of Modern America*, 194-199.
[2] U. S. Industrial Commission, *Report* (Wash., 1900-1902), XIX,
308.

for his consolidation.   He had won the admiration of
Wall Street by a recent handling of Jay Gould who had
been attempting a raid on the Kansas and Pacific of
which Villard was then receiver.   Though it had been
a long fight, it had ended in Villard securing a fair value
for the property intrusted to him.   His triumph over
"that most unscrupulous and most dreaded machina-
tor" gave him a position in American financial circles
which enabled him to achieve one of the most spectacular coups of the time, the "blind pool" as it is called in
Wall Street history.[1]

The Northern Pacific had come into money, having
sold $40,000,000 worth of bonds.   Villard, fearing it
would invade his territory by continuing its line down
the Columbia to the sea, decided to control the situation
by buying into the Northern Pacific and assuring himself a place on its board.   This must be done secretly.
In February, 1881, he sent a confidential circular to fifty
persons, asking them to subscribe to a fund of
$8,000,000 for an object which he would disclose later.
Within twenty-four hours twice the amount was assured.   When the plan was finally revealed to the chosen
fifty they at once subscribed an extra $12,000,000.   As
Villard was now able to buy a controlling interest, the
Northern Pacific management was obliged to allow him
the representation he sought.   The president resigned
and in September, 1881, Villard succeeded to the office.
He at once proceeded with great energy to spend the
money in the treasury to complete the Northern Pacific.
In 1883 the ceremony of driving the last spike took
place in western Montana.[2]

The completion of the Northern Pacific might well
have shattered James J. Hill's dream of a route to Puget
Sound, but Hill was not perturbed.   To one of his

[1] Hedges, *Henry Villard and Railways of Northwest*, chap. iv.
[2] Henry Villard, *Memoirs* (Boston, 1904), II, 300, 309-312.

partners he wrote, "I think the time is at hand when railway property generally will be tested by its capacity to pay net earnings. . . . I think the Northern Pacific will have its greatest trial when . . . its finances are no longer sustained by sales of bonds, but all payments must be made from earnings . . . ."[1] The man who uttered this true prophecy headed the fourth transportation realm, that centering in St. Paul. A born transportation man, he was a new type of railroad leader, one who held that "earnings and not stock quotations make a road great." Hill—"that Hill," as he was called in the Northwest—was an Irish-Canadian's son who as a boy had aspired to make India his home and establish a steamship line on the Brahmaputra. In 1856, when he was eighteen, he started from his home in Ontario, but got no farther than St. Paul, then a town of scarcely five thousand, where he took a job in a firm handling Mississippi River freight. In less than twenty years he became one of the influential business men in the American Northwest; certainly no one equaled him in a knowledge of its resources.

In 1878 Hill, grasping his chance, entered railroading. In association with N. W. Kittson and two other Canadians (later Lord Strathcona and Lord Mount Stephen) he bought up the St. Paul & Pacific Railroad, a short Minnesota line which started from St. Paul and ended in the northern prairies. Under Hill's management the road was virtually reconstructed, and its lines were developed into an integrated system. Before the end of 1878 it reached the international border where it connected with a Canadian road to Winnipeg. By 1887 it had penetrated westward to Great Falls, Montana. Two years later the system, renamed the Great Northern, had 2770 miles in operation across Minnesota, North Dakota and Montana. In 1893 Hill realized his

[1] J. G. Pyle, *The Life of James J. Hill* (Garden City, 1917), I, 337.

ambition by extending the road over the Cascade Range to the Pacific tidewater.[1]

Under his management the Great Northern alone among the transcontinental lines weathered every financial storm.   Moreover, while the other roads in that section had been given land grants or governmental financial assistance, Hill had no such aid.   At the outset practical men had ridiculed the notion of a railroad traversing the far northern country, climbing mountain ranges, crossing hundreds of rivers and extending for great stretches through wild and uninhabited regions. But Hill was more farseeing than his critics.   The strength of the Great Northern lay in its low first cost, its conservative financial structure and the shrewdness of its management.   He personally supervised the construction; he selected the routes with favorable grades; he saw to it that the cost of operation should be less than that of any other railroad in the section.

Last but not least, he knew that his line was not worth a penny more than the Northwest itself.   "Make it desirable for people to come here, make it easy for them to carry on their business, and we will get the freight," he said.   "We consider ourselves and the people along our line as co-partners in the prosperity of the country we both occupy; and the prosperity of the one should mean the prosperity of both, and their adversity will be quickly followed by ours." [2]   Hence the settlers of the Northwest had his real concern.   He helped in the building of communities; he opened banks and made possible the erection of schools and churches; he guided agricultural projects and taught cattle breeding, soil replenishment and the drainage of lands.   It was largely due to his unceasing interest in all that pertained to getting the most out of the soil that the "Hill country"

[1] Pyle, *Life of James J. Hill*, I, chaps. vii-xx.
[2] Pyle, *Life of James J. Hill*, I, 297.

developed more evenly and with fewer tragedies than any other large-scale land enterprise of these years. It added to the country's resources a vast new zone of production.

Equally notable, though not immediately so successful, were the attempts to rehabilitate public lands hitherto classified as waste. The area affected comprised the Mountain and Pacific region, aggregating fully two fifths of the entire country, Alaska excluded. The inhabitants of these eleven states and territories numbered 1,751,000 in 1880, nearly half of them in California. The second most populous state was Colorado, and the most thinly settled section was the territory of Wyoming, where there were but 16,500 over ten years of age.

Hitherto the miner and the cattleman had been the principal ones to profit by the resources of this great region. In 1877 Congress had passed a somewhat ambiguously worded act by which tracts of 640 acres of desert land were offered at $1.25 an acre to individuals on condition that irrigation be attempted within three years.[1] No one perceived the inadequacies of this legislation and the need for constructive action more clearly than John Wesley Powell, head of the federal geological survey of the Rocky Mountain region, who in 1878 submitted an official report on the possibilities of developing the arid public lands.[2] Already famed for his exploration of the Colorado River and his thrilling descent of the Grand Canyon, Major Powell was a man who spoke with authority.[3] He pointed out that the so-called desert country contained a goodly percentage of public lands which could be made arable by appro-

[1] Thomas Donaldson, comp., *The Public Domain* (Wash., 1884), 415.
[2] J. W. Powell, *Report on the Lands of the Arid Region of the United States* (2d edn., Wash., 1879).
[3] See Nevins, *Emergence of Modern America*, 284.

priate treatment. Too much attention, he said, had heretofore been paid to the chemical constituents of soils, too little to those physical conditions by which moisture and air are supplied to the roots of growing plants. He insisted that nearly all soils are suitable for agriculture when properly supplied with water. This went against a popular superstition that alkalines permanently ruined land; Powell claimed that they could be washed out. Illustrations already existed, he said, of what could be done. The most important undertakings were in the Mormon settlements of Utah where, through what he termed "coöperative labor," great tracts had been artificially watered and were producing abundantly.[1] An equally noteworthy example was Union Colony, near Greeley, Colorado, which under the direction of a board of trustees had successfully irrigated a wide area.

If such enterprises were to be conducted on a large scale and without severe losses and delays, Powell believed that Congress should enact regulations which would give would-be settlers the advantage of accumulated experience. To this end he outlined legislation which embodied suggestions for the scientific and orderly development of the public lands and also gave attention to the social and educational necessities of settlers. If, he said in part, the irrigable lands could be offered in quantities to suit purchasers and a colony system were provided for poor men who wished to coöperate; if the timberlands should be opened in ways that he proposed, and pasturage lands were offered under a colony plan, a land system would be provided for the arid region adapted to the wants of all persons desiring to become actual settlers.

Unfortunately, Powell's recommendations won no immediate response from Congress. A painful experience

[1] For the early development of irrigation in Utah, see Cole, *Irrepressible Conflict*, 91-92.

under the act of 1877 proved necessary before the federal government adopted a more adequate policy in regard to land redemption. The eighties witnessed a veritable irrigation boom in the arid region. Companies were formed to take up land, irrigate it and invite settlement. The country was flooded with agents offering securities in this or that scheme. The rosiest possibilities were presented: sure wealth for investors, quick prosperity for settlers. There were no warnings that time, money and courage were needed; that the best of the projects were freighted with difficulties, many of them incalculable. In response to the offerings not only were large amounts of stock sold, but throngs of people were soon finding their way across the plains—sometimes hundreds of miles from a railroad—to land which they expected at once to see blossoming like the rose.

These coöperative undertakings, as they were misleadingly called, quickly showed the same weaknesses as stock companies in many other economic fields of the time. Just as in oil, coal, ore and certain manufacturing industries, the promoters often had little knowledge of how to put their undertakings on a solid basis and frequently little desire to do anything more than to reap profits from stock sales. And just as in other undertakings, many rushed in not as bona-fide farmers but as speculators, eager to make a quick turnover. Every unsound and dishonest exhibit in the use of capital, common in the country, manifested itself in these irrigation schemes.[1] Weld County, Colorado, where the success of the Greeley colony naturally attracted capital, soon became threaded with more canals than the water supply could take care of. Grave disturbances, intense bitterness of feeling and large losses of crops resulted.

[1] F. H. Newell, *Report on Agriculture by Irrigation in the Western Part of the United States, at the Eleventh Census: 1890* (Wash., 1894), 91.

It was not until the great drought of 1890, however, that the one-sided character of many of the contracts for water held by farmers was demonstrated. These contracts contained a clause which could be interpreted as relieving the company from responsibility if it failed to furnish the quantity of water agreed upon. Such a failure might, and did when the great drought came, mean not only the destruction of entire crops but also the impoverishment of farmers who had mortgaged their lands to pay for water rights. This default sometimes involved a foreclosure by the company. "Apparently," said Frederick Haynes Newell, who at that time was studying irrigation for the federal government, "it is in the power of a company failing to furnish water to foreclose a mortgage and obtain possession of the land." [1] The overdevelopment, bad management, and unsound and often dishonest financing in a great number of the irrigation schemes resulted, in the ten years following Powell's report, in giving irrigation companies as bad a reputation as gold and silver mining companies had.

Though Congress was not yet stirred to action, the experience of the 1880's led the several states and territories to attempt to develop more adequate legislation. Thus, California in 1887 passed a law for establishing irrigation districts. These districts could be formed on petition of the people. They were to be governed by a board of directors which had a right to sell bonds for development. Each district was to work out its own system of selling and controlling water. But of the forty-some districts formed between 1887 and 1892, only two were really successful. The chief difficulty was that the local men chosen to raise and supervise the spending of money had little or no business judgment; there was less of dishonesty than of inexperience. As

[1] Newell, *Report on Agriculture*, 95.

Newell said, the districts, as a rule, had been as well managed as other corporations conducted by untried officials.[1] It was the story familiar all over the country in every line of endeavor—of a few men undertaking hopefully to launch enterprises of whose nature they knew nothing, and of innocent people who had no idea what qualifications they should demand of those who conducted the enterprises in which they invested.

Wyoming dealt more successfully with the problem. Her law of 1890, founded on the experience of other commonwealths, was generally considered the best and most practical which had been so far adopted. It recognized what virtually no state up to this time had recognized: that the first step in any sound irrigation scheme is to know how much water is available for a given territory. It further took into account what was called the "duty of water," that is, how much land, say, an inch of water could be expected to irrigate.[2] The statute required that it be decided who had a right to water and provided agents to see that the proper persons were served. Every settler had a paper showing the order of his priority, just how much he was to receive, and the number of acres on which the water was to be used.

Meanwhile, in 1888, the federal government had begun a series of surveys of the arid region. The purpose was to measure the flow of streams, big and little, and to estimate the volume of water that could be depended upon over a given period. The work was in charge of Frederick Haynes Newell, a graduate of the Massachusetts Institute of Technology, who had had large field experience in the Southwest under Major Powell's direction and who had just been appointed assistant hydraulic engineer of the United States geological survey. Under Newell's direction the investigation went on for a

[1] Newell, *Report on Agriculture*, 37-39.
[2] Newell, *Report on Agriculture*, 12.

number of years, winning for him the title of the "Father of Irrigation." His first and most important report, that of 1894, to which reference has already been made, embodied all the experience of the settlers, favorable and unfavorable. It showed that, if there had been exploitation and injustice, there had also been an accumulation of important practical knowledge. It showed too that, whatever the failures and difficulties, there had been a good deal of real achievement. The number of bona-fide irrigators by 1890 had increased to 52,584, and the number of irrigated acres from less than one million in 1880 to over three and a half.

The discussions in Congress during these years, often bitter and highly contentious, and the interest stirred up by a succession of irrigation conventions, beginning with one at Salt Lake City in September, 1891, led in 1894 to the passage of what is known as the Carey act.[1] By its terms a state in the arid region could make a contract with the United States, by which the latter bound itself to grant, free of cost, up to a million acres of desert land if the state would see to it that this land was irrigated, reclaimed and occupied within ten years after the passage of the act. The engineering plans for each enterprise must be approved by an official state commission, also the charge which was to be made for water rights. The results fell short of the expectations. Less than a million two hundred thousand acres in all were applied for, and only the state of Wyoming so carried out the agreement that it actually received the patent for the lands.[2] Despite the disappointing results of the Carey act interest in irrigation continued to increase in the Great

[1] U. S. Statutes at Large, XXVIII, pt. i, 422-423; Loomis Havemeyer, ed., Conservation of Our Natural Resources (N. Y., 1930), 152-154.

[2] This patent was for only eleven thousand three hundred acres. Institute for Government Research, The U. S. Reclamation Service (Service Monographs, no. 2), 6.

West. According to the census of 1900, which was taken in 1899, both the number of irrigators and the amount of irrigated land had doubled in the years since 1890.

The great achievement of this twenty-year period was that it taught the thoughtful and intelligent among legislators, developers and settlers what was necessary to establish and conduct irrigation projects. This knowledge had come mainly from two sources. One was the successful demonstration made by men, singly or in groups, who had redeemed a few desert acres by continuous effort. The other was the scientific work done under the direction of such men as Powell and Newell. It was this work which gradually convinced Congress that, if any great stretches of the arid region were to be redeemed by irrigation, larger undertakings than those possible through coöperative labor or private capital were necessary. It was gradually becoming clear to those who were studying the problem that the federal government itself must go into the business of irrigation.[1]

Quite apart from the problems involved in administering the desert lands, the government at Washington encountered many other difficulties in its disposition of the public domain. Surveyors, paid at exorbitant rates, often gave the government dishonest service. Instances occurred of the willful destruction of monuments in order to make resurveys necessary. The land laws were not scrupulously observed. Homestead and bounty lands were alienated with little attention to either the spirit or the letter of the law. Railroads, which had been granted a total of over one hundred million acres, failed to live up to their contracts. Cattlemen pastured their herds upon the public lands; they even fenced the

[1] For the action later taken, see H. U. Faulkner, *The Quest for Social Justice* (*A History of American Life*, XI), 4.

land and endeavored to keep homesteaders off with force. The country was denuded of timber by lawless lumber companies, and valuable minerals were extracted from the public domain without shadow of right and sometimes in collusion with government officials. Bold attempts were constantly made to seize tracts consigned by treaty to the Indians.

These and other abuses were bluntly disclosed in 1885 by W. A. J. Sparks of Illinois, President Cleveland's appointee as commissioner of the general land office.[1] With characteristic vigor Cleveland proceeded to deal with these evils. The general land office established the practice of carefully scrutinizing applications to see whether homestead and preëmption claims were well founded. In a proclamation of August 7, 1885, the President ordered the removal of all unlawful fences and commanded the military to see that the order was obeyed. Within a year enough fences were taken down to restore to the open country more than a million acres.[2] He also directed prosecutions against some of the more flagrant instances in which railroads had not lived up to their contracts.

In a similar manner Cleveland bestirred himself to protect the Indians from encroachments by land-hungry whites. On March 13, 1885, he warned the motley crowd of "individuals, associations of persons, and corporations," which had organized to enter and settle the Oklahoma lands in the Indian Territory, to give up their enterprise on pain of being removed by military force.[3] A month later he returned to the Indians certain tracts of the old Winnebago reservation and the Sioux reservation in Dakota Territory which his predecessor

[1] Secretary of the Interior, *Annual Report for 1885*, I, esp. 90-91, 167-178, 182-183.

[2] Richardson, comp., *Messages and Papers*, VIII, 308-309; Secretary of the Interior, *Annual Report for 1886*, I, 30.

[3] Richardson, comp., *Messages and Papers*, VIII, 303-304.

Chester A. Arthur had restored to the public domain. Arthur's order, he declared, had been "illegal and in violation of the plighted faith and obligations of the United States." [1] In July he commanded all whites who were grazing cattle on the Cheyenne and Arapaho lands in Indian Territory to "depart and entirely remove therefrom with their cattle, horses, and other property." [2]

Cleveland, however, recognized the need of a more constructive solution of the problem of Indian lands. The upshot was the passage of the Dawes severalty act in 1887 which, among other things, opened much reservation land to white occupancy.[3] In other respects also his protective oversight of the public land brought desirable results. With just pride he reported to Congress on December 3, 1888, that "over 80,000,000 acres have been arrested from illegal usurpation, improvident grants, and fraudulent entries and claims, to be taken for the homesteads of honest industry . . . it is a recompense for the labor and struggles of the recovery." [4]

While the principal attention of this generation was devoted to making the Great West habitable for white settlers, in some of the older states attempts were also made to turn waste land into productive acreage. The largest undertaking, and the one which from the point of view of the future proved the most significant, was in Florida. Under a federal statute of 1850 Florida had been given title to all the overflowed public lands which it might drain.[5] To carry on the work an internal-improvement fund had been set up. Steady progress was made, but the Civil War wrecked much that had

[1] Richardson, comp., *Messages and Papers*, VIII, 305-307.
[2] Richardson, comp., *Messages and Papers*, VIII, 307.
[3] See Schlesinger, *Rise of the City*, 371-372.
[4] Richardson, comp., *Messages and Papers*, VIII, 795.
[5] Caroline M. Brevard, *A History of Florida* (J. A. Robertson, ed., Fla. State Hist. Soc., *Publs.*, no. 4), II, 180.

been accomplished. For eight years after the war the fund had averaged only a bit more than thirteen thousand dollars a year from the sale of lands.

The nation-wide recovery from the hard times of the 1870's enabled Florida to resume the work with redoubled energy. In 1880 the state elected a new governor, William D. Bloxham. Bloxham's slogan was "drainage." He joined forces with a millionaire, Hamilton Disston, a Philadelphia saw manufacturer, who had gone to Florida to fish and hunt and had become fascinated by the problem of developing the country. Particularly did the draining of the Everglades attract him. Bloxham made a bargain with Disston: if he and his associates would construct a system of drainage around Lake Okeechobee, the huge shallow lake on the north side of the Everglades, alternate sections of the land reclaimed would be deeded to them. At the same time the governor persuaded Disston to buy outright four million acres of swamp land north of Okeechobee for a million dollars, most of it in cash. By this means he saved the internal-improvement fund from bankruptcy.[1]

Disston proceeded to work out a colonization scheme for his tract. Half of the land he sold to foreigners, principally Englishmen. When the settlers arrived, they found that little more had been done than to stake out their water-soaked acres. As a result only a few remained, in and around Lake Kissimmee, to struggle with the drainage problem. Gradually they succeeded in reclaiming extensive tracts. The rest of the two million acres Disston sold through land companies. Various grades of land were offered: twenty-five cents an acre for the overflowed, ten dollars for the dry.

A more substantial development resulted from the enterprise of H. A. DeLand, who had made a fortune in soda and saleratus in Fairport, New York. During a

[1] Brevard, *History of Florida*, II, 182-186.

A cypress shingle-yard in Florida

Helena, Montana

Seattle, Washington

New Regions Beckon

sight-seeing trip to Florida in 1876 he had been cap-
tivated by what is now Volusia County. Here he
bought a great tract from the internal-improvement
fund, laid out a town with streets sixty feet wide,
planted trees, started an academy and sold land to settlers. They arrived in great numbers, many of them
Swedes. Like all newcomers to Florida in that day,
they planted a single crop: oranges. In 1885, just as
their trees were about to bear, there came a killing frost,
ruining most of the plantings and ruining DeLand himself, for he had guaranteed settlers ten per cent on their
investment as soon as the groves came into bearing. Unlike most promoters, he met the obligation though it
took nearly everything he had.[1] Notwithstanding this
catastrophe a considerable number of the sturdy Swedes
remained. They replanted their groves, setting their
trees deeper and devising methods of fighting frost; and
while the trees were growing they sought for a paying
supplementary crop. This they found in celery, which
soon became one of Florida's most profitable vegetable
products.

Discouraging as the results of Disston's speculative
and DeLand's sound undertakings were, they did not
stop drainage or development in Florida. Orange groves
continued to be planted, and by 1893 Florida was shipping five million boxes of oranges a year. It was not
agriculture alone that attracted people, however. Many
came to work the phosphate deposits lying east of
Tampa. A tract which turned out to be about forty
by twenty-five miles in extent was opened in the late
eighties. But, as was characteristic of all pioneer undertakings in the country, many of the first comers knew
nothing about the business they were entering. People

[1] Information given the author in an interview in 1926 with Dr.
Lincoln Hulley, president of John B. Stetson University at DeLand,
Florida.

rushed to the phosphate mines as they did to the irrigation projects of the West and the drainage ventures of Florida. A large number were ruined in "the phosphate boom," but, as always, a few of the more sturdy stuck. The period of trial and experiment passed, the miners and manufacturers learned their business, and phosphates became another of Florida's important products. As a result of this varied development the state's population grew by a hundred thousand from 1880 to 1890. By the end of another decade Florida contained nearly three hundred thousand inhabitants.

The degree of success resulting from these varied efforts to people the sparsely settled parts of the country was in part reflected in a growth of the total population of the United States from fifty million in 1880 to seventy-six million at the century's close. The Great West became organized into self-governing commonwealths. Washington, Montana and the Dakotas entered the Union in 1889, Idaho and Wyoming in 1890, and Utah, her case prejudiced by the Mormon practice of polygamy, finally in 1896.[1] With the system of states extending in an almost solid array from sea to sea, with railroads and other means of communication binding them together, with a vast population undivided by tariff walls or other political barriers to the free exchange of goods, the stage was set for a gigantic industrial development such as the United States had never before known.

[1] F. L. Paxson, *History of the American Frontier* (Boston, 1924), chap. lviii.

CHAPTER III

CONSOLIDATING NATIONAL COMMUNICATIONS

AN essential part of the country's equipment for carrying on business on a nation-wide scale was the telegraph. Already in 1880 its receipts totaled over sixteen and a half million dollars. Of this amount thirteen million were taken in by one company, the Western Union, which that year paid an eight-per-cent dividend.[1] The Western Union was the most nearly perfect franchise undertaking in the country. It had originated in a combination of more than fifty companies a few years before the Civil War.[2] The effect on the business had been immediate. Patents were pooled, duplications were cut out, and the service rapidly improved. In 1866 the company had moved its headquarters from Rochester to New York City. It continued to grow by the double means of absorbing competition and extending its lines. In 1878, when Norvin Green was made president, the mileage of the Western Union was 76,955 with 194,233 miles of wires.[3] Green was an energetic Kentuckian who got his start in life by helping to operate a floating grocery on the Ohio and the Mississippi; then he had turned successively to medicine and state politics and finally to the telegraph business. As

[1] Seventy-six other companies reported to the census. Their combined receipts amounted to less than $4,000,000, of which $1,500,000 went to a concern called the Atlantic and Pacific. *U. S. Compendium of the Tenth Census* (1880), pt. ii, 1310-1325.

[2] A. C. Cole, *The Irrepressible Conflict* (*A History of American Life,* VII), 7-8.

[3] President of the Western Union Telegraph Company, *Annual Report for 1878,* 8.

president of the Southwestern Telegraph Company he had been active in promoting the formation of the Western Union, becoming its vice-president.

Great as was the organization over which he now came to preside, it by no means satisfied his ambition. He set out to make it a complete monopoly. By 1881 two important competitors disputed the field with him: the American Union and the Atlantic and Pacific. Raising the Western Union's capitalization to $80,000,000, he absorbed them both at a cost of $23,400,000. Fifteen and a half million of the new stock was distributed as a dividend to the Western Union stockholders.[1] In carrying out this refinancing he was aided by Jay Gould.[2]

The contracts under which the company operated were of enormous value. Nine tenths of them were with railroads. The roads not only conferred the right to put up poles and wires along their routes, but they provided free transportation of men and materials. Moreover, nine thousand of the more than twelve thousand telegraph offices were supplied by the railroads. In return for these advantages the Western Union furnished free wire service to the rail companies. It was with reason that President Green said in the report of his stewardship, made in 1882, that by his renewal of many of these contracts, most of them for long terms, the "company has been greatly strengthened."[3]

His success was no doubt a powerful factor in deciding the American Union and the Atlantic and Pacific companies to sell. This accomplished, Green told his directors, "Successful competition with your Company is improbable if not actually impossible." Stating that

[1] President of the Western Union Telegraph Company, *Annual Report for 1881*, 5.

[2] *Appletons' Annual Cyclopædia*, n.s., VII (1882), 119.

[3] Norvin Green, President to the Board of Directors, *Remarks, September 13, 1882* (n.p., n.d.), 3.

the company "has attained such magnitude and strength, that it is no longer necessary to buy off any opposition," he added, "Competition may be a popular demand, and it may be good policy on the part of your Company to indulge competing lines between the principal points. This would not materially interfere with remunerative dividends . . . ." [1] In 1883 the Western Union transmitted forty million messages over four hundred thousand miles of wire. [2]

The public did not view the completion of the Western Union's control of the nation's telegraphs with Green's satisfaction. It felt that, though it received efficient service, both the profits and the rates were too great. As a matter of fact, the profits rose from about three and a half million in 1878 to over seven in 1882, but tolls per message were reduced by only seven tenths of a cent. Moreover, there was a widespread doubt as to the wisdom of allowing private monopolistic control of an instrument so essential to the economic life of the country.

Irritation against the Western Union was increased by a spectacular strike. [3] At ten minutes past noon on Thursday, July 19, 1883, practically the entire telegraph operating force in all the cities between New York, New Orleans and Omaha, as well as many in Canada, left their instruments. The business of the whole country was seriously disorganized. The strike dramatically demonstrated the place the telegraph had assumed in the world of business. "The function of the telegraph in our highly organized commercial and social life," said Harper's Weekly, "has come to be as general

[1] Green, Remarks, 5.
[2] U. S. Senate Committee on Education and Labor, Report (1885), I, 186, 868-869, 961.
[3] Senate Committee on Education and Labor, Report, I, 103-106; Nation (N. Y.), XXXVII, 68, 88, 108, 110, 127, 130, 132-133 (July 26, Aug. 2, 9, 16, 1883).

and as important as that of the mail.   In some respects
it is even more of a necessity. . . . Not only is it an indispensable instrumentality in ordinary exchanges, but it
is absolutely necessary for the safe and sure administration of the railways themselves." [1] The employees made
out a good case for their action.   "The company has
shown in its dealings with the operators something of
the same grasping and unscrupulous spirit that it has
betrayed in its stock operations," said the editor of
Harper's Weekly.   This the public generally believed,
but the company had the upper hand.   Slowly the
strikers saw that they were losing and, after a month,
they returned to work.

If they had suffered the company had also suffered.
It was held responsible for the strike because of unfair
treatment of its employees.   This new source of resentment, added to the older ones, caused increasing demands that the telegraph be taken over by the government or, if not, that there should be a governmental
postal telegraph.   The demand for one or the other
began to appear in the programs of many protesting
and reforming groups: the Farmers' Alliances, the National Grange, the Knights of Labor, the American Federation of Labor, the International Typographical
Union, the People's party and the Prohibitionists as
well as many boards of trade. [2] Bills for the establishment of a postal telegraph were submitted to Congress.
By the end of the century seventy-five bills advocating
such an adjunct to the post office had been introduced
and seventeen different investigating committees had reported in its favor.   But the movement made no further
progress.

[1] Editorial, *Harper's Wkly.*, XXVII, 467 (July 28, 1883).
[2] U. S. Industrial Commission, *Report* (Wash., 1900-1902), IX,
890-896.

Postmaster-General John Wanamaker argued the case for government ownership in 1892 in these words:

> The mail and telegraph are the life current of business, and to a large extent of social life, and the private monopoly of either system must result in creating a preferred class, to which high rates may not be objectionable. The humbler citizen must do without. It was said long ago that the telegraph was a monopoly, and so is the postal system; but the difference is that one is operated for private gain and the other for public good. The Government follows a settler across the plains and into the mines and establishes a post-office, in order that his family may have letters and newspapers and be more content in a frontier home. The telegraph goes where it can find paying business only; and so it falls out that only a sixtieth part of the people of the United States, owing, not to the need, but to the inconvenience and charges, employ the telegraph. . . . The fact is that in some respects the telegraph seems to get farther and farther away as the capital and the power of the corporation increase.[1]

To thinking people all this was obvious, but congressmen generally felt too beholden to the Western Union to take an action which it opposed. A member of the Industrial Commission, after hearing abundant testimony, declared, "A liberal use of the franking privilege gives the corporation power in legislation"; and he quoted a former president of the Western Union as saying, "The franks issued to Government officials constitute nearly a third of the total complimentary business." [2]

Though the agitation failed to attain its major objective, it helped to stimulate competition on the part of

---

[1] Quoted in testimony of A. L. Randall, U. S. Industrial Commission, *Report*, IX, 243.

[2] U. S. Industrial Commission, *Report*, XIX, 676.

the few remaining independents.   The company, operated as an adjunct of the Baltimore & Ohio Railroad,
became so strong a rival that Jay Gould, now named by
press and public as the financial head of the Western
Union, paid five million dollars for it and made a fifty-
year contract for the use of its lines.[1]   But the most
active competitor was the Postal Telegraph Company
which had charge of the land lines set up by the Commercial Cable Company.

The Commercial Cable Company, founded in 1883,
was owned by John W. Mackay and James Gordon
Bennett, editor of the *New York Herald*.   In 1884 it
had laid two transatlantic cables in competition with the
service which the Western Union had undertaken two
years before by leasing for fifty years two cables from
the American Telegraph and Cable Company.[2]   Mackay
had plenty of money left for the development of land
lines, for he owned two fifths of the bonanza mines of
the Comstock lode in Nevada.[3]   Bennett, his partner,
helped by giving the lines the great and growing news
business of the *New York Herald*.   They could also
depend upon considerable patronage from those who
wanted to "encourage competition."

A disastrous rate war followed the Postal Telegraph
Company's entry into the field in 1886—so disastrous
that within a year its president, Albert Brown Chandler,
was willing to listen to overtures from the Western
Union for a peace treaty.   Few men had had so long an
experience in the business as Chandler.   After learning

[1] President of the Western Union Telegraph Company, *Annual Report
for 1888*, 5; *Appletons' Annual Cyclopædia*, n.s., XII (1887), 273.

[2] This lease would have expired in 1932 but in 1930 the Western
Union purchased the cable company. Anon., *Short History of the West-
ern Union Telegraph Company* (issued by the Western Union Telegraph
Company in mimeographed form, n.p., n.d.), 4.

[3] For the Comstock lode, see Allan Nevins, *The Emergence of Modern
America* (*A History of American Life*, VIII), 136-137.   In one year,
1874, Mackay and his partner, James G. Fair, had taken $150,000,000
out of the ground.

telegraphy as a boy in a West Randolph, Vermont, office, he never later left the telegraph. In 1863 he had entered the United States military telegraph service, occupying what was called the "President's Room," the room to which President Lincoln resorted night after night to read line by line copies of all messages received and sent—his way of finding out how the war was really going.[1] After the war Chandler had shuttled in and out of the Western Union and the Atlantic and Pacific, and was president of the latter in 1881 when the Western Union acquired it in its campaign to establish a monopoly. With his extensive experience in the business Chandler fully appreciated the dangers to the Postal Telegraph Company of cut-throat competition with the Western Union.

The understanding worked out in 1887 did not include a division of business or an interchange of stock or property. It was an agreement to follow the same schedule of rates, and henceforth to give up those competitive practices which, Chandler said, were "equivalent to paying for the obtaining of business. . . . Under the system of rebates," he told the Industrial Commission, "the meanest would get the largest favor." It went to "the one who insisted on having the largest rebate that could be allowed, or else he was 'going to give his business to the other company.' "[2] By establishing uniform rates and sticking to them the telegraph companies themselves cured an abuse which had by 1887 grown to such proportions on the railroads that the federal government undertook to regulate it.

One abuse not ended by the peace treaty was the franking privilege. The Western Union had long granted this favor. "Our property," Norvin Green

[1] Interview of A. B. Chandler with author. See also Ida M. Tarbell, *The Life of Abraham Lincoln* (N. Y., 1900), II, 105-106, 141.

[2] Quoted in testimony of A. B. Chandler, U. S. Industrial Commission, *Report*, IX, 195.

once remarked, "is more or less subject to the action of national, State, and municipal authorities, and the judicious use of complimentary franks among them has been the means of saving to the company many times the money value of the free service performed." [1]   If Chandler's testimony before the Industrial Commission is to be believed, the Postal Telegraph Company for many years restricted franks to members of Congress who enjoyed what he called "reciprocal relations which entitled them to free service."   Later, however, "perhaps under the necessity of meeting our great competitor as much as for any other reason," it extended the privilege to other congressmen as well as to aldermen, mayors and judges.   By the close of the twenty years the evil was more widespread than at the beginning.

The truce with the Postal Telegraph left the Western Union virtual master of the field.   The period between 1882 when President Green saw it apparently free from competition and 1887 when it recognized the Postal Telegraph as an ally had been hard on profits.   They had declined from over seven and a half million in 1883 to under four million in 1886.   The public, however, had benefited, for the average toll fell from 38 cents in 1883 to 31.3 in 1886.   It was never again to go higher than 32.5, and that for but a single year: 1891.   After 1887 profits recovered steadily, rising to six million in the last year of the century.   But this was profit on an enormously increased business.   In 1886 the Western Union sent a little over forty-three million messages, in 1890 nearly fifty-six million, and in 1898 more than sixty-two. [2]

The Western Union's struggle for supremacy had been complicated in the late seventies by the appearance

---

[1] U. S. Industrial Commission, *Report*, XIX, 676.
[2] President of the Western Union Telegraph Company, *Annual Report for 1898*, 6.

of an entirely new form of communication, an invention by which one spoke directly over a wire to an auditor at a distant point.[1] The Western Union had regarded it at first as a mere "electrical toy." On one occasion it declined the opportunity to buy Alexander Graham Bell's rights to his invention for one hundred thousand dollars.[2] But when the public began to take the telephone seriously, the company revised its judgment. Too late to take advantage of Bell's offer, it espoused the claims of a rival inventor, Elisha Gray, and in December, 1877, launched the American Speaking Telephone Company with a capital of three hundred thousand dollars. By every means fair and foul the interlopers fought the Bell interests. Not only did they possess the advantage of wealth and of experience in organization, but they used their political influence to prevent communities from giving franchises to the Bell Company. They could, and did, prevent Bell wires from going along many a highway and street, and, as for getting into a railroad office, that was out of the question.

Then something happened which they had not foreseen. The Bell group found a leader, experienced in management, unafraid, and fully convinced of the great future of the telephone. This was Theodore N. Vail, a young man of thirty-one, who had held the important position of general superintendent of the railway mail service of the United States, which he had completely reorganized.[3] One of the first acts of the new general manager was to bring suit against the Western Union for infringement of the Bell patents. The Western Union made a spirited resistance, but when finally the

[1] Nevins, *Emergence of Modern America*, 88-89; A. M. Schlesinger, *The Rise of the City (A History of American Life,* X), 93-97.
[2] H. N. Casson, *The History of the Telephone* (Chicago, 1910), 58-59.
[3] A. B. Paine, *In One Man's Life* (N. Y., 1921), chaps. xii-xv.

testimony was all in, their own lawyers convinced them that their case was hopeless, that they had been infringing on Bell's patents, and that the sensible course was to settle.

By this time the American Speaking Telephone Company, pushed as it had been by men controlling not only ample capital but many franchises and connections invaluable in the business of communication, had set up some fifty-six thousand telephones in fifty-five cities. Moreover, its service was more satisfactory than that of the Bell system because of its control of the Edison transmitter, an invention which cleared up the static on the wires. But even with such advantages it could not go on if the Bell patent was valid. Hence in November, 1879, it concluded a settlement by which it recognized Bell as the inventor of the telephone and consented to retire from the business. The Bell Company agreed to buy the telephone system of the Western Union and to pay for seventeen years a twenty-per-cent royalty on all rentals and royalties.[1]

There could not have been a finer bit of advertising for the Bell system than its victory over the Western Union. Everybody now was struggling for stock. It sold as high as one thousand dollars a share the day after the agreement was announced.[2] When the American Bell Telephone Company, as it was now called, made its returns to the census takers of 1880, it reported total assets of over $9,500,000 and an authorized capital stock, common and preferred, of $10,000,000, of which $7,350,000 had been issued. It had a big progeny, reporting to the census one hundred and forty-seven companies, most of them small.[3] A significant item was the number of people to whom the telephone was giving

---

[1] Paine, *In One Man's Life*, chap. xxiii.
[2] Paine, *In One Man's Life*, 142.
[3] *U. S. Compendium of the Tenth Census*, pt. ii, 1332-1333.

Popularizing the Telephone

work as managers, accountants, electricians, linemen, operators and the like. The employees numbered well over three thousand.[1] Indirectly the telephone also gave employment to workers in the established industries: carpenters, plumbers, mechanics, miners, etc.

The rapid growth of the telephone stimulated attack on the Bell patents.[2] The Bell Company fought out thirteen lawsuits of which five were carried to the federal Supreme Court. It encountered five hundred and eighty-seven other lawsuits of various natures; but with the exception of two trivial contract suits it never lost a case. Besides, it was beset by promoters and stockjobbers who, in one period of three years, started a hundred and twenty-five competing companies in open defiance of the Bell patents. Unlike the Western Union, their main object was not to conduct a legitimate telephone business, but to sell stock to the public. Although few of these companies ever sent a message, the face value of their stock was $225,000,000.

The most startling of these attacks as well as the most significant for a student of business methods in the eighties and nineties was a suit brought in September, 1885, by the federal attorney-general's office, charging that, when Bell made his application for a patent, he knew of the prior invention of the telephone by a German, Philip Reis.[3] This Reis invention was familiar to the courts and to scientists. In Lord Kelvin's words, it was "not in any sense a speaking telephone." It did transmit sound, but, as Edison said, the man at the other end must know what was coming if he was to understand the words.[4] There was a second charge: that Bell's attorneys had bribed patent-office officials to turn

---

[1] U. S. Compendium of the Tenth Census, pt. ii, 1338.
[2] Casson, History of the Telephone, 88-89, 100.
[3] Catherine Mackenzie, Alexander Graham Bell (Boston, 1928), 257-275; Paine, In One Man's Life, 157-158.
[4] Casson, History of the Telephone, 95.

over Bell's specifications to them and that they had doc-
tored them to meet certain claims which they feared
would invalidate his patent.

In the absence of Attorney-General Augustus H. Garland, the solicitor-general had brought this suit on
twenty-four hours' notice, without consulting the patent
office and certainly without knowing anything of the
history of the Bell patent.   The plaintiff was the Pan-
Electric Company, a Tennessee corporation already convicted of infringing the Bell patents.   Another thing the
solicitor-general did not know was that the attorney-
general had himself refused to bring the suit.[1]   The liti-
gation might have gone the way of all its predecessors,
with little more than annoyance and expense to the defendants, if the *New York Tribune* at this juncture
had not brought to light the fact that the attorney-
general had been the legal adviser of the Pan-Electric
from its start and held a block of its stock.   Not only
was Garland a stockholder, but so were three United
States senators, also various other gentlemen in public
office.

The newspapers, notably the Republican press, made
the most of this scandal in President Cleveland's official
household.   The *World,* the *Sun,* the *Evening Post*
and the *Tribune* demanded that Garland be dismissed
and the suit dropped.   The *Times,* loyal to Cleveland,
insisted that the proceedings go on and turned its guns
on the Bell Company.   It was a "greedy monopoly"
based on a patent "fraudulently amended."   It played
up the Jay Gould prejudice, which might have been pertinent if the Western Union or certain railroad systems
had been involved, but which was baseless in the case
of the Bell Company.   It further charged a "criminal
and corrupt league of an insolent corporation with venal
newspapers."   "This case must be tried," thundered

[1] Allan Nevins, *Grover Cleveland* (N. Y., 1932), 294.

the *Times*, "in spite of the outcry kept up by certain newspapers in the pay of the Bell Telephone Company."[1] It was not until the Supreme Court gave a decision favorable to Bell in 1888 that the *Times* ceased its clamor.[2]

The growth of the telephone company in spite of all attacks was due largely to the astuteness of Theodore Vail's management. He established a great engineering department to study all imaginable mechanical improvements. He gave the greatest attention to every detail of the service and insisted on the fairest and most courteous treatment of patrons. To meet public irritation at the danger and inconvenience of the multiplication of overhead wires, he began to test the feasibility of underground lines as early as 1882 in a series of trials near his Massachusetts home. So satisfactory were the results that cables at once began to go underground. All sorts of wrappings for the wires were tried, most of them failures, but by 1890 the type now in use was discovered: the paper-wound cable. By 1898 several hundred thousand miles had been put underground.[3]

Vail also improved the quality of the wire. Bell had "made iron talk," but iron was not always a reliable conductor and the distance it would carry was limited. Vail, hearing of a hard-drawn copper wire, tried it out. With copper wire one might connect cities, as he had insisted from the start. In face of the strongest opposition of his associates he strung a double wire of the new material in 1884 between New York and Boston.[4] It marked the birth of "long distance."

A new company, the American Telephone and Tele-

[1] Mackenzie, *Alexander Graham Bell*, 269-270.

[2] Mackenzie, *Alexander Graham Bell*, 275.

[3] Casson, *History of the Telephone*, 128-134; Paine, *In One Man's Life*, chap. xxx.

[4] Casson, *History of the Telephone*, 170-172; Paine, *In One Man's Life*, 169-172.

graph Company, was organized in 1885 with a capital of $100,000.[1] Its immediate purpose was to build and own long-distance lines for the American Bell Company, but its remoter aim was to unite under one leadership all the telephone companies in the United States. This vast ambition was partially achieved in 1900 when, re-organizing with a capital of $250,000,000, it took over the American Bell Telephone which since 1888 had been paying dividends of from fifteen to eighteen per cent, giving two shares for one.[2] Thirty-five subsidiaries entered the merger.

Many small towns, particularly in the rural parts of the West, continued to maintain their own local telephone service, however.   Indeed, their number increased after the expiration of the basic Bell patents in 1893.   No fear of their ultimate fate kept communities from setting up their own plants.   When a company did not come their way or, coming, proved too expensive, small-town folk took the matter into their own hands.   Nor was it unusual for a group of farmers to buy receivers, insulators and batteries and to string wires, using the home of their leader as an exchange.[3]   When the Industrial Commission made its survey, it found that at the very time the American Telephone and Telegraph Company was capitalizing itself at $250,000,000, small Wisconsin towns were forming local companies, giving a fifty-dollar share to each receiver and no share to anybody not renting an instrument. With the service costing about $1.00 a month for a home and $2.50 for a business, one company paid a dividend of 75 cents a month.   In New York City at that time patrons paid $240.00 a year for service.[4]

[1] Paine, *In One Man's Life*, 179-181, 349-351.
[2] John Moody, *The Truth about the Trusts* (N. Y., 1904), 373.
[3] Bureau of the Census, *Telephones and Telegraphs, 1902* (*Special Rep.*), 9-11.
[4] Casson, *History of the Telephone*, 178-179.

But the Wisconsin company could not give a connection outside its own limits, while from a New York telephone the user could talk to Chicago—five minutes for $9.00. The great telephone trust was on its way. As from the start, it was in the hands of those who had built it, with the same financial backers, conservative men, not stock manipulators. Far different in its business ethics from the Western Union, and much newer in the field, it joined with the great telegraph trust to form a system of lightning communication which embraced the entire land and gave greater unity to the nation's economic life.

CHAPTER IV

ELECTRICITY INVADES INDUSTRY

APART from giving the country a comprehensive system of swift communication, electricity provided this generation with a vital new source of light and power. Inventors on both sides of the Atlantic had earlier glimpsed the possibilities, but until the late seventies little definite progress had been made. Before the problem of electric lighting could be solved, however, it was necessary to devise an efficient dynamo. Charles F. Brush, a young Ohio engineer and graduate of the University of Michigan, found the answer. His invention had the stamp of quality put upon it in a contest of dynamos held in 1877 at the Franklin Institute of Philadelphia, the judges deciding it to be the most effective for practical purposes.[1]

The next step was to invent a light. This Brush accomplished by hitching his dynamo by wires to two sticks of carbon placed in a vertical relation to each other and driving a current through them. The result was a brilliantly luminous arc formed of particles of carbon leaping from one rod to the other. Moreover, by the new system sixteen lamps could be maintained on a single wire. Brush's arc light was so satisfactory that the Telegraph Supply Company of Cleveland, which had been backing his experiments, immediately

[1] J. W. Hammond, The History of the General Electric Company, chap. i. It was in connection with his work on the news bureau of the General Electric that this history of the concern was prepared. The author died in 1934, and his manuscript has never found a publisher. It is based not only on a full knowledge of printed materials but also on the private records of the concern's consolidation and an acquaintance with the important characters involved.

placed it on the market.   The enterprising John Wanamaker promptly put it in his department-store windows
on Chestnut Street, Philadelphia.   "The Blue Moon,"
as the new light was popularly called, was chiefly useful,
however, for outdoor illumination.   Rapidly it spread
from town to town.[1]   Cleveland put up towers two
hundred and fifty feet high; in San Francisco the California Electric Light Company was incorporated in
1879 with a capital of five hundred thousand dollars.[2]

The Telegraph Supply Company overlooked no opportunity to push its new product.   Hearing that
Wabash, Indiana, was considering the installation of
gas lights, it persuaded the town council to try the Brush
system.   Four lamps, each of three-thousand-candle
power, attached to cross-arms on the dome of the court-
house two hundred feet above the ground, were to provide light for the whole city.   There was great public
interest in the affair, an interest which the Telegraph
Supply Company carefully nurtured.   Before the lights
were turned on at eight o'clock in the evening of
April 17, 1880, the town was filled with strangers,
among them representatives of all the big and little
Middle Western papers as well as some from the East.
"Your correspondent," wrote the *Chicago Tribune* reporter,

went up into the dome, right under the light, where
he beheld a scene of magnificent splendor.   For a mile
around, the houses and yards were distinctly visible,
while the far-away river flowed like a band of molten
silver. . . . Wabash enjoys the distinction of being the
only city in the world lighted by electricity.[3]

[1] See A. M. Schlesinger, *The Rise of the City* (*A History of American Life*, X), 98-99.
[2] Hammond, History of the General Electric Company, 94.
[3] Hammond, History of the General Electric Company, 104.

But Brush's was not the only successful arc-light system in the field by 1880. Elihu Thomson, who had been one of the judges in 1877 to declare Brush's dynamo the best on the market, now had devised an equally efficient mechanism. As a teacher and lecturer in the Philadelphia Central High School and the Franklin Institute he had long been interested in electrical experimentation. One of his devices which had particularly excited the public was a small, direct-current, arc-light dynamo. From this he in time developed a system which by 1879 was so successful that business men who saw a great future for electric lighting began to buzz about him.[1]

Among others were men from New Britain, Connecticut, who persuaded Thomson to let them organize a company around the patents of himself and his fellow inventor Edwin J. Houston, also of the Central High School. This company, the American Electric, with a capital stock of $87,000 locally subscribed, set out in the fall of 1880 to manufacture Thomson-Houston dynamos and arc lights. After three years' experience in New Britain, Thomson and his active partner, E. W. Rice, exercised the right their contract gave them to withdraw when convinced that the products were not being energetically pushed. They then joined a new concern organized by Charles A. Coffin, a shoe manufacturer of Lynn, Massachusetts. Coffin himself knew little about electrical matters at the time, but he had a genius for organization and the ability to surround himself with the best technical men in the field. The new company, organized in 1883, was called the Thomson-Houston Electric Company. It started with a capital of $250,000 which nine years later was increased to $10,-000,000. In the year 1892, when it was consolidated

[1] K. T. Compton, "An American Faraday," *Technology Rev.*, XXXIII, 183-184.

with the Edison General Electric Company of New York, its profits were $2,700,000. Coffin's faith in electricity as a money-maker had been richly justified.

The arc lamp which Brush, Thomson and others were developing was ill adapted for indoor use because the light could not be subdivided. The problem of subdivision was one that men had been working on for many years. The solution came with the invention of a practicable incandescent bulb in 1879 by Thomas A. Edison who had already to his credit many other useful electrical devices.[1] While the arc light and the dynamo behind it had been making such great strides, Edison had been busy improving his phonograph and seems not to have concerned himself with the possibilities of electric illumination until September, 1878, when he visited Ansonia, Connecticut, to find out what a well-known dynamo inventor, William Wallace, was up to. Here he saw eight electric lights operated by dynamos which in turn were run by river power.

"I have let the other inventors get the start of me in this matter somewhat," he told a newspaper reporter on his return to New York, "because I have not given much attention to electric lights, but I believe I can catch up to them now." "If you can make the electric light supply the place of gas, you can easily make a great fortune," the reporter suggested. "I don't care so much for a fortune," Edison replied, "as I do for getting ahead of the other fellows."[2] He lost no time in preparing to "get ahead of the other fellows." With characteristic energy he prosecuted endless experiments in his laboratory at Menlo Park, New Jersey. Before he had quite

[1] See Allan Nevins, *The Emergence of Modern America* (*A History of American Life*, VIII), 87; and Schlesinger, *Rise of the City*, 95, 97, 99-101, 302.

[2] Interview in *N. Y. Tribune*, Sept. 28, 1878, quoted by George Westinghouse, jr., "A Reply to Mr. Edison," *N. Am. Rev.*, CXLIX (1889), 655.

reached his goal, Henry Villard, who had contracted with John Roach for a steamer for his Oregon Railway and Navigation Company, ordered Edison's incandescent lighting system installed.   Roach opposed it, but Villard insisted.   It was the first electric plant on a sea-going vessel.[1]

In January, 1880, Edison took out his patent, but it was not until the eve of the national election that he was ready to give an impressive public demonstration of what he had accomplished.   "If Garfield is elected," he told his lieutenant, "light up that circuit; if not, do not light it."[2]   Garfield was elected, the switch was closed, and a long row of lamps beamed out along the street in front of Edison's residence.   Not the least important point in the exhibit was the fact that the power was carried not by overhead wires but by underground mains.

Edison was soon turning out bulbs in quantity at Harrison, New Jersey, the first factory for the purpose in the country.   At the same time he was busy improving the supplementary equipment: the dynamo, underground conductors, installation, fixtures, meters—everything, in fact, necessary for setting up a commercial lighting system such as was being contemplated in a down-town section of New York City.

The Brush arc light had already been established in a section of Broadway and had been adopted by certain business concerns; but Edison and his backers believed that his system was superior.   The great banking house of Drexel, Morgan & Company was now willing to organize the Edison Illuminating Company and let it demonstrate what it could do.   In order to be close to the generating plant, known as the Pearl Street Station, Edison moved to New York, setting up his office at 65

[1] Henry Villard, *Memoirs* (Boston, 1904), II, 290.
[2] Hammond, History of the General Electric Company, 141.

Edison in 1879

Fifth Avenue, an office occupied by him until his death. Practically everything used in the plant was developed by Edison himself. He not only invented, but watched with untiring attention the processes of manufacture. "I used to sleep on piles of pipes in the station," he once said with reference to the tubing for the conductors. "I saw every box poured and every connection made on that whole job. There wasn't anybody else who could superintend it."

The Pearl Street Station was ready to operate on September 4, 1882. Nobody knew as well as Edison that the least slip might ruin the whole undertaking, imperiling life as well as property. But, as he later said in telling the story, "I swallowed my heart and gave the word." [1] The current was turned on and it worked —worked not only in the district to be illuminated, but at the banking house of Drexel, Morgan & Company which had found the money for the experiment; on the stock exchange where shares ran high; at the offices of the *New York Times* and the *New York Herald*, and in scores of smaller places. There was no question after September, 1882, that the incandescent light was a success. [2]

What the country now had was two systems of electric illumination carried on from central generating plants. The chief limit to the future of these lights lay in the current itself. The field of distribution by direct current was restricted in practice to one or two miles. This meant that in a city of considerable size there must be many generating plants. Plans for New York called for about sixty separate stations, each equipped with small engines and generators and each generator supplying a certain area from its own inde-

---

[1] Hammond, History of the General Electric Company, 181.
[2] F. L. Dyer and T. C. Martin, *Edison; His Life and Inventions* (rev. edn., N. Y., 1929), I, chaps. xvi-xvii.

pendent circuit.   Satisfactory service to scattered communities seemed to be commercially out of the question.[1]

To remedy this grave defect, inventors began to give attention to developing the alternating current. Basing his experiments on earlier discoveries by Faraday and Henry, an eccentric Frenchman named Gaulard, backed by a sporty Englishman Gibbs, demonstrated in 1884 that, by means of a crude "secondary generator," or transformer, an electric current could be sent many miles.[2]   Elihu Thomson at once appreciated the importance of the discovery and began experimenting. By 1887 he had an alternating-current dynamo of his own on the market.[3]   The most aggressive protagonist of the new system, however, was George Westinghouse of Pittsburgh. He was known at this time chiefly as the inventor of railroad brakes and signals.[4]   Hitherto he had worked little in electricity, his only practical application of the current being to the control of his braking and signaling devices. But when he heard of what Gaulard and Gibbs had done he at once took fire. With such a current the future of electricity for power and light exceeded anything he had dreamed. Purchasing the American rights of Gaulard and Gibbs, he set his brilliant staff to work. By 1886 they were ready to put on the market an electric-light system using the alternating current.[5]

The use of the alternating current for commercial purposes met the strongest scientific opposition in both

[1] C. E. Skinner, "Lighting the World's Columbian Exposition," *Western Pa. Hist. Mag.*, XVII, 15.

[2] Waldemar Kaempffert, ed., *Modern Wonder Workers* (N. Y., 1924), 524-525.

[3] Hammond, History of the General Electric Company, 370.

[4] See Nevins, *Emergence of Modern America*, 98-99.

[5] H. G. Prout, *A Life of George Westinghouse* (N. Y., 1921), 102. An able young engineer, William Stanley, jr., was chiefly responsible for the type of transformer that Westinghouse installed in his first alternating-current station, the one at Buffalo in 1886. Kaempffert, ed., *Modern Wonder Workers*, 525-526.

America and England.   Here it was Thomas A. Edison;
there it was Sir William Thomson (later Lord Kelvin).
The objection which excited the public was the constant
danger to human life.   But back of this objection was
the tremendous pressure brought against the alternating
current by those who had great sums invested in private
and public plants using the direct current.   Westinghouse was quite within the facts when he wrote, "the
struggle for the control of the electric light and power
business has never been exceeded in bitterness by any of
the historical commercial controversies of a former day.
Thousands of persons have large pecuniary interests at
stake, and, as might be expected, many of them view
this great subject solely from the stand-point of self-
interest." [1]

Edison, cast in an unfamiliar rôle, led the fight against
the alternating current.   To such lengths did the controversy go that experiments on living animals were performed before public audiences.   "In 1889, I witnessed
the execution of a horse and a calf in the Edison Station
of Columbus staged before the Ohio State legislature,"
says Dr. Charles E. Skinner.[2]   The purpose was to demonstrate the greater danger of the alternating current
as compared with the direct.   One of the most important
contributions to the discussion was a paper by Edison
in the *North American Review* for November, 1889, in
which he voiced his personal desire to prohibit the use
of the alternating current.   To this article Westinghouse
made a well-argued and temperate reply.   He could
speak calmly because by this time the alternating current
was rapidly outstripping the direct in central stations
for incandescent lighting.

The possibility of replacing the early small generators
by one central plant and of carrying the power long

---

[1] Westinghouse, "A Reply to Mr. Edison," 654.
[2] Skinner, "Lighting the World's Columbian Exposition," 18.

distances put an entirely new face on problems of electric illumination.   It meant the consolidation of interests and it meant refinancing on a large scale.   It set men with money to working with fresh energy to secure control of street franchises in all the larger cities and, incidentally, added greatly to the burden of municipal corruption.[1]   Central electric power stations increased from eight in 1881 to 2774 in 1898.[2]   Some of these involved interesting experiments in municipal ownership.   The electric-light plant which Chicago built in 1887 had become the largest municipal lighting system in the world by 1898 and had nearly paid for itself out of the difference between its operating expenses and what it would have cost the city to buy the same amount of current from a private company.[3]   At the same time Allegheny, Pennsylvania, was paying its municipal plant a fourth less than Pittsburgh across the river was paying a private company.

One of the most picturesque fights to control a utility in the public interest occurred in Detroit, led by Mayor Hazen S. Pingree, "Potato Patch Pingree," as he later was called because of the gardens he started during the Panic of 1893 in the town's vacant lots.   Pingree found, when he entered office in 1889, that Detroit was paying nearly twice as much for electricity as her neighbors, Cleveland, Buffalo and Grand Rapids.[4]   He determined to end this by establishing a municipal plant.   Having secured an honest commission and an able Scotchman, Alex Dow, as manager, he contracted for equipment

[1] See Schlesinger, *Rise of the City*, 389-392.

[2] Bureau of the Census, *Central Electric Light and Power Stations, 1902 (Special Rep.)*, 106-107.

[3] U. S. Industrial Commission, *Report* (Wash., 1900-1902), XIX, 683.

[4] This was true also of gas.   Pingree remedied the abuse in the case of gas by forcing a new franchise through the council, which presently resulted in as low a rate as that in the other cities.   G. B. Catlin, *The Story of Detroit* (Detroit, 1923), 598-599.

with a company which had no foothold in the town. For two years there was a battle, marked by injunctions, charges of bribery, and misrepresentations from the intrenched gas and electric companies, long enemies but now united in their purpose to prevent the government's intrusion into their field. When Dow finally had his plant running, he furnished light at one half less per year, including interest, depreciation and allowance for taxes, than the city could have secured by contract with a private company at the time the plant was built.[1] Such results could be attained with efficient nonpolitical management, but this was not so easy to insure, as experience in other places showed.

The development of electricity for light and power forced a multitude of changes in all sorts of industries. For example, there was the water-gas industry, which represented an investment of something like $69,000,-000 when electricity began effectually to supplant it. To save itself, it sought new uses, emphasizing heating rather than lighting. In 1890 the Bacchus stove was first put on the market and in four years the demand for it exceeded the supply. Similarly, there was a big investment in the manufacture and sale of oil lamps and gas fixtures. To take advantage of the coming of the incandescent light the trade sought to adapt its equipment to the new luminant. It saw that the wires were at first carried along the brackets of gas chandeliers and the lamp adjusted below the gas socket. If the electricity went off, the customer still had his gas jet. Presently attractive designs for "electroliers" were being made and were in great demand.[2] Electrical appliances

[1] Catlin, *Story of Detroit*, 601-607; U. S. Industrial Commission, *Report*, XIX, 683.
[2] Bureau of the Census, *Central Electric Light and Power Stations, 1902*, 101; E. W. Byrn, *The Progress of Invention in the Nineteenth Century* (N. Y., 1900), 60-61.

multiplied until in 1898 it was estimated that there was a capital of $1,900,000,000 invested.

Side by side with electric lighting there developed electric traction, threatening horse, steam and cable roads in the city streets. As early as 1847 Moses G. Farmer had built an experimental two-passenger car at Dover, New Hampshire, operated by means of a current carried from batteries to a motor connected with one of the axles. Twenty-eight years later a poor mechanic, George F. Greene, built a similar railway at Kalamazoo, Michigan. By the mid-seventies there had been developed out of the work of many experimenters a continuous-current, self-exciting, stationary dynamo which could be used for power. This opened up new possibilities. The problem now was how the power the dynamo provided could be transmitted so as to drive a train on rails.[1]

Impetus was given to the search by the first commercial electric railway, installed by the eminent German inventors, Werner and Wilhelm Siemens, at the Berlin Exposition of 1879, which carried passengers successfully day after day. The heads of the great American electric companies were soon pushing their inventors and engineers to attack the problem. Henry Villard, president of the Edison Electric Company, was counseling Edison; Charles A. Coffin was urging Elihu Thomson. Edison exhibited an electric locomotive in 1880 at Menlo Park and delighted in giving visitors a ride in the car. But his experiment came to nothing commercially; nor did the later efforts of Edison, or those of Stephen D. Field, a nephew of Cyrus W. Field, who ran a train in Chicago in 1883.[2]

[1] F. J. Sprague, "Electric Traction in Space of Three Dimensions," Md. Acad. of Sciences, *Journ.*, II, 166-171.

[2] T. C. Martin, "History and Development of Electric Traction," Bureau of the Census, *Street and Electric Railways, 1902 (Special Rep.)*, 160-167.

The real advances were made by young, energetic inventors experimenting on their own initiative. One was Leo Daft, an Englishman engaged in manufacturing motors at Greenfield, New Jersey, who in 1883 turned out a locomotive which was used to pull a car over the Saratoga and Mt. McGregor Railroad. Another was Charles J. Van Depoele, a Belgian who had set up a plant in Chicago for making electric-light dynamos and in the fall of 1883 showed an electrically driven car at the Chicago Interstate Fair. It was Daft who in 1885 built the first road which for more than a year actually carried passengers for fares. This was in Baltimore on a branch of the Baltimore Union Passenger Railway and was successful enough to induce the New York street railways to allow him to experiment on their tracks. Van Depoele was even busier in the West than Daft in the East. South Bend, Minneapolis, Appleton in Wisconsin, Fort Huron, Michigan, all gave him orders to set up his system.

Although Daft and Van Depoele were recognized as the two most promising electric-traction engineers in the country, neither had demonstrated that an installation superior to the existing horse and cable-operated roads was possible. That soon followed through the work of the man since known as the "Father of the Electric Railway," Frank J. Sprague. He was one of the many who as boys had become infatuated with electricity. Winning a scholarship in the Naval Academy at Annapolis, he had kept up his interest and in his first long cruise in the late seventies made what he called "fifty-seven varieties of inventions." No sooner was he back than he tried to replace the old oil lamps in the navy with incandescent lights. He then went abroad on leave of absence to visit electrical exhibitions in Paris and London. He overstayed his leave, but made so important a report on what he had seen that his superiors permitted him to escape court martial.[1]

While in London Sprague began to plan for the operation of street railways by electricity, and one of the ideas for which he applied for a patent on his return was the trailing trolley; but in this Charles Van Depoele had anticipated him.[2] This overlapping of inventions had from the beginning been one of the confusing and provoking features of the development of both electric traction and electric lighting, just as it had been of the telegraph and the telephone. Patent wars were waged incessantly, entailing heavy court expenses and much suspicion and mutual recrimination. An outstanding electric engineer of the time, Benjamin Garver Lamme, who came fresh from the Ohio State University into the Westinghouse concern, remarked that it was a common experience of technicians to discover that what appeared to them original ideas had been patented years before but never used. "It is surprising too, at times," he declared,

to note how many people think of almost the same thing at the same time, and how their ideas are yet, unquestionably, independently conceived. One instance occurred in my experience of four different people coming to me, within about one month, with the same scheme, to ask my opinion. Upon investigation, I found that they all had devised the scheme independently; and what is more interesting, it was not a scheme for which there was any particular call at that time.[3]

Whatever the patent complication, Sprague always found a way out. Committed to the ambition of developing a practical system of electric traction, he left

[1] Sprague, "Electric Traction," Md. Acad. of Sciences, *Journ.*, II, 178-179.
[2] Kaempffert, ed., *Modern Wonder Workers*, 120-121.
[3] B. G. Lamme, *Benjamin Garver Lamme, Electrical Engineer; An Autobiography* (Mansfield Dudley, ed., N. Y., 1926), 140.

the navy in 1883 and, after a few months with Edison, organized the Sprague Electric Railway & Motor Company with a capital of one hundred thousand dollars on paper. He was allowed to try out his developments on the New York street railways, but the financiers, though they came to look, went away unconvinced. Sprague's chief satisfaction in these fruitless experiments seems to have been that one day Jay Gould was so scared by the blowing out of a fuse that he jumped off the train, never to return.[1]

Eight years had passed since the Siemenses ran their train in Berlin. Yet there were but nine commercial installations in Europe and ten in the United States. "These installations," says Sprague,

> were characterized by the utmost diversity of practice— high and low electrical pressures, series and multiple arrangement of motors, traffic rail conductors and conduits, third rails, slotted tubes, single and double overhead wires carrying trolleys with flexible cable connections, as well as upward-pressing arms carried on the cars.

The motors also varied in construction and control. Ordinarily each car had but one motor, carried either on the front platform or in a dummy car, and connected to the driven axle by belt or chain. "Nowhere," he adds, "was there an installation which in extent or character of equipment could form the basis of general commercial exploitation or command the confidence of capital."[2]

In 1887 Sprague's opportunity came to prove that he had, as he believed, a practical system: a contract for a street railway in Richmond, Virginia. The terms were fantastic. Completion was called for in ninety days

---

[1] Sprague, "Electric Traction," Md. Acad. of Sciences, *Journ.*, II, 190.
[2] Sprague, "Electric Traction," Md. Acad. of Sciences, *Journ.*, II, 192-193.

of a route twelve miles long (including a hill a mile long), with a central plant of three hundred and seventy-five horse power, an overhead line, and forty cars with eighty motors. This was nearly as many motors as were then giving uncertain railway service throughout the world. If the result was satisfactory the Sprague Company should be paid one hundred and ten thousand dollars. It took more than ninety days, but by the fall of 1887 experimental trains were taking the hills and corners of Richmond, something that in the opinion of John Stephenson, the veteran street-railway builder of the day, an electric train could never do. By February, 1888, the road was in commercial operation, and financiers were looking it .over.[1]

Chief among these was Henry M. Whitney, president of a Boston street railway for which he was considering new equipment—cable probably—but, before he decided, he journeyed to Richmond to see what Sprague had accomplished there. In particular, he wished to ascertain whether the system could operate a large number of cars simultaneously. To clear away any doubt Sprague determined upon a dramatic demonstration. The visitor was asked if he would like to see an attempt made at midnight to move a large number of cars then bunched at the terminal. On Whitney's assent, Sprague relates,

> orders were given at the central station to put on extra safety catches, to run the potential up to 500 volts, and to keep the engines going no matter what happened. At the appointed time, on signal the motormen of the 22 cars started as rapidly as they could get clearance headway, but although the potential drop was so great that the car lights could hardly be seen, every car got away and was soon hustling out of sight.[2]

[1] Kaempffert, ed., *Modern Wonder Workers*, 124-125.
[2] Sprague, "Electric Traction," Md. Acad. of Sciences, *Journ.*, III, 6-7.

The test was conclusive. On his return to Boston Whitney presented the case so eloquently to the board of aldermen that he obtained permission to put in a composite line, one part, near the old Providence Depot, of conduit construction, and the remainder, to Allston, of overhead construction. Sprague motors were used on all the cars. Sprague's achievement was celebrated far and wide. Other cities quickly followed the example set by Richmond and Boston.[1] The intense popular interest was picturesquely shown in the case of New Orleans. There a mass meeting, called in favor of replacing the mule with the new system, had as its slogan:

Lincoln Set the Negroes Free!
Sprague Has Set the Mule Free!
The Long-Eared Mule No More Shall Adorn Our Streets.

These successes induced the Edison Electric Company to absorb the Sprague Company. But when Sprague saw that the merger meant changes in his system of which he did not approve and also the dropping of his name from his machines, he resigned. He could not give up his interest in electric traction, however. By 1895 he had developed a new idea, a means of making up long trains by a combination of car units, without regard to number or sequence, some but not all of them equipped with motors. By the new scheme it was possible to control the trains from either end of any car through master switches connected to the common train line.[2] He had hit on the "multiple-unit" system which soon became almost universally used in electric traction.

As Sprague found himself absorbed, so did Van Depoele who by 1887 had installed electric roads in perhaps twenty American cities. When Charles A. Coffin

---

[1] See Schlesinger, *Rise of the City*, 92-93.
[2] Sprague, "Electric Traction," Md. Acad. of Sciences, *Journ.*, III, 19.

told Elihu Thomson early in 1888, "We ought to get into street car electrification" and asked, "Who has done the pioneer work?" Thomson replied, "Van Depoele." [1] Coffin immediately sought him out, bought his company, paying for its patents on a royalty basis as was his custom, and added Van Depoele to the engineering staff. It was Van Depoele who solved, not only for the Thomson-Houston Company but also for Sprague in Richmond, one of the most troublesome problems connected with the installation of motors: the sparking of the commutator. The metal brushes or blocks hitherto used to take care of the annoyance had yielded poor results. "Try carbon," suggested Van Depoele. Though everybody was skeptical carbon worked. Elihu Thomson was to say later that "the carbon brush was the most important invention ever made in the electric railway field." [2]

From the first the Thomson-Houston Company was highly successful in electric railways. This was due less perhaps to the excellent quality of its equipment and the care and integrity of its installations than to the salesmanship of Coffin and his method of financing local plants, a method which he had used with success in electric lighting. His practice was to take the bonds of newly formed concerns in part payment for equipment. As a result, the holdings were scattered all over the country and companies rapidly multiplied.

In its many new applications electricity had come to touch the life of the people at countless points. It was the modern miracle, lighting homes and public places, carrying the human voice great distances, propelling passenger cars through city streets, lifting swift elevators in high office buildings, and promising innumerable benefits as yet undeveloped. As in other economic fields,

[1] Hammond, History of the General Electric Company, 435.
[2] Hammond, History of the General Electric Company, 458.

however, once the period of crude experimentation passed, this new instrumentality of social well-being had tended to fall under the control of a few great capitalists. Increasingly the electrical industry became a component part of the consolidated national business order.

CHAPTER V

THE RISE OF THE INDUSTRIAL TRUST

THE trend toward combination was quite as strong in manufacturing as in the electrical industry or in the field of communication. It was forced mainly by what was called overproduction, but which might more correctly be called underconsumption.[1] Through the use of machinery the manufacturer had learned how to double, treble or even more greatly multiply his output. He had been taking full advantage of every new labor-saving device with little or no regard to its effect on either markets or labor. Where the efficient broom maker had formerly kept seventeen men busy making five hundred dozen brooms in a week, he now had nine men turning out twelve hundred dozen. Carpet manufacturers were using one man where thirty years before they had used from ten to twenty. Where once a first-class journeyman made from six hundred to a thousand two-pound cans by hand, now with a machine he turned out from two thousand to twenty-five hundred. A fifty-per-cent displacement of labor was not unusual.[2]

This output was thrown on the market before the labor displaced had been absorbed. This meant, for a time at least, cutting off the purchasing power of those who had lost their jobs. In general, there was little scientific attempt to measure demand. Production outstripped consumption alarmingly in some instances. As

[1] As David A. Wells remarked at the time, "In a certain sense there can be no overproduction of desirable products so long as human wants for such products remain unsatisfied." *Recent Economic Changes* (N. Y., 1889), 71.
[2] U. S. Commissioner of Labor, *First Annual Report* (1886), 82-84.

a case in point, the output of the iron industry in five states doubled between 1885 and 1888. This was the result of improved processes, for the number of furnace stacks declined.[1] Under the pressure of a wanton production the weaker producer went to the wall, thus still further curtailing purchasing power.

Behind the manufacturer, pushing him to build or enlarge plants regardless of existing capacity, were men who, having idle capital to invest, were willing to go into iron or glass or wire or textiles or any other line that promised big profits. What they were seeking was not active business but, in the words of David A. Wells, to convert their wealth "into the form of negotiable securities paying dividends or interest with regularity, and on the recipiency of which the owner can live without personal exertion or risk of the principal." [2] Frequently, though perhaps less often than was popularly supposed, the marketing of such securities was a pure speculation on the part of those who had formed the company or corporation. They organized to sell stock, not to mine iron or run a railroad; stock promoters and speculators fed on the avidity with which many people seized a new issue without scrutinizing what was behind it. Without a greedy and gullible public they could not have lived.

Overproduction sooner or later forced prices too low for profits, causing bankruptcy of the weak, temporary losses for the strong, short or long periods of unemployment and general business instability. In every considerable industry attempts were made to correct this instability. The favorite form was the pool. In essence, this was a voluntary secret agreement of all or of a majority of the units of an industry to produce and handle their product according to a fixed set of

[1] Wells, *Recent Economic Changes*, 140.
[2] Wells, *Recent Economic Changes*, 75.

rules.   The agreement and its regulation differed in almost every case; so also did the results.

The most substantial pool in 1878 was that of the salt producers of Michigan, known as the Michigan Salt Association.[1]   The industry had gone up and down since it was started in 1859, largely according to its degree of success in curbing overproduction. Public opinion agreed that the combinations had improved the grade of salt by the system of inspection they had established and, as long as they lasted, had brought "order and stability" into the business.   Also, the public had paid a little higher for its salt.   But no association had long endured.   When it was seen that the producers were making money, capital pushed in, price-cutting followed, and there was a gradual return to unchecked competition.   As an observer characterized one such disastrous period, "It was a Donnybrook Fair in the salt market.   When you saw a head, you hit it." [2]   The plight of the individual Michigan manufacturer was the worse because the great salt districts of New York and Ohio were well organized.

As an escape from this unprofitable warfare, and also as a treaty-making power with the Ohio and New York districts, the leaders of the industry in 1876 formed the Michigan Salt Association.   It was a stock company in which the amount of stock held by any concern was limited to one share for each barrel of its average daily capacity.   The association's business was the manufacturing and marketing of salt.   Each member was obliged to make an annual contract to turn over to it his full product or to lease his plant to the association. A seven-per-cent dividend, together with the losses and expenses of handling, was deducted from the proceeds of

[1] J. W. Jenks, "The Michigan Salt Association," W. Z. Ripley, ed., *Trusts, Pools and Corporations* (rev. edn., N. Y., 1916), 1-21.
[2] Jenks, "Michigan Salt Association," 11.

sales before a division of profits was made. The agreement was limited to five years.[1] When at the end of that time the association expired, it was continued for a second five-year period; again, in 1886, it was reorganized for a third five-year period.

The association was fortunate in securing an efficient management, one experienced enough to detect weaknesses or raids, and flexible and shrewd enough to take care of them. Controlling about eighty-five per cent of the output, it did not hesitate, when challenged, to squeeze out a troublesome competitor. The public interest in cheaper salt was, on the whole, satisfied. Among other things, the association prevented a practice which under full competition had regularly raised prices to consumers and cut them for producers, the practice whereby large dealers bought great quantities of salt in the summer when it was cheap and plentiful and stored it until winter when it became scarce. They could demand a high price from which they alone profited. Under the new arrangement they received a small commission for each barrel sold.[2]

A looser and much less enduring form of pool was that of the makers of cordage, binding twine, rope of all kinds. Cordage was an inviting industry since it required little capital and fed a constantly growing market. Since 1860, pools had been formed from time to time to limit the overproduction which the inrush of fresh capital and consequent cutting of prices below the profit mark caused. They rarely lasted over three years. "Breaking up, fighting and getting together again" was their story. The plan customarily followed was later explained to the Industrial Commission by J. M. Waterbury, a member of the pool existing in 1880:

[1] Jenks, "Michigan Salt Association," 7-9.
[2] Jenks, "Michigan Salt Association," 14-16.

Well, all manufacturers would meet and agree to divide the business of the country upon certain percentages, and when they had agreed on the percentages the rule was that each manufacturer should make his returns monthly to a supervisor, and if his business ran beyond his percentage he paid in to the supervisor so much per pound on the excess beyond his percentage; and then those that went below that percentage drew out from the supervisor an amount as much per pound as they went below their percentage. The supervisor acted as a clearing house for the manufacturers.[1]

The member which profited most by this agreement was the long-established Plymouth Cordage Company in Massachusetts, which in 1936 remained an independent concern after one hundred and twelve years of continuous operation. It was its policy to exceed its allotment and cheerfully pay the fixed amount on this surplus, which was distributed to those who fell short of their quota. The result was that at each renewal of the arrangement its percentage grew greater while that of some of its less enterprising competitors dwindled. By 1885 the Plymouth Company's allotment, originally ten per cent, had risen to twenty.[2]

Not all the minor pools formed around 1880 were as loose in construction as the cordage pool. The American Wall Paper Manufacturers' Association, which included practically every factory in the country, fixed prices and maintained them at a high point. The administration was in the hands of a commissioner. Each company furnished security for its performance of the agreement; those which failed to live up to the terms were fined. An interesting feature of the wall-paper pool was the attempt to drop the middlemen and deal

[1] U. S. Industrial Commission, *Report* (Wash., 1900-1902), XIII, 126.

[2] Plymouth Cordage Company, *One Hundred Years of Service* (Plymouth, Mass., 1924), 39-40.

directly with customers.   This had the unexpected effect
of causing many middlemen to go into the business for
themselves.   The pool broke down because certain manufacturers secretly sold goods at less than the scheduled
prices.

Pools proved an unsatisfactory instrument for establishing order and stability in a business because they
suffered from two basic defects.   In the first place, they
violated underlying principles of both common and
statute law, and hence could not be enforced in the
courts.   The only guarantee of good faith came from
the creation of deposits, the imposition of fines and other
more or less cumbersome devices.   The second difficulty
lay in the fact that, under the circumstances, pools could
be but temporary expedients.   They could afford no cer-
tainty for stability of prices or of industrial policy over
any extended period.[1]

Industry, however, had not been depending solely on
the pool as an instrument of stability.   As a means of
avoiding the shortcomings of that device, business magnates often obtained control of some element essential
to the life of an industry.   The railroads, the telegraph,
the telephone had such a whip hand in their exclusive
franchises.   Control of raw materials would accomplish
the same end, but usually nature had scattered raw materials so widely and so prodigally as to make it exceed-
ingly difficult for any man or group of men to monopolize the supply. An exclusive patent afforded an advantage which might temporarily give a monopoly; but
here nature interfered in another way, endowing many
men with inventive capacity.   A patent which created a
monopoly was usually followed quickly by other inventions which performed the same function, sometimes
more efficiently.   An advantage much sought by industry was a privileged relation to transportation.   If a

[1] Ripley, ed., *Trusts, Pools and Corporations*, xvi.

manufacturer could ship his raw material and his product at a lower rate than his competitor, he could undersell him and finally bring him to terms. Though public opinion was strongly opposed to such discriminations, not until the mid-eighties did the opposition crystallize in a federal statute defining and forbidding them.[1]

The most brilliant illustration of the supremacy possible through a control of shipping rates was the practical monopoly of the petroleum industry which since 1872 had been developed by an oil-refining and marketing concern of Cleveland, Ohio, known as the Standard Oil Company.[2]   Yet considering the remarkable abilities of John D. Rockefeller, who headed the Standard, it may well be asked whether the company had needed to resort to unfair methods of competition in order to gain preëminence in the field.   Rockefeller was a man who gave himself entirely to his business, saw it as a whole, its tiniest detail as well as its largest possible ramification.   He knew how to select and handle his associates, knew what to tell them and what to conceal.   He took deep satisfaction in economies, hated waste whether in small or great things.   Combined with these qualities was a genius for organization which it would be difficult to parallel in the history of American industry.   With such an equipment nothing could have prevented him from becoming one of the leaders, probably the greatest, in the oil business.

But Rockefeller detested and feared free competition and the disorder and uncertainties which attended it. It interfered with stable prices and profits; it glutted the crude and refined markets; it was wasteful.   He had seen no way to bring order and stability into the industry but for him and those with him to take over the entire

---

[1] See later, 100-101.
[2] See Allan Nevins, *The Emergence of Modern America* (*A History of American Life*, VIII), 397-400.

John D. Rockefeller

oil-refining and marketing business of the country. By this means it could be run economically, efficiently and profitably for those in the combination. This could be done most expeditiously by getting special rates from the railroads. It was fair to ask them, he held, because the Standard would be the biggest and the most regular shipper. Aided by these special advantages over competitors, the Rockefeller group had acquired, through stock purchase or through direct or indirect property purchase, some seventy-four refining concerns, including many of the most successful in their districts.[1] Contracts limiting the quantity of oil to be refined had also been made with certain firms strong enough to refuse to sell. In 1878 the Standard Oil Company was manufacturing over ninety per cent of the output of the country.

In securing mastery of the refining industry the Standard had been aided by its success in carrying out one of the most farsighted policies in its history, that of controlling the pipe lines which carried oil from the wells to the railway shipping points as well as to the tanks in which surplus was stored. So great had become its power over transportation facilities that in 1879, on representation of the Petroleum Producers' Union, the state of Pennsylvania, which produced the bulk of the world's oil, brought suit in equity against the Pennsylvania Railroad and the several pipe lines which Standard owned or controlled.[2] The upshot was an indictment in April of John D. Rockefeller and seven of his associates. The indictment charged a conspiracy to secure a monopoly of the oil business through the control of transportation.

This indictment, together with the demonstration of the methods employed by the Standard, naturally at-

---

[1] Ida M. Tarbell, *The History of the Standard Oil Company* (N. Y., 1904), I, chaps. iv-vi.

[2] Tarbell, *Standard Oil Company*, I, chaps. vii-viii.

tracted public attention.   It was an object lesson in success, also in evasion, for the men were never brought to trial.   There were repeated postponements, sought by the defendants "on advice of counsel."   An investigation in New York state at the same time interfered. Moreover, so the producers believed, the railroads brought such pressure to bear on the state authorities to drop the prosecution that they were glad to seize any pretext for delay.   The independents finally tired of the struggle and in 1880 a settlement was arranged.   With it the Petroleum Producers' Union came to an end.

Meanwhile the Rockefeller group took steps to consolidate their control of the various companies they had acquired in order to obviate competition.   To overcome the objections inherent in the pool, they devised a novel form of industrial organization: the trust.   It was an old legal device fitted to new conditions.   Adopted in 1879 and revised in 1882, the plan provided for a board of nine trustees to which all the capital stock of the constituent companies was assigned, the original shareholders accepting "trust certificates" in lieu of their former evidences of ownership.[1]   The trust was an improvement upon the pool both as regards effectiveness and stability.   Its success soon prompted other industries to adopt a similar form of organization.   As the sequel was to show, however, trusts were vulnerable legally because the agreements upon which they were based were matters of record.   Hence they could be moved against by the courts under the common law.

Efforts by competing companies to escape the effects of the transportation monopoly which the Standard had established continued.   The most ambitious scheme was to build a pipe line to the seaboard by which an independent producer could ship crude oil directly from the wells without favor of the railroads.   An attempt to

[1] Tarbell, *Standard Oil Company*, II, 135-137.

lay such a line from the oil regions to Baltimore had been made in 1876 by the Pennsylvania Transportation Company, the chief engineer being General Herman Haupt, the Civil War bridge builder. The project attracted great attention, but failed through a combination of railroad opposition and bad financial management.[1] The idea continued to be cherished, however, and in the fall of 1878 the Tidewater Pipe Company was organized to lay a conduit from the Bradford (Pennsylvania) oil field, by this time the center of production, over the Allegheny Mountains to a point where it would connect with the Reading Railroad. That road, which heretofore had carried no oil, was glad to get the freight until the line could be finished.

The right of way was quickly obtained, but as soon as work began the railroads and the Standard interests manifested strong opposition. This took the form of ridicule, of assertions that oil could not be pumped over the mountains, of rumors of financial weakness and of guerrilla-like efforts to break the right of way. But it did not prevent the completion of the project. In late May, 1879, the time arrived to test the question whether or no nature could be flouted and oil be forced over the mountain barrier. It was an exciting occasion. The westernmost pump was started on the twenty-eighth. The oil flowed up and on about as fast as a man could walk, being attended on its way by both believers and doubters. In seven days it covered the distance of a hundred and nine miles and reached the junction point with the Reading.[2]

There was no question thereafter in the minds of either the Tidewater Pipe Company or the Standard that pipes rather than rails would carry the oil of the future. Bitterly the railroads fought the interloper.

[1] Tarbell, *Standard Oil Company*, I, 174-178.
[2] Tarbell, *Standard Oil Company*, II, chap. ix.

Rates were lowered on the oil-carrying roads until they were far below cost. The pipe line, completing its way to the seaboard after its successful demonstration, encountered the same guerrilla tactics that it had fought on its first lap. Not until 1886 did the Tidewater pipe line reach New York City. But by that time the company was no longer a free agent. It had attempted to protect its business by acquiring refineries of its own and developing its own markets. The Standard Oil Company had so vigorously opposed it that in 1883 a division of interests was effected which gave the Standard eighty-eight and a half per cent of the business and the Tidewater the rest.[1]

This "gentlemen's agreement" between the Tidewater and the Standard did not end the struggle of the independent companies. A fringe of irreconcilable producers, refiners and local pipe-line men persisted in efforts to do business in an industry which was being swamped by an ever greater production of oil. As a form of mutual help they organized the Producers' Protective Association in 1887. Late in the year a shutdown was tried for a few months, but, like all such efforts at artificial control, it benefited in the end only the stronger concerns. In 1888 and 1889 coöperative oil companies were organized to furnish pipe lines and storage tanks to take care of the independent producers' output, accommodations which the Standard alone was then giving. The Standard thwarted this effort by buying control of the companies.[2] This marked a new departure, for up to 1887 the Standard had not been an oil producer. Now, however, the difficulty of controlling the industry to its liking forced it into production. The last step was taken to complete integration.

Enough producers remained, however, to keep up the

[1] Tarbell, *Standard Oil Company*, II, 300-302.
[2] Tarbell, *Standard Oil Company*, II, chap. xv.

fight.   To achieve a closer-knit organization, they formed in 1891 the Producers' Oil Company with a capital of six hundred thousand dollars.   Over a thousand producers subscribed to the stock, also the few independent refiners left in the oil region.   The two interests joined in building a pipe line from the wells to the refineries; but the problem remained of getting the refined product to the seaboard, for the railroads declined shipments at reasonable rates.   Again necessity forced a solution.   Under the leadership of Lewis Emery, jr., of Bradford, one of the most aggressive and resourceful of the independents, they undertook the laying of double pipes to the seaboard, one line for crude oil and one for refined.   They encountered all the difficulties, even to physical violence, which had beset the first seaboard line, but in 1893 they attained their object.[1]   The eventual outcome of this struggle was an entirely independent company, the Pure Oil Company, a ten-million-dollar concern into which in 1900 the three interests which had united their resources, the producers, the refiners and the pipe-line owners, were consolidated.   It was an aggregation as completely integrated as the Standard Oil Company itself, owning and controlling its crude oil, its refining, its transportation on land and sea and its marketing facilities at home and abroad.[2]

Next to petroleum, the trend toward combination evidenced itself most strikingly in iron and steel.   It was the industry upon which all others directly or indirectly depended.   For the fifty million people of the United States it was of vital importance that iron and steel be produced as cheaply and efficiently as possible.   The price of these products affected the cost of practically everything the people bought—tools of all sorts, wagons

---

[1] Tarbell, *Standard Oil Company*, II, 167-170.
[2] Tarbell, *Standard Oil Company*, II, 189-191.

and plows, the stoves on which the women cooked—
as well as freight rates on the shipments of farmers,
merchants and manufacturers. In 1878 the leading iron-
producing region was Michigan. The value of the
yield was something over six million a year. Next came
Pennsylvania with a little over four million, followed
closely by New York state.[1]

But while these were the most productive centers,
other fields were about to undergo rapid development.
There was the immensely rich Vermilion Range in
Minnesota, discovered in 1868, but so inaccessible that
not until 1875 could a capitalist be induced to build the
sixty-mile railroad necessary to carry the ore to a shipping point on Lake Superior. He was Charlemagne
Tower, a Pennsylvania millionaire, who sank some
four million dollars in the project before the first cargo
was shipped in 1884. In the same year a second Minnesota district, the Gogebic, began to send ore to market.[2] Coal, a necessary ingredient in the making of steel,
lay plentifully at hand, for already in 1880 the near-by
bituminous fields of Illinois were yielding over six million tons a year. The old Northwest, however, was no
longer the farthest outpost of the industry. Several
Western states were making iron and steel products by
1880, including California, Kansas, Missouri, Texas
and Wyoming.[3] The year 1881 saw the opening of
the first furnace of the Colorado Coal and Iron Company at Pueblo.[4]

[1] *U. S. Compendium of the Tenth Census* (1880), pt. ii, 1242.

[2] H. N. Casson, *The Romance of Steel* (N. Y., 1907), 52-55; G. L.
Goodale, comp., *Chronology of Iron and Steel* (R. J. Speer, ed., Pittsburgh, 1920), 205.

[3] *U. S. Compendium of Tenth Census,* pt. ii, 1136-1137.

[4] Goodale, comp., *Chronology of Iron and Steel,* 198, 218. In 1892
the Colorado Coal and Iron Company was reorganized under the name
of the Colorado Fuel and Iron Company. In 1902 John D. Rockefeller
bought a large interest in the Colorado Fuel and Iron Company and
became active in its management. J. T. Flynn, *God's Gold* (N. Y.,
1932), 433.

At the same time a rich area was being developed in the South, around Birmingham in Alabama. Within a radius of a few miles there existed large deposits of iron ore, of coal, of dolomite, of lime—all the elements needed for the industry. The Confederacy had made steel and iron in this district during the Civil War. Despite various attempts to develop the industry in the years following, little success was attained until the 1880's. Then the Alabama Coal Company began operation on a large scale. Eight new concerns—rolling mills, furnaces, mining companies—opened in the Birmingham district between 1880 and 1884.[1] The demand for the pig iron they turned out was greater than the mills could supply. Abram S. Hewitt, an authority on iron and steel matters, said in 1883 that the Birmingham district was "the only place on the American continent where it is possible to make iron in competition with the cheap iron of England." He added, "I think this will be a region of coke-made iron on a grander scale than has ever been witnessed on the habitable globe."[2]

Not only had the American iron and steel industry the advantage of these well-distributed and apparently inexhaustible supplies of ore and coal, but it seized and adapted to its purposes the many revolutionary technological advances which came from English and German experimenters. In 1881 Captain William R. Jones, general superintendent of Andrew Carnegie's first steel plant, the Edgar Thomson, at Braddock, Pennsylvania, which had amazed American and English competitors by its output, told the British Iron and Steel Institute why in his judgment his works could produce five hundred and fifty-five tons to a Britisher's four hundred and

---

[1] Ethel Armes, *The Story of Coal and Iron in Alabama* (Birmingham, 1910), 283.
[2] Armes, *Story of Coal and Iron*, 301.

twenty. One reason was that, "while your metallurgists, as well as those of France and Germany, have been devoting their time and talents to the discovery of new processes, we have swallowed the information so generously tendered through the printed reports of the Institute, and have selfishly devoted ourselves to beating you in output."[1] The other reasons were the employment of young ambitious men, a strong but pleasant rivalry between plants, a working force of mixed nationalities, the eight-hour day, and the use of the most up-to-date machinery.[2]

The demands on the industry for increased production, particularly of steel, grew annually. Thus, in 1870 less than 30,500 tons of Bessemer steel rails had been made in the United States. Ten years later the output was over 850,000 tons, in 1890 nearly 1,900,-000. In 1880 about fifty per cent of the rails used were iron, but by 1890 less than one per cent. Just as steel was taking the place of iron in rails, so it was supplanting iron in bridge building. It had first been used structurally in the Eads Bridge across the Mississippi at St. Louis, completed in 1874. Four years later a bridge entirely of steel was opened across the Missouri River at Glasgow. By 1890 it was generally accepted as the material from which a bridge should be made, replacing iron as iron had in its turn replaced wood.[3] Another new use appeared in the form of structural steel for the modern style of office buildings known as skyscrapers.[4] The transformation of the American navy from wood

[1] B. J. Hendrick, *The Life of Andrew Carnegie* (Garden City, 1932), I, 309-310. Such was the interest of the British Institute in what was going on in America that in 1890 they met in the United States for the first time and later published a report of their observations and proceedings.

[2] Goodale, comp., *Chronology of Iron and Steel*, 199.

[3] Goodale, comp., *Chronology of Iron and Steel*, 217.

[4] See A. M. Schlesinger, *The Rise of the City* (*A History of American Life*, X), 282-283.

to steel provided a fresh source of demand. In 1887 the Bethlehem Iron Company signed a contract for the first American-made armor plate—6700 tons at $536 a ton. The next year the Bethlehem Iron Company began the first steel shaft for propellers of United States warships.[1]

A stalwart set of ironmasters, with highly developed and well-placed plants, many of them dating from before the Civil War, led the industry. In the East were the Cooper Hewitt Works at Phillipsburgh, New Jersey, outgrowth of Peter Cooper's ironworks, established at Trenton in the thirties; the Pencroyd Iron Works, near Philadelphia, founded in 1852 by Percival Roberts, a man as deeply interested in the art of iron making as in his tonnage; the Cambria Iron Works of Johnstown, Pennsylvania, and those of Jones & Laughlin in Pittsburgh, two concerns in successful operation since 1853. The Cambria had provided at least two men of unique value to the industry: Captain "Bill" Jones whom Carnegie in 1871 had placed in charge of his first steel mill, and John Fritz who since 1860 had headed the Bethlehem Iron Company. In the West the most important single concern was the Illinois Steel Company, the outgrowth of a mill built in 1857. There were great numbers of smaller plants; the census of 1880 gave the number as 1005.[2] In the South the Tennessee Coal, Iron and Railway Company was organized in 1881.

The stronger concerns, forced into a struggle for materials and markets, faced a necessity for quickly adopting new processes and of taking on new lines of production. All this required money in sums which the business itself rarely could supply. As a result, they found themselves obliged to employ not only new operations but also new financial methods. A furious contest en-

[1] Goodale, comp., *Chronology of Iron and Steel*, 212.
[2] *U. S. Compendium of Tenth Census*, pt. ii, 936.

sued which ended in the swallowing up of many of the 1005 smaller plants.   The most significant man in this bitter warfare was Andrew Carnegie, easily by 1878 the dominating figure in the iron and steel business. He was less an ironmaster than a master promoter and money-maker, a type which was to render the old-fashioned ironmaster secondary in the industry.   His success was due in part to his ability to pick men.   He once suggested as his epitaph: "Here lies the man who was able to surround himself with men far cleverer than himself."   Along with this astuteness went his foresight in safeguarding supplies of essential raw materials.

Carnegie exercised both talents in 1882 when he made certain of the permanency of his coke supply by buying out and taking into his business Henry C. Frick.   Frick had gained control of most of the coke ovens of the Connellsville district in Pennsylvania by taking advantage of the bargains in coal lands which the depression of the seventies had thrown on the market.   By 1882 he controlled four fifths of the output of coke.[1] Carnegie acquired a large share of the H. C. Frick Company, but allowed Frick to remain master of it.

The two men made a remarkable team.   Carnegie was the inspiring leader, imaginative and warmly human.   Frick was the cold, hard-headed man of affairs. He filled Pittsburgh with hordes of laborers brought from every obscure village of eastern and southern Europe, and was a determined foe of trade unionism. Under the leadership of these men and their associates the Carnegie company made rapid strides.   In 1892 the Carnegie Steel Company, Limited, was formed with a capitalization of $25,000,000.[2]   In the quarter-century from 1875 to 1900 the Carnegie interests paid profits

[1] J. H. Bridge, *The Inside History of the Carnegie Steel Company* (N. Y., 1903), 170-173; Hendrick, *Life of Andrew Carnegie*, I, 294.

[2] Casson, *Romance of Steel*, 116; Bridge, *Inside History of Carnegie Steel Company*, 254-256.

aggregating $133,000,000; in the single year 1900 the profits amounted to $40,000,000, of which Carnegie's personal share was $25,000,000.[1]

Other companies made similar progress.   The Illinois Steel Company benefited greatly from its enterprise in early acquiring ownership of exclusive supplies of ore. The Colorado Fuel and Iron Company enlarged its capitalization in 1892 to thirteen million dollars.   By that time the Tennessee Coal, Iron and Railway Company had attained gigantic proportions, being the biggest single possessor of coal and ore lands and iron furnaces in the country.   By the close of the century the United States led the world as a steel producer, its output almost doubling that of Great Britain.

In other fields of economic life similar processes of combination and integration were at work.   For many years the whisky distillers had been perplexed by over-production and price-cutting competition.   Agreements to restrict production had been tried without success. A temporary wave of prosperity struck the industry from 1879 to 1881 because crop failures abroad caused a heavy demand and higher prices for American whisky. But at the same time new capital rushed into the field, the number of distilleries increased, and, with the falling off of the European demand, the producers found themselves in greater distress than before.[2]   The upshot was the formation in 1881 of a pool, the Western Export Association, which was intended to limit the output.

This and later similar attempts failed to stabilize the industry; and in the spring of 1887 the leading distillers, taking a leaf from the experience of the Standard Oil Company, formed a trust.   The organization was called the Distillers' and Cattle Feeders' Trust.[3]   The

[1] Bridge, *Inside History of Carnegie Steel Company*, 94-102, 295.
[2] J. W. Jenks, "The Development of the Whiskey Trust," Ripley, ed., *Trusts, Pools and Corporations*, 22-25.
[3] Jenks, "Development of Whiskey Trust," 26-35.

new plan enabled those in authority to reduce production at the source instead of exporting the surplus at a loss, as had been done under the old pools.   The trust put prices high enough to pay good dividends to the members and to accumulate a financial war chest to wage battle with independent distillers.   But the scheme of the allied distillers was soon disturbed.   Higher prices brought new people into the industry.   Distilleries, big and little, multiplied, vastly complicating the price-cutting campaigns on which the trust depended to clean up all outsiders.   Nevertheless the combination maintained its predominant position.[1]

In the same year that the whisky trust was formed, the National Cordage Company was organized under the leadership of what was called the Cordage Big Four. These four concerns in and near New York City, the largest of them Waterbury & Company, controlled over forty per cent of the industry.   The device by which they expected to whip the other sixty per cent into their amalgamation was control of the world's supply of manila hemp, the raw material of rope making.   This supply was handled by four or five firms in the Philippines, and with these firms the National Cordage Company contracted for practically their entire stock.   Armed with these contracts, it gave its competitors the choice of entering the combination and enjoying its advantages or of staying out and paying a higher price for raw material.[2]   Soon nearly seventy per cent of the industry had joined the combination.

The only important concern which refused was the Plymouth Cordage Company.   A bitter fight followed. The National attempted to secure stock control of the Plymouth by running up prices, but the majority of the stockholders thwarted this maneuver by forming them-

[1] Jenks, "Development of Whiskey Trust," 45.
[2] U. S. Industrial Commission, *Report*, XIII, 127.

selves into a voting trust.   Its next attack was on the
company's supply of raw materials.   On one occasion
the National held up in New York Harbor a cargo of
hemp ordered by the Plymouth.   When the latter sought
to take it by a writ of replevin, the National anchored it
at sea beyond the three-mile limit, and hence outside
the jurisdiction of the court.   Only threats of immediate
criminal proceedings brought the hemp to Plymouth.[1]
By such determined resistance the Plymouth was able
to retain its independent existence and, at the same time,
share in the high prices which the rope trust succeeded
in maintaining.

Both the preferred and common stock of the National
Cordage Company were on the exchange.   J. M. Waterbury, the president, later testified before the Industrial
Commission that his first application to the stock-
exchange committee had been to list only the preferred
stock, but the commitee, after questioning him, asked
him "to list the whole thing." "So," continued Waterbury, "the common stock was listed at the request of the
Stock Exchange committee at that time, because they
thought we had a pretty sound scheme of consolidation." [2]   From the first, National Cordage stock was a
favorite, and the speculation in it ran high.   Purchasers,
of course, did not know that the enhanced prices which
the rope combination was exacting were having much
the same result as in the case of the whisky trust.   They
were investing capital to build a fresh crop of competition and were putting money into the coffers of existing
plants for enlargement and for defense funds.

The centripetal trend which we have been following
aimed at the control of an entire industry, that is, a
monopoly, or at a complete integration of essential parts
in order to insure safety against attack by ruthless com-

[1] Plymouth Cordage Company, *One Hundred Years of Service*, 42-43.
[2] U. S. Industrial Commission, *Report*, XIII, 127.

petitors. The success attained inspired outsiders with the notion that, if an industry did not consolidate itself, they should shoulder the task. The greatest of these promoters in the closing decades of the century was "Judge" W. H. Moore, head of the Chicago legal firm of the Moore Brothers, which had long specialized in corporation law.

Their first important venture was the reorganization of the Diamond Match Company, involving an increase of the capitalization from $3,000,000 to $7,500,000 and later to $11,000,000. Into this organization went practically all the saw mills and factories on which the trade depended. But matches require boxes, and the Moores followed their first promotion with a second, the merger of the leading manufacturers of strawboard into a seven-million-dollar corporation. In 1890 they brought several Eastern cracker manufacturers together into the New York Biscuit Company with a capitalization of $9,000,000. Eight years later followed the National Biscuit Company which, with a capital of $55,-000,000, commanded a monopoly control of ninety per cent of the cracker-biscuit companies of the country. By this time they were being besieged with requests to organize companies "from the marshes of Maine to the Pacific Coast." [1]   The Moores insisted on economy, efficiency and centralized management in the mergers they effected, and possessed a knowledge of the intricacies of corporation law which generally enabled their clients to steer clear of the courts.

A less spectacular promoter, but one so active that he became known as the "Father of Trusts," was Charles R. Flint, jr. Unlike "Judge" Moore, Flint was a merchant and banker, but, like him, he believed that combination was a necessary and inevitable step in industrial evolution. The trust he defined as "an alliance

[1] U. S. Industrial Commission, *Report*, I, 963.

of work, brains and money," of "labour, intelligence and capital." [1]   In his mind it had nothing in common with "corners" or the creation of a monopoly. If he is to be believed, he always advised against consolidation when there were no advantages of importance to be secured. He was critical of overcapitalization, of bankers who indorsed securities without knowing whether they were sound, of a public which bought recklessly for speculation, not investment. Combinations meant to him better business, better service to the people. No promoter of the time made out a better case for consolidation or warned more frankly of possible abuses. He organized or helped organize combinations in starch, rubber and other commodities. [2]

By 1890 at least fifteen great trusts and combinations had been formed in addition to those with which the period began. [3]   Among the more important of those which have not been discussed were the American Cottonseed Oil Trust in 1884, the National Linseed Oil Trust in 1885, and the National Lead Trust and the Sugar Refineries Company, both in 1887. "In an incredible number of the necessaries and luxuries of life, from meat to tombstones," declared one contemporary,

> some of the inner circle of the "fittest" has sought, and very often obtained, the sweet power which Judge Barrett found the sugar trust had: It "can close every refinery at will, close some and open others, . . . artificially limit the production of refined sugar, enhance the price to enrich themselves and their associates at the public expense, and depress the price when necessary to crush out and impoverish a foolhardy rival." [4]

[1] C. R. Flint and others, *The Trust: Its Book* (J. H. Bridge, ed., N. Y., 1902), chap. v.

[2] See Flint and others, *The Trust*, 207-226, for excerpts from Flint's testimony before the Industrial Commission in March, 1900.

[3] John Moody, *The Truth about the Trusts* (N. Y., 1904), 453-467.

[4] H. D. Lloyd, *Wealth against Commonwealth* (N. Y., 1894), 4-5.

To this despondent observer it seemed that the letters, U. S. A., were rapidly coming to signify the "United Syndicates of America." It looked as though nothing could stop the movement.

CHAPTER VI

NATIONALIZING THE RAILROADS

THE part the railways played in making a monopoly of the Standard Oil Company was not exceptional in the business life of the country. It was simply the completest and best advertised illustration of their power. So keen was the competition for freight on rail lines that large shippers were usually able to make their own terms, obtaining not only discriminatory rates but also the use of sidetracks and other special accommodations. Such allowances were oftentimes sufficient of themselves to drive competitors from the field. Nor was it the big shippers alone who secured favors. Smaller manufacturers who could bring influence to bear, threaten or cajole, also received special treatment. Sometimes this was accorded "from a desire to relieve individuals from the consequences of previous unfair concessions to rivals in business." [1]

The system, if such it could be called, was never accepted even by the railroads as anything but an unsafe and, in the end, unsatisfactory way of doing business. The secrecy which they enjoined in granting favors evidenced their uneasiness as to what would happen if the shipper who considered himself wronged should appeal to the courts. "There was not the least doubt," said the interstate-commerce commission in its initial report in 1887, "that had the case been properly brought to a judicial test these transactions would in many cases have been held to be illegal by the common law . . . ." It added, however, that "proof was in general difficult,

[1] Interstate Commerce Commission, *Annual Report for 1887*, 5-6.

91

the remedy doubtful or obscure, and the very resort to a remedy against the party which fixed the rates of transportation at pleasure, . . . might prove more injurious than the rebate itself." [1]   Parties affected by it, therefore, generally preferred to direct their efforts to securing similar favors for themselves.

But, as in the case of the Standad Oil Company, not all shippers acquiesced.   There were always some left over from each battle who pulled themselves together and prepared for a new attack.   Popular sentiment was, to an increasing extent, with them. This was due to sympathy with the underdog; to resentment at the arrogance of the railroads; and to a profound conviction that, though the ownership of rail stocks and bonds was private, the roads themselves were public highways created by the state for public use and with an obligation to carry persons and freight on equal terms. [2]

Though the most discussed complaint against the railroads was their alliance with Big Business, it was not the only one.   Among the grievances tabulated by the Cullom Senate committee in 1886 were the charges that rates were fixed without regard to the actual cost of service, being based on "what the traffic will bear" and on the necessity of paying dividends on "watered stock and interest on bonds improperly issued"; that local rates were too high as compared with through rates; that both local and through rates were unreasonably high at noncompeting points; and that unreasonable discriminations existed between localities similarly situated.   Condemning the management of the railroad business as "extravagant and wasteful," the committee pointed particularly to the costly practice of granting

[1] Interstate Commerce Commission, *Annual Report for 1887*, 7.

[2] For the so-called Granger laws, passed in the 1870's and based on this principle, and for the action of the Supreme Court in upholding such legislation, see Allan Nevins, *The Emergence of Modern America* (*A History of American Life*, VIII), 174-176.

passes and to the heavy expenditures entailed in the
"reckless strife for competitive business." It held that

> the effect of the prevailing policy of railroad manage-
> ment is, by an elaborate system of secret special rates,
> rebates, drawbacks, and concessions, to foster monop-
> oly, to enrich favored shippers, and to prevent free
> competition in many lines of trade in which the item
> of transportation is an important factor.

Such favoritism and secrecy, it said, "introduce an
element of uncertainty into legitimate business that
greatly retards the development of our industries and
commerce." [1]

To cure some of the worst abuses, the railroads from
time to time tried pooling devices.[2] These represented
an effort at self-government on their part. Pools were
to put an end to all the conscienceless bargaining with
shippers. Quickly, however, the evils so notorious
under free competition reasserted themselves in the pools.
Mutual distrust, the bad faith of some companies, the
eagerness of all to increase their allotments in future
arrangements, the brief duration of the agreements—
such factors as these combined to render the pools inef-
fective. As the public saw it, the device, which had
been adopted to remedy the evil of unregulated competition, was as bad as the evil itself.

No recital of benefits, no emphasis on attempts at
self-correction, no insistence on the economic value of
the roads quieted the popular distrust. What people most
feared was the growing division of the United States
into transportation satrapies, ruled by men of force,
daring and a passion for order, who believed the suc-

[1] Senate Select Committee on Interstate Commerce, *Report* (Wash.,
1886), 180-181.
[2] E. R. Johnson and T. W. Van Metre, *Principles of Railroad Transportation* (N. Y., 1916), 294-303.

cess of their plans was so important for the country as to justify a disregard of all law and rules of fair dealing, or who were greedy for wealth regardless of human cost. Yet there were sound reasons for these consolidations besides the sinister ones the public harbored. Economy and convenience made them inevitable, a logical response to popular demand as well as to considerations of profit and power. In many instances, absorption was the only means of keeping alive short roads which were dying of traffic starvation. The mine or oil field or industry on which they depended had become exhausted, or a more economical route with wider connections had invaded the territory. Consolidation, however, usually took the form of raids ending in capture. The sharp warfare attracted the attention of the public, while the slower process of economic development went unnoticed.

An orgy of speculation in rail securities raged in the early eighties, induced by the return of prosperity after the six years of dark depression following the Panic of 1873. An important, if temporary, factor in the return of good times was a crop failure in Europe in 1879, which caused forty per cent of the American wheat output to be exported at higher prices than had been known in many years.[1] The immediate effect of the boom in foodstuffs was to increase the acreage put into cereal crops and to lengthen the mileage of railroads to carry them. Industry recovered along with agriculture. For the first time since the Civil War the United States resumed specie payment.[2] Europe was again eager to invest in American securities. The market was flooded with money.[3]

[1] D. A. Wells, *Recent Economic Changes* (N. Y., 1889), 6-8.
[2] See Nevins, *Emergence of Modern America*, 305.
[3] Between July 1 and November 15, 1879, the favorable balance of trade paid in gold amounted to $59,000,000. J. D. Richardson, comp., *A Compilation of the Messages and Papers of the Presidents* (Wash., 1896-1899), VII, 558.

The favorite investment was rails, and the promoters obliged the investing and speculating public with a spate of issues.   In 1880 over seven thousand miles of railway were built, about equal to the excited building of 1871 which had hastened the Panic of 1873.   In 1881 nearly ten thousand miles were added, and in 1882 over eleven thousand five hundred.   A well-informed contemporary student of railroads declared in 1884 that this new mileage had not cost over thirty thousand dollars a mile, but that it was capitalized at seventy thousand.[1] One feature of the dizzy financing was the payment of huge stock returns.   In 1880 the Louisville Nashville and the Chicago & Rock Island railroads each declared hundred-per-cent dividends.   All told, the rail corporations in this single year distributed to their shareholders something like forty million dollars.

Some there were who warned that this state of affairs could not last.   They remembered the fevers of ten years before and the long convalescence that followed.   Certain capitalists began to put their money into trust companies.   It was noted, too, that Americans, not foreigners, were active in the market now.   But the mass of professional and amateur speculators would not heed the increasing signs of impending disaster.   In 1883 the crops were not so good, and the country was ravaged by rate wars in East, West and South.   The New York Central and the West Shore cut passenger charges to a cent a mile.   The war extended to the Pennsylvania, the Erie, the Delaware & Lackawanna and the Baltimore & Ohio.   As earnings sharply declined, dividends began to be cut.

Rapidly through 1884 the wind came out of the inflated structure.   Europe commenced to call back gold.

---

[1] Frank Parsons, *The Railways, the Trusts, and the People* (C. F. Taylor, ed., *Equity Series;* Phila., 1906), pt. i, 109, quoting *Poor's Manual for 1884.*

In early April the price of wheat fell, bringing on a panic in Chicago. A prominent Wall Street speculator, James R. Keene, was caught in the market and crashed. In May came the disastrous failure of Grant and Ward. The nation was shocked less by the financial irresponsibility of Ward than by the appalling proof that a man of the inestimable services and undoubted honesty of ex-President Grant could be used for the purposes of conscienceless speculators. "The failure," said the *Nation,* "is the most colossal that ever took place among merely private firms in the United States and one of the most disgraceful." [1] This event was followed closely by a defalcation of some three million dollars by John C. Eno, president of the Second National Bank of New York. Money lost in Wall Street speculations was the explanation. Though the loss was made good, it took more than this to overcome the shock to confidence. Wild rumors filled the air. A run closed the doors of the Metropolitan Bank whose president, George I. Seney, was deep in railroad speculation. Then began one of those mad stock-exchange stampedes that leave so many casualties. Stock firm after stock firm, bank after bank, shut down. Bank failures, which had fallen from 10,478 in 1878 to 4735 in 1880, rose to 10,968 in 1884. [2]

Meantime exports declined. America had sold a bill of about $686,000,000 worth of agricultural products in 1880; it amounted to less than $536,000,000 in 1884 and fell to $485,000,000 in 1886. [3] By the end of 1884 it was already clear to the country that its suddenly gained prosperity was shattered, notably in the case of railroad values. No better proof of the recklessness of railroad financing and management ex-

[1] Editorial, *Nation,* XXXVIII, 415, 455 (May 15, 29, 1884).
[2] U. S. Commissioner of Labor, *First Annual Report* (1886), 67.
[3] U. S. Industrial Commission, *Report* (Wash., 1900-1902), XIX, 188.

isted than the fact that in 1886 one hundred and eight roads with a trackage of eleven thousand miles were in the hands of receivers.   It was to be long before values touched the levels of 1881 again.   The quotations of twenty-eight rail stocks which, averaging seventy-three in 1878, had risen to one hundred and fourteen in 1880-1881 and to one hundred and sixteen in 1881-1882, dropped in 1884-1885 to seventy-five.   Although in five of the next thirteen years they averaged around one hundred, it was not until 1898-1899 that they were back where they had stood in 1881-1882.[1]

The depression of 1884-1885 heightened the popular resentment which had long been gathering against the railroads and their practices.   For some years the separate states had tried various methods of dealing with the problem.   The favorite expedient in the Middle West had been to pass laws setting up official commissions with authority to fix rates, but such legislation was often hastily framed and proved disappointing in practice.[2]   Massachusetts had preferred to endow its commission merely with investigative powers and the authority to give publicity to its findings.   It depended upon the force of public opinion to correct abuses.   By 1880 some fourteen states had adopted the Massachusetts plan, though some of them only after a long fight.

In the case of Peik v. the Chicago & Northwestern Railway the United States Supreme Court had gone so far as to hold that, until Congress took steps to regulate interstate commerce, a state commission possessing mandatory powers might fix rates on shipments passing beyond state limits.[3]   But even in such states difficulties arose as regards rail corporations chartered in other commonwealths.   The state courts had little or no control

[1] U. S. Industrial Commission, *Report*, XIX, 29.
[2] Nevins, *Emergence of Modern America*, 168-169, 371-372.
[3] A decision in 1876, 94 *U. S. Reports*, 164.

over them.   "They come into a State," James B.
Weaver of Iowa complained in Congress in 1880,

> for the purpose of making money, carrying on trans-
> actions with citizens of the State, and why should they
> not be compelled to go into the State courts, there to
> adjudicate matters arising between themselves and citi-
> zens of the State?   They are citizens of the State for
> all other practical purposes; but, when a controversy
> arises under the law as it now stands, the corporation
> has only to go into the State court and there set forth
> the fact that it is a foreign corporation, organized under
> the law of Massachusetts or of some other State, and
> the cause is removed to the Federal court.[1]

Each year it became more obvious that the question
must be nationalized, that it was too complicated for
state handling.   Jealous as the states were of their pre-
rogatives, some of them began to turn to the federal
government.   Thus in 1880 the Mississippi legislature
begged Congress to "provide, by appropriate legislation,
some adequate means of . . . regulating the tariff and
freight rates on all railroads and navigable streams in
the United States."[2]   Discussion of the question in committees and on the floor of Congress took more and more
time and showed both reluctance and confusion.   To
some members such as Judge J. H. Reagan of Texas the
solution seemed simple.   Reagan fathered a bill to forbid
certain practices which any right-minded person could
not but agree were unfair—such were rebates, drawbacks, pooling—and to order equal rates and opportunities.   Enforcement of the law was to be in the hands
of the courts instead of a special commission.   The bill
passed the House in 1878, but it died in the Senate.[3]

[1] *Appletons' Annual Cyclopædia*, n.s., V (1880), 140-141.
[2] *Appletons' Annual Cyclopædia*, n.s., V, 528.
[3] L. H. Haney, *A Congressional History of Railways in the United States, 1850-1887* (Univ. of Wis., *Bull.*, no. 342), 288-290.

Five years later the principle of federal regulation was strongly urged upon Congress by Chester A. Arthur. He was the first President of the United States after the Civil War to challenge the absolute power that individuals and corporations were exercising in society and to assert boldly that Congress could not tolerate such abuses:

> While we can not fail to recognize the importance of the vast railway systems of the country and their great and beneficent influences upon the development of our material wealth, we should, on the other hand, remember that no individual and no corporation ought to be invested with absolute power over the interest of any other citizen or class of citizens.   The right of these railway corporations to a fair and profitable return upon their investments and to reasonable freedom in their regulations must be recognized; but it seems only just that, so far as its constitutional authority will permit, Congress should protect the people at large in their interstate traffic against acts of injustice which the State governments are powerless to prevent.[1]

The sentiment remained strong among some members, however, that it was best to allow the states and the railroads to control their own affairs and that Congress should keep hands off.[2]   This, of course, was the view of the railroad "experts and officials" who, as Reagan complained, thronged the committee rooms and corridors and often appeared on the floor of the House with their attorneys, "the ablest in the United States, all of them paid out of the people's money . . . ."[3]   But the same conviction was shared by not a few of the economists of the day.   So thorough a student of the railroad

[1] Message of December 4, 1883, Richardson, comp., *Messages and Papers*, VIII, 185.

[2] *Appletons' Annual Cyclopædia*, n.s., V, 184.

[3] *Appletons' Annual Cyclopædia*, n.s., X (1885), 210.

and its relation to social well-being as Edward Atkinson considered federal regulation a futile attempt to overcome hardships which "can only be remedied by the slow progress of events," not by "meddlesome statutes." [1]

Though the desire for regulation steadily increased in Congress, definite action was held up by differences of opinion as to ways and means. Thus in 1885 the Senate and the House each passed a bill, but the two branches could not agree upon a common measure. Two events in 1886, however, brought matters to a head. One was the scorching condemnation of railway abuses made by the Senate committee of which Shelby M. Cullom of Illinois was chairman. [2] The other was a decision of the Supreme Court which, reversing its view in the Peik case, forbade individual states to fix rates on shipments passing beyond their borders. [3] By declaring unconstitutional state regulation of interstate commerce, the Wabash decision made federal regulation imperative.

On February 4, 1887, after fifteen years of discussion, the interstate-commerce law was enacted by a vote in the Senate of 43 to 15, in the House of 219 to 41. [4] The act, modeled in part on an English statute of 1854, forbade discriminations and the pooling of traffic, made it illegal to charge more for a short haul than for a long haul over the same line "under substantially similar circumstances and conditions," provided for a uniform system of railway accounting and required the roads to file their tariffs for public inspection. Oversight of these regulations was placed in a commission of five members, none of whom could be taken from the ranks of railroad men or own rail securities. This body, however, could not fix traffic rates or enforce its own decisions; nor did

[1] *Appletons' Annual Cyclopædia*, n.s., IX (1884), 686.
[2] See earlier, 92-93.
[3] Wabash, St. Louis and Pacific Railway Company *v.* Illinois, 118 *U. S. Reports*, 557.
[4] Haney, *Congressional History of Railways*, 292-310.

its powers cover transportation wholly within one state. The commission could order a violator to desist from illegal acts and levy a fine of five thousand dollars; but if the carrier declined to obey, the commission could enforce obedience only through equity proceedings in the federal courts.[1]

On the whole, the measure was fairly well received. Everybody but railroad managers welcomed the publication of tariffs and a uniform system of accounting. The clause on the short and long haul excited criticism from those who thought it meant always charging equal mileage regardless of conditions: "one hundred times as much for one thousand miles as for ten miles." *Harper's Weekly* reported an "earnest uprising" of business men in Cincinnati against "a provision which the Interstate Commerce Bill does not contain, and which no railway reformer ever committed the absurdity of proposing."[2] The chief protest from business and railway interests, however, centered on the pooling clause. On the other hand, those towns and individuals which had suffered from the discrimination of pools rejoiced. The *Chicago Tribune* felt that the pool managers were only getting what they deserved, so "odious" had been their "discriminations in favor of individuals and places."[3]

The severest complaint of the public was the failure to put teeth into the law. The necessity of appealing to the courts to compel obedience to the commission's orders involved a process too slow to satisfy harassed shippers and towns which saw their neighbors prospering while they were dying. "It is the shadow and not the substance of governmental control," cried the *Chicago Herald*; but it conceded: "it is a step in the right

[1] *U. S. Statutes at Large*, XXIV, 379-387.

[2] J. F. Hudson, "The Inter-State Commerce Bill," *Harper's Wkly.*, XXXI, 42 (Jan. 15, 1887).

[3] Digest of newspaper comment on interstate-commerce bill in *Public Opinion*, II, 251 (Jan. 8, 1887).

direction." In a similar spirit the *Cincinnati Commercial-Gazette* and the *New York Evening World* acclaimed the statute as "the beginning of a National railroad policy." The *New York Evening Post* hailed it as the most important piece of legislation since the resumption of specie payment. Even the *New York Sun,* which deplored such "an extraordinary measure of paternal government," predicted: "A good deal of rascality will disappear with secret rates and rate cutting; much money which now goes to pool commissioners and clerks will be saved." [1]

Obviously the success of the new law depended on the make-up of the commission which should administer it. One objection urged by those who opposed regulation by a commission—Reagan of Texas was the most outspoken—was that men free from the influence of rail corporations could never be found. Another was that, if they could be found, they would prove too ignorant of railway management to handle the problems which everybody had now come to recognize as extraordinarily complex. The appointments which President Cleveland made, however, disarmed such criticisms. At the head of the commission he placed Thomas M. Cooley, a distinguished lawyer, a Republican with twenty-one years' service on the Michigan supreme court and a man who had had experience as receiver for a large railroad system. Following Cooley in order of naming were William R. Morrison, an Illinois Democrat and tariff reformer, whose eight terms in Congress had covered the entire period of railway agitation; Judge Augustus Schoonmaker, a New York Democrat known to Cleveland as a civil-service reformer; Aldace F. Walker of Vermont, a Republican who had fathered the Vermont railroad commission and had been at close quarters with a corrupt railroad ring in New England; and Walter L.

[1] Digest of newspaper comment in *Public Opinion,* II, 250-251.

Bragg, a Democrat who was chairman of the radical railway commission of Alabama.

The appointments were well received—"very respectable citizens," said the *New York Sun*. The *New York Evening Post* declared Cleveland's critics "only break silence to applaud." [1] Some criticism was offered, however, because no trans-Mississippi representative had been named. "Mr. Cleveland ought to study geography before he appoints another Commission," it was suggested. But the fact that he had emphasized competence for the duties of the office above sectional considerations won for the commission at the outset a large measure of public confidence.

At last the rail transportation of the country was to be dealt with as a national problem. At last the government of the United States had decided no longer to allow the roads to exploit the people in the name of "progress." But the work of applying the law was like cutting a path through a jungle, so complicated were many of the cases which flooded the new body. Based as most of them were on some form of privilege which benefited one group or locality at the expense of another, the practices had been so long in existence that disturbing them was deemed an invasion of rights. Moreover, there was the greatest difficulty in getting all the facts, in understanding their relations when collected, in deciding whether or no the shipping was conducted "under substantially similar circumstances and conditions." Sometimes the commission faced the dilemma of doing actual harm by applying what was the plain meaning of the law. Untangling established customs, even when they were obviously unjust, necessitated a long train of readjustments too complex for prompt action.

When a decision was made, it might be years before

[1] Digest of newspaper comment in *Public Opinion*, II, 537, 539 (April 2, 1887).

it was enforced. Thus in 1888 the independent shippers from the oil regions of Pennsylvania to the seaboard complained to the commission that the rate on transporting oil in barrels had suddenly been increased from fifty-two cents to sixty-six. This violated the practice of charging the same rate whether the oil was carried in barrels or tank cars. The new rate had obviously been forced on the railroads by the Standard Oil Company in order further to embarrass the independents. The hearings occurred in May, 1889, but the commission delayed its decision until December, 1892, much to the dissatisfaction of the independent oil men. One complaint against the commission from the beginning had been that it moved too deliberately. Yet it is difficult to see how it could have hurried, considering the intricacies and the number of the novel problems heaped upon its shoulders. The decision in the oil case, when it came, pleased the complainants. The railroads were required to make the rates equal whether the oil went in barrels or tanks, and to furnish tanks if shippers gave reasonable notice. Two years later the commission ordered the payment of nearly one hundred thousand dollars to the injured shippers. The railroads refused to recognize the obligation and took the matter into the courts. Long after the end of the century the shippers were still trying to collect the damages.[1]

From the time the commission was established it faced increasing resistance to the discharge of its functions.[2] The old evils reappeared in a new guise. Rebates and special concessions were hidden by deceitful methods of accounting. Though pooling was not resorted to, railroads attained much the same result through traffic associations, which regulated charges and punished diso-

[1] Ida M. Tarbell, *The History of the Standard Oil Company* (N. Y., 1904), II, 281-282.

[2] Johnson and Van Metre, *Principles of Railroad Transportation*, 499-508.

ROSWELL MILLER, PRESIDENT OF THE CHICAGO,
MILWAUKEE, AND ST. PAUL RAILROAD.

JOHN M. EGAN, PRESIDENT OF THE CHICAGO,
ST. PAUL, AND KANSAS CITY RAILROAD.

JAY GOULD,
P

GEORGE COPPELL, CHAIRMAN OF THE BOARD OF
DIRECTORS OF THE DENVER AND RIO GRANDE
RAILROAD.

SIDNEY DILLON, PRESIDENT OF THE UNION
PACIFIC RAILROAD.

J. PIERPONT
MO

THOMAS F. OAKES, PRESIDENT OF THE
NORTHERN PACIFIC RAILROAD.

GEORGE C. MAGOUN, CHAIRMAN OF THE BOARD
OF DIRECTORS OF THE ATCHISON, TOPEKA,
AND SANTA FE RAILROAD.

HENRY VILL
DIRECTOR

Railway Presidents and Other Participants in the Conference at th

MISSOURI   A. B. STICKNEY, CHAIRMAN OF THE BOARD OF DIRECTORS OF THE CHICAGO, ST. PAUL, AND KANSAS CITY RAILROAD.   ALLEN MANVEL, PRESIDENT OF THE ATCHISON TOPEKA, AND SANTA FE RAILROAD.

L,   RUSSELL SAGE, PRESIDENT OF THE IOWA CENTRAL RAILROAD.   WILLIAM J. PALMER, PRESIDENT OF THE DENVER AND RIO GRANDE WESTERN RAILROAD.

E BOARD OF
PACIFIC   C. P. HUNTINGTON, PRESIDENT OF THE SOUTHERN PACIFIC RAILROAD.   JAMES J. HILL, PRESIDENT OF THE GREAT NORTHERN RAILROAD.

. Pierpont Morgan in New York City on December 15, 1890

bedient members.   Not until 1897 was it possible to secure a decision from the Supreme Court that such associations were illegal, and then the decision was based on the provisions of the Sherman antitrust law of 1890, not on the interstate-commerce act.[1]

The powers of the commission were constantly in dispute, and were often rendered worthless by court decisions.   Though the interstate-commerce law itself apparently affirmed that the commission's findings of fact must be accepted by the court as "prima facie evidence as to each and every fact found," the federal courts would not issue decrees without permitting a retrial of the merits of the case.   To no effect, the commission insisted that controversies about rates were questions of fact and not of law, to be determined by specialists rather than by the courts, and that the latter should simply decide whether the proper legal forms had been observed.   Time and again the court overruled the decisions of the commission, steadily reducing its effectiveness.   Meanwhile the railroads failed to remain at peace with one another.   Many persons, forgetful of the cutthroat competition of the years before 1887, argued that the antipooling clause was to blame by placing the railroads at the mercy of the most ruthless companies.

Thus the practical workings of the interstate-commerce act fell far short of the expectations of its friends. Yet decided gains had been made.[2]   The right of federal regulation, long disputed, was established in law; the principle of publicity was kept alive; and a somewhat better adjustment of transportation charges was secured. Most significant of all, experience under the law indicated clearly the changes which should be made to secure

[1] U. S. *v.* Trans-Missouri Freight Association, 166 *U. S. Reports*, 290.
[2] Johnson and Van Metre, *Principles of Railroad Transportation*, 508-509.

effective regulation. This was an important legacy left by this generation to the next.[1]

The dust and smoke of battle excited by rail abuses and the contest over regulation should not be allowed to obscure the constructive services which the roads were quietly performing. It was not difficult for congressmen who believed the government should let the railroads alone to grow dithyrambic over their achievements. Since the close of the Civil War they had helped bind together a country which, without them and their ally, the telegraph, would have remained a collection of practically isolated units. The mileage grew from approximately 93,000 in 1880 to over 163,500 in 1890. Within the single decade as extensive a trackage was laid as the three leading countries of Europe had constructed in fifty years.[2] Though by 1890 the most urgent needs had been met, the total mileage was brought to over 193,000 by 1900.

Improvements in service went along with increased mileage. In 1882 freight rates stood at 1.24 cents a ton per mile, half of what they had been ten years before. By 1890 they had fallen to ninety-three hundredths of a cent and by 1898 to seventy-six hundredths.[3] The substitution of steel for iron rails went on apace. In 1880 only about three tenths of the roads were so equipped, ten years later close to eight tenths.[4] With more durable rails came heavier locomotives. From a weight of 102,000 pounds in 1881 they grew to 230,000 by the close of the century.[5] A brilliant example of improved locomotive was Number 999,

[1] See H. U. Faulkner, *The Quest for Social Justice* (*A History of American Life*, XI), 116.

[2] Johnson and Van Metre, *Principles of Railroad Transportation*, 26, 31-32.

[3] U. S. Bureau of Statistics, *Statistical Record of the Progress of the United States, 1800-1906* (Wash., 1906), 33.

[4] U. S. Industrial Commission, *Report*, XIX, 291.

[5] U. S. Industrial Commission, *Report*, XIX, 292.

placed in service in 1893 by the New York Central. It celebrated its debut by making a world's record of one hundred and twenty-two and a half miles an hour.[1] Freight cars also grew in size and stability; tracks became more solid; bridges were made stronger. Through the widespread adoption of George Westinghouse's automatic air brake and other safety appliances the railroads sought valiantly to reduce the hazards of travel. Nevertheless between 1891 and 1895 the annual average of casualties was over six thousand killed and more than thirty-five thousand injured.

The spread of the railroad to all parts of the country had been attended by a decline of water transportation. In the Mississippi Valley the rivalry between river and rail had been most dramatic and expensive. But, in spite of the long resistance, the river had been bridged in the 1870's and was soon paralleled on both sides by railroads which carried freight not only more rapidly but more reasonably. Between 1880 and 1900 the freight shipped from St. Louis by water fell from a million tons to two hundred and forty-five thousand.[2] Traffic by way of the Erie Canal, once the chief carrier between the seaboard and the Middle West, suffered a similar decline. Of the tonnage carried by rail and canal in New York state, the canals alone in 1878 handled over twenty-seven per cent, but by 1885 only about seventeen and by 1895 less than ten. This decline occurred in spite of the fact that the rate by lake and canal from Chicago to New York was considerably lower than that by lake and rail or by rail alone.[3]

The steady eclipse of inland water traffic was due in

[1] No. 999 is carefully preserved and still shown at expositions and fairs along the route of the New York Central.

[2] U. S. Industrial Commission, *Report*, XIX, 435.

[3] The water rate on wheat, for instance, in 1878 was 9.15 cents; by all rail it was 17.70. In 1885 it was 5.87 cents by water and 14.00 by rail; and in 1895, 4.11 cents by water and 12.17 by rail. Bureau of Statistics, *Statistical Record of Progress of United States*, 34.

part to the persistent hostility of rail lines to carriage by river, canal or lake. However bitterly they might fight one another, they joined forces to resist water transportation.[1] In the case of the Erie Canal the New York Central let it be known that it would sever connections with any road accepting freight from the waterway—a policy which cut New England off from benefits which she might otherwise have enjoyed.[2] The legitimate advantages of transportation by rail, however, dealt the greatest blow to water routes. A railroad was not only swifter, but it gave a wider distribution. It could go into parts of the country otherwise inaccessible; it was simple to run a rail to a new wheat area, a new mine, a new oil well. Loading and unloading freight was much easier and less expensive from a car than from a boat. Transfer from rail to rail was easier than transfer from boat to boat. No longer was it necessary for a town to plant itself on a river bank, a lake front or an ocean harbor. Growing cities like Denver and Indianapolis proved that a railroad center was as advantageous as a water site.

Nature itself was against the river as a steady traffic bearer. Ice blocked the Mississippi to navigation for a considerable part of the year in the important reaches of the North. St. Paul had to allow for a closed season of four months during which the river men sat idle. Few of them like that young clerk on the wharves, "Jim" Hill, used their enforced leisure to store up information, particularly about anything that might help the development of the newly opened country.[3] And if it was not ice, it might be floods, or the water might be

---

[1] W. Z. Ripley, ed., *Railway Problems* (Boston, 1907), 313.

[2] Senate Select Committee on Interstate Commerce, *Report* (*Testimony*) (Wash., 1886), 367.

[3] J. G. Pyle, *The Life of James J. Hill* (Garden City, 1917), I, chap. ii. See also earlier, 21.

too low for navigation and boats be tied up, capital rotting away.

Water transportation suffered also because of the failure to improve its methods, its equipment and its connections. If the water companies had been as energetic and resourceful as the railway companies, the story might have been different. There was little excuse for damp and dirty pits on lake and canal boats, which resulted in injury to wheat cargoes. Similarly, inadequate storage at receiving points often exposed freight to the mercy of rain and thieves. A federal commission, appointed to study the reasons for the decline of water traffic, compared this lack of enterprise with the situation in Germany where a number of cities had made a larger investment for terminals and for the storage of freight and the handling of boats than in the whole of the Mississippi River above New Orleans.[1]

Only in the carriage of heavy nonperishable goods was water transportation able to hold its own. Timber, which was being cut so lavishly in Wisconsin and Minnesota, could be conveyed most profitably by river. This was a great and growing business. In 1880 over two hundred million feet were cut in the region of the St. Croix; ten years later the cutting was more than four hundred and fifty million. In the upper Mississippi region, above St. Anthony's Falls, the logging from 1881 to 1890 amounted to three and a half billion.[2] Practically all this timber was cut in the winter, hauled to a logging point on the stream and lashed into rafts which, before the end of the century, were towed down the river by steamboats. A raft three hundred feet long was a good bulk in 1880, but before many

[1] National Waterways Commission, *Final Report* (Wash., 1912), 66-74.
[2] C. E. Russell, *A-Rafting on the Mississippi* (N. Y., 1928), 336-337.

years they had grown four or five times as long with a width of two hundred or more feet. If ever a great natural resource was put to a good use it was this lumber. It was replacing sod houses on the plains of Nebraska and building cribs for corn, shelters for animals, stores for trading and schools and churches throughout the Middle West.

Coal was another commodity which lent itself to water transport. When coal could be carried two thousand miles from Pittsburgh to New Orleans at a dollar a ton, the rivers got the freight unless it was a rush order. Likewise the Great Lakes, though losing wheat to the railroads, gained as carriers of coal and also of ore. This was made possible by the opening in September, 1881, of a new lock in the St. Mary's Canal, one five hundred and fifteen feet long and eighty feet wide, which accommodated ships of sixteen-feet draft. The old locks, which had been but three hundred and fifty feet long and seventy wide, had taken care of vessels which drew only twelve feet or less of water. It was the inauguration of one of the most important commercial highways of the country, for it gave the Lake Superior iron and copper regions readier access to the world.[1] Five years after it was opened more tonnage was passing through the St. Mary's Canal than through the Suez Canal. The United States government at once began work upon deepening and widening the channel.[2]

The success of the St. Mary's Canal led to discussion of similar waterways in other parts of the country. There was talk of a canal across Cape Cod, of one connecting the Hudson with the East River, of another from Lake Huron to Lake Ontario. But the plan which

[1] S. L. Goodale, comp., *Chronology of Iron and Steel* (J. R. Speer, ed., Pittsburgh, 1920), 199.
[2] Goodale, comp., *Chronology of Iron and Steel*, 208.

seemed in 1884 the nearest to realization was a route across Nicaragua in Central America. Here there were already sixty miles of navigable river and a lake forty miles long. A treaty with Nicaragua authorizing the United States to undertake the necessary construction was announced to Congress by President Arthur on December 1, 1884. The "rich territory on the Pacific," he said in his message, "is for the ordinary purposes of commerce practically cut off from communication by water with the Atlantic ports, the political and commercial advantages of such a project can scarcely be overestimated." [1]   The government's interest in the project had undoubtedly been stimulated by the fact that five years before a French company, headed by Ferdinand de Lesseps, builder of the Suez Canal, had obtained the right to dig a waterway across the Isthmus of Panama.[2] To the average business man, however, an interoceanic route meant simply a check on the transcontinental rates charged by the railroads.

When President Cleveland entered office a few months after Arthur submitted the treaty, he promptly withdrew it from the Senate. "Maintaining, as I do," he declared, "the tenets of a line of precedents from Washington's day, which proscribe entangling alliances with foreign states, I do not favor the acquisition of new and distant territory or the incorporation of remote interests with our own." [3]   Nevertheless Congress on February 20, 1889, was induced to charter a private company to undertake the project. The Maritime Canal Company, as it was called, began excavation at Greytown on the Atlantic side in 1890, but it was forced to sus-

[1] Richardson, comp., *Messages and Papers*, VIII, 238.
[2] J. B. Henderson, jr., *American Diplomatic Questions* (N. Y., 1901), 73-75.
[3] Message of December 8, 1885, Richardson, comp., *Messages and Papers*, VIII, 327.

pend operations three years later by the Panic of 1893.[1]
Meantime the de Lesseps enterprise had also met disaster.
The ultimate accomplishment of an isthmian canal had
to await the early years of the new century.[2]

[1] Henderson, *American Diplomatic Questions*, 75-80.
[2] See Faulkner, *Quest for Social Justice*, 147-148.

CHAPTER VII

CLASHING ECONOMIC PHILOSOPHIES

THE vast and, for the most part, unregulated economic development led to the production of great private fortunes such as America had never before known. In 1892 the *New York Tribune* and the *New York World* undertook separately to show just how many millionaires there were in the country.[1] The *Tribune* found 4047, the *World* 3045. The largest number in each list derived their wealth from trade and transportation. The *Tribune* listed 1752 under this heading. Merchandising accounted for 986; banking for 294; railroads for 186; brokerage for 56; local utilities for 35; telegraphs and telephones for 12. In agriculture there were but 84, and over half of these were cattle raisers in the West. No millionaire husbandman was listed. There were, besides, 65 millionaire lawyers, "presumably corporation lawyers," commented the *Tribune*. "But of course they have invested in real estate and securities, that is, have been speculators." Included in the list were odd but understandable fortunes: three made in the circus business, and one in the Tweed Ring in New York City.

These huge accumulations had come about under the system of *laissez-faire* or unlimited competition. As James Bryce pointed out in his luminous commentary on the national scene, one of the dogmas of the American was "his right to the enjoyment of what he has

[1] G. P. Watkins, *The Growth of Large Fortunes* (Am. Econ. Assoc., *Publs.*, ser. 3, VIII, no. 4), 141-147. See also A. M. Schlesinger, *The Rise of the City* (*A History of American Life*, X), 218-219.

earned." [1] This attitude was a natural outgrowth of
the earlier conditions of pioneer life with its abundance
of opportunities for every man. In the irrepressible
spirit of frontier individualism such men as Andrew
Carnegie found the secret of American success—the rule
that the prize should fall "to the freest and therefore to
the best man." Luck, said Carnegie, played a negligible
part:

> "What men call luck,
> Is the prerogative of valiant souls." [2]

Yet nearly every year saw fresh challenges to the
inherited dogma. From Germany, shortly after the
Civil War, had come Marxian socialism, finding its supporters in Northern industrial centers among persons of
German origin.[3] The doctrine in its American version
proposed to abolish the right of private property in the
more essential branches of production, distribution and
transportation and to substitute therefor a system of
public ownership with economic self-government. This
meant no more private ownership of gold and silver
mines, of oil or coal; no more railroad satrapies; no
more Carnegies, Rockefellers, Hills or Goulds. It meant
the direction of the nation's resources by those who were
willing to give their best, not for private gain but for
the public welfare.

In 1877 the various local socialist groups joined together to form a national organization under the name,
the Socialist Labor party of North America. For fifteen

---

[1] James Bryce, *The American Commonwealth* (London, 1888), II,
404.

[2] Andrew Carnegie, *Triumphant Democracy* (N. Y., 1886), 211, 239.
Though objecting to governmental "interference," business men saw no
inconsistency in demanding governmental help in the form of tariffs and
the like.

[3] See Allan Nevins, *The Emergence of Modern America* (*A History of
American Life*, VIII), 382-383.

years this body led an obscure and precarious existence.[1]
It was handicapped by a membership largely immigrant
in character. Devoting itself to propaganda, it employed a terminology unfamiliar to American ears. Not
until 1892 did it nominate a presidential ticket and then
only in six states. It polled 21,500 votes in 1892,
36,000 in 1896 and 82,000 in the congressional elections of 1898.[2] By this time it had discovered a militant leader in the person of Daniel De Leon, a West
Indian Jew, but his efforts to gain the support of the
powerful organized-labor bodies of the time came to
naught.

What the ordinary unhappy and ignorant person
culled from socialism was a vague scheme for dividing
the country's wealth. What would happen when it
was divided few of them went so far as to speculate.
At all events, it would tone down the fortunes of the
immensely rich. The answer of the *laissez-faire* school
was in figures. Suppose that the 4047 millionaires averaged three million apiece, there would be $12,141,-
000,000 to divide. Divide this sum by 62,979,766,
the number of inhabitants in 1890, and about $192
would be left to hand out to each. This was not income, but capital—money invested in cotton raising,
grain elevators, packing and provisions, oil producing,
lumber—which otherwise would provide employment
and produce more wealth.

E. L. Godkin, editor of the *Nation*, discussed the
question in the *Forum* in June, 1894, from yet another
angle. "The notion," he said, "that there is a reservoir
of wealth somewhere, either in the possession of the
Government or the rich, which might be made to diffuse
'plenty through a smiling land' . . . is probably the

---

[1] Morris Hillquit, *History of Socialism in the United States* (N. Y.,
1903), pt. ii, chap. iii.
[2] Hillquit, *History of Socialism*, 283-284.

most mischievous delusion which has ever taken hold on the popular mind."[1] Noting that the census of 1890 had estimated the total national wealth at somewhat over sixty-five billion dollars, he continued:

> Evenly divided, this would give $1,039 per caput, or a little more than $5,000 per family. . . . If the laborer spent his $5,000 at once in making himself comfortable, he would . . . be plunged at once into a very hopeless kind of poverty. But suppose he invested it; it would not yield him over, say, six per cent at present rates of interest. This would make his income $300 a year, or about $6 a week. It is evident that he could on this make no material change in his style of living.[2]

No well-posted socialist, however, would have acknowledged paternity of such crude ideas. Nor was the socialist program the most radical one with which this generation was confronted. To the left of socialism stood anarchism. Anarchism proposed to abolish both capitalism and the political state. In their stead it offered a system of loosely federated voluntary groups, each owning its means of production, living as it willed and exchanging its products with societies similarly constituted. Though the main impulse to anarchism came from European thinkers, and though its five or six thousand adherents in the United States were mostly of German immigrant stock, the development of the philosophy owed something also to the writings of Americans, notably Josiah Warren (who died in 1874) and his able disciple, Benjamin R. Tucker.[3]

Even less than socialism did anarchism interest the American public. Other things aside, it greatly restricted

---

[1] "Who Will Pay the Bills of Socialism?" reprinted in E. L. Godkin, *Problems of Modern Democracy* (N. Y., 1896), 237-238.

[2] Godkin, *Problems of Modern Democracy*, 235-236.

[3] Eunice M. Schuster, *Native American Anarchism* (Smith College, Studies, XVII), 93-105, 138-143.

its appeal because of the terroristic methods which most of its leaders espoused. A convention of delegates from twenty-six states at Pittsburgh in October, 1883, declared the object of the movement to be "the destruction of the existing class government by all means, *i.e.*, by energetic, implacable, revolutionary and international action."[1] Messages of encouragement were received from anarchistic groups in England, France, Holland, Italy, Spain and Mexico. The occasion first brought into prominence such figures as Johann Most, August Spies and R. A. Parsons. Whatever chances the cause had of winning new converts were shattered by the outburst of public rage three years later when Chicago anarchists were popularly blamed for the killing of policemen and bystanders in the Haymarket riot.[2]

If imported panaceas made little dent on the average American mind, the case was different with panaceas of domestic origin. It was in the eighties that Edward Bellamy and a host of other novelists began to dazzle the public with romances based on the coming of an ideal society.[3] People looking at conditions about them could see the evil results of the all-pervading industrialism; some of them were ready to believe that Bellamy and his kind had found a practicable way out. The schemes portrayed by these writers, while differing from one another in points of detail, bore striking resemblance to socialism or communism. That these terms were never employed probably indicates the purely American background of their thinking.

Bellamy as he wrote his book became so entranced by the plausibility of *Looking Backward* (1888), and later so impressed by the popular acclaim it excited, that he proceeded to expound his views at greater length in a

[1] Hillquit, *History of Socialism*, 237-238.
[2] See later, 161-165.
[3] See Schlesinger, *Rise of the City*, 261-262.

second romance, *Equality,* published in 1897. In it he took particular pains to explain the system of civic training which was necessary to fit men and women to take part in a state in which all land and industry were socialized. Bellamy's perfect society educated the youth of the country during the first twenty-one years of their life. The next three years were given to various kinds of unskilled labor. This was the period in which they demonstrated their aptitudes, also in which the quality of their intelligence was tested. Then followed an apprenticeship in the particular trade, art or profession which had been chosen or assigned. At every stage there was strict grading. To the best men went the choicest positions—not choicest in "credits," as he called the annual income which each person received from the government, but choicest in opportunity to use talent, to do creative work or to win honors from the state. Bellamy was realist enough to know that the fallible human beings of his own day could not hope to operate so complex a social mechanism unless they were prepared for the task by an elaborate course of discipline and training.

The most original American solution for the ills of society was the one offered by Henry George in *Progress and Poverty: an Inquiry into the Cause of Industrial Depressions and of Increase of Want with Increase of Wealth.* In 1879, when he published this work, he was forty years old. Born in Philadelphia, he had shirked the conventional education which his father desired to give him and at seventeen had gone to sea. After a voyage of some fourteen months which took him to Melbourne and Calcutta, he returned to Philadelphia where he set out to learn the printing trade. But the call of the sea was too strong and soon he was sailing around South America on his way to San Francisco. Here for several years he led a somewhat erratic but

always industrious and observant life.[1] Perhaps if
George had been able to establish himself either as a
printer, gold miner or newspaper editor, all of which he
tried; in fine, if he had not failed in whatever he undertook, his mind would not have set itself so tenaciously
on the problem of the uneven distribution of wealth.
As it was, he was deeply and unfavorably impressed
with the orgy of land speculation which California was
experiencing and which tended to center great estates in
a few hands. In 1868, on a business trip to New York
City, he saw the problem in a different aspect and returned to California much struck by the "shocking contrast between monstrous wealth and debasing want" in
the nation's metropolis.

In *Progress and Poverty* George formulated the bold
conclusions to which his reflections had led him. He
challenged the generally accepted notion that capital was
the basic factor in creating wealth. When orthodox
economists are asked where capital comes from, he said,
they reply that it is the wealth piled up each year over
and above what is needed to keep the country going.
But where does wealth come from? He answered that
it is the fruit of labor applied to the land. God gave
man the land, but man has to use his hand and brain in
its cultivation before he can feed and clothe and shelter
himself. It is the partnership of the two, land and
labor, which produces wealth. Any surplus is called
capital, and this capital labor uses to increase wealth.
Instead of capital being necessary to labor, it is labor
which creates capital. Capital is a dead weight without
labor.[2]

How, George asked, has it come about that capital
now holds itself superior to labor? Is not the chief

---

[1] Henry George, jr., *The Life of Henry George* (N. Y., 1900), chaps.
i-vi.

[2] *Progress and Poverty* (N. Y., 1879), bk. i. As George used the
term, land included natural resources of the earth like minerals and timber.

reason that capital, seeing that land is necessary to labor, gains possession of the most advantageous sites? Capital holds these lands undeveloped for a rise in value. Labor, by opening adjacent territory, gives them the increasing value for which capital is waiting. When finally the lands are opened to development, capital reaps a profit out of all proportion to its contribution. This George called the "unearned increment." This capture of the land by capital has made labor dependent on capital. But since God has given the land to all, it cannot justly be alienated any more than air or sunshine.[1]

George's solution was to free the land, return it to the people as a whole. The mere limitation of land holdings would be of no avail, for land differs so widely in fertility and location that one tract will make its owner wealthy while another tract of equal size will barely earn its owner a living. Hence George proposed to tax land in such a manner as to do away with all advantages not due to the owner's exertions. This should be the one and only tax, the "single tax." The revenue yield, he contended, would be so great as to make all other taxes unnecessary. At the same time, the plan would make it unprofitable for owners to let real estate lie idle, tend to multiply the number of home owners and throw open abundant opportunities for the employment of labor.[2]

The only comfort that socialists and other opponents of the existing economic system got from George was his powerful arraignment of the effects of capitalism. "So long," he wrote, "as all the increased wealth which modern progress brings goes but to build up great fortunes, to increase luxury and make sharper the contrast between the House of Have and the House of Want,

[1] *Progress and Poverty*, bk. vii.
[2] *Progress and Poverty*, bks. viii-ix.

progress is not real and cannot be permanent. . . . The tower leans from its foundations, and every new story but hastens the final catastrophe." [1] But he did not agree that capitalism was doomed. He did not believe the world could operate to cure poverty and secure progress save through capitalism, and in the single tax capitalism possessed the panacea.[2] "So far from being a work of communistic tendencies," the *Nation* declared of *Progress and Poverty*, "the reader will find in it arguments to overthrow nearly all the communist theories of the present day." [3]

The book excited widespread attention both at home and abroad. George had launched his doctrine at a lucky moment, for the cry to return the land to the people was being heard in more than one country. "Land and liberty" was the slogan of the Nihilists of Russia. The demand for the nationalization of Irish lands was rocking Great Britain. In America he won disciples not only among the underprivileged but also among men of wealth and influence. Many of the latter took easily to a program which promised to relieve them of taxes on factories, personal property, imports and incomes.

Progress and Poverty, said the *New York Herald*,

is not merely the most original, the most striking and important contribution which political economy has yet received from America, but it is not too much to say that in these respects it has had no equal since the publication of "The Wealth of Nations," by Adam Smith, a century ago, or, at least, since Malthus formulated his theory of population and Ricardo his theory of rent.

---

[1] *Progress and Poverty* (edn. of 1882), 9.
[2] *Progress and Poverty*, bk. x, chaps. iv-v.
[3] This and the later press comments quoted are reprinted at the beginning of the tenth edition of *Progress and Poverty* (N. Y., 1882).

The *Methodist* declared the work so able that no one intending to speak or write on such a subject could afford to neglect it. The *Nation,* though condemning George's position as unsound, praised his spirit of candor and engaging literary style. In a more hostile tone the *Examiner and Chronicle* of New York called *Progress and Poverty* the most pernicious treatise on political economy that had been published in many a day, all the more pernicious because every page bore traces of learning and culture. It was left for Professor Goldwin Smith in the *Bystander* to stress a practical difficulty to the successful working of the single tax. After observing that George's remedy placed the entire land under the state, he pointed out that "the Government, into the hands of which the vast proceeds of the confiscation are to be put, is one which, in the case of the United States, the projector himself describes as a den of brigands."

Removing from San Francisco to New York in 1880, George devoted himself with apostolic zeal to the propagation of his cause. Early in the eighties he made speaking tours in Ireland on behalf of the Irish Land League and in England for the Land Reform Union, winning an immense following among wage-earners. Ramsay MacDonald, then a youth, has told of the effect *Progress and Poverty* made on his mind. There is no question but that the book helped to prepare the way for the later British Labor party. In a similar spirit American labor welcomed George as a champion. A contemporary student found thousands of workers, who had never before looked between the covers of a book on economics, reading *Progress and Poverty*.[1] Probably to most of them, however, George appealed less as the bearer of a specific doctrine than as a vague symbol against injustice and oppression.

[1] R. T. Ely, *The Labor Movement in America* (N. Y., 1886), 284.

In 1886 the United Labor party of New York City decided to enter the mayoralty race and persuaded George to become its candidate. The campaign was fierce and spectacular. Against him the old parties nominated the strongest opponents they could muster. Abram S. Hewitt headed the Democratic ticket. Though he had earlier formed a favorable opinion of *Progress and Poverty*, he now told the voters that George's victory would be "the greatest calamity that could menace the prosperity of the city." Theodore Roosevelt, who probably had not read the book—later he spoke of George as "an utterly cheap reformer"—was the Republican candidate.[1] Hewitt won by some twenty-two thousand votes. George ran ahead of Roosevelt by about eight thousand. George himself believed that he had been counted out, and there were those even in the opposing camps who agreed with him. Two years later the single-taxers made a foray into national politics under the name of the United Labor party; but their presidential ticket attracted so few votes that they did not try a second time.[2]

By entering politics George had confused his fight: the single tax was no longer a shining sword in the hand of a knight with a single purpose. The causes of his supporters were his causes. In turn he fought for free trade, the shorter day, recognition of unions. His course undoubtedly antagonized many who might otherwise have been at least tolerant friends. In an effort to unite his followers, he and his colleagues founded the Anti-Poverty Society for the purpose of disseminating "the truth that God has made ample provision for the need of all men . . . and that involuntary poverty is the result of the human laws that allow

---

[1] Allan Nevins, *Abram S. Hewitt* (N. Y., 1935), 465-467; H. F. Pringle, *Theodore Roosevelt* (N. Y., 1931), 111-115.

[2] Edward Stanwood, *A History of the Presidency* (Boston, 1898), 463-465, 485.

individuals to claim as private property that which the Creator has provided for the use of all." [1]

George wore himself out writing books and articles, lecturing, sticking to his work in spite of the warnings of his physician until in 1897, in the midst of a second campaign for the mayoralty, he died. But there was too much vitality in his ideas for them to die with him. They were never more alive than in 1898. There is no place in the thinking world where he is not still read, where he has not followers. He is inextricably woven into the liberal thought of the world. [2]

George taught as a self-trained economist. Few professional economists were willing to go the whole distance with him. Nevertheless, among the younger teachers in the universities there were strong stirrings of revolt against the cold logic of the classical school of economics. [3] Their most influential spokesman was Richard T. Ely who, fresh from studying in Germany, joined the Johns Hopkins faculty in 1881. As one of his students later recorded, Ely impressed it on his classes that Adam Smith, Ricardo and John Stuart Mill

> wrote about the world as it had been in the days of our grandfathers, when there were no railroads, when large-scale industry was not known, huge aggregations of capital had not appeared, and the industrial revolution had just begun. . . . Text-books talked about the universality of competition; Professor Ely told us that competition was coming to an end. They outlined laws of rent, of profits, of demand and supply that were inoperative. They pictured a society of struggle, while Professor Ely showed us a world of

[1] George, *Life of Henry George*, 492 n.

[2] In John Dewey's opinion, "It would require less than the fingers of the two hands to enumerate those who from Plato down rank with him." See Dewey's introduction to H. G. Brown, comp., *Significant Paragraphs from Henry George's Progress and Poverty* (Garden City, 1928), 1.

[3] See Schlesinger, *Rise of the City*, 226-228.

Richard T. Ely   Henry George

Political Economists

monopoly, an economic feudalism that was fast taking the place of the theoretical world of freedom and equal opportunity.[1]

To Ely economics was a science of human relations, and the first duty of the economic order was to humanize itself by giving labor a fairer share of the joint product of capital and labor and by making conditions of life more tolerable for the many. By adherents of the *laissez-faire* school his teachings were denounced as socialistic; by socialists, impatient of ameliorative methods, they were condemned, in Karl Marx's phrase, as "soft-mouthed slobber." [2] Many of Ely's students were to become distinguished leaders in American public life. The most eminent of them, Woodrow Wilson, before he left Johns Hopkins planned to write with Ely a history of American economic thought. Though Wilson's later absorbing activities prevented the idea from being carried out, he never lost interest in the project.[3] Lyman Abbott opened the columns of the *Outlook* to Ely. The head of the Chautauqua movement, Bishop John H. Vincent, invited him to conduct graduate work at Chautauqua for six weeks each summer and to write a book on economics for the Chautauqua Literary and Scientific Circle.[4] Ely undoubtedly indicated the middle path toward social improvement which most thoughtful Americans of the time preferred to take.

The clashing economic philosophies had a profound effect on the attitude of the public toward the rapidly changing organization of business and financial life.

[1] F. C. Howe, *The Confessions of a Reformer* (N. Y., 1925), 28.

[2] This was Marx's characterization of reformers and humanitarians. V. G. Simkhovitch, *Marxism versus Socialism* (N. Y., 1913), 279.

[3] Davis R. Dewey was also to have participated in the enterprise. R. S. Baker, *Woodrow Wilson; Life and Letters* (Garden City, 1927), I, 180-181.

[4] See Schlesinger, *Rise of the City*, 172-173.

Though the more extreme proposals seemed utopian and irrational to the bulk of the people, the yeast continued steadily to work throughout these twenty years. It fed the country's unrest, and convinced more and more, even of the *laissez-faire* school, that there must be regulations and reforms if the existing economic system was to maintain an even keel. Two classes in particular, neither of which wished to overturn the capitalist order but merely to modify and correct it, led in this unrest: the farmers and the wage-earners.

CHAPTER VIII

THE FARMERS ORGANIZE

THE forward thrust of industry and finance tended to focus the attention of the country on the newer problems of development and to obscure the central position which agriculture continued to hold in the national economy. In numbers the farmers far exceeded any one of the four classes into which the census of 1880 divided the country's wealth producers. Out of 17,392,099 engaged in "gainful and reputable occupations" 7,670,-493 were in agriculture. This was almost exactly twice as many as in manufacturing and mining and over four times as many as in trade and transportation.[1] The value of what these farmers sold, consumed and had on hand was estimated at nearly two and a quarter billion dollars.[2]

The drive to people unsettled land, particularly in the region west of the Mississippi, resulted during the eighties in enlarging the number of farms in the United States from 4,008,907 to 4,564,641.[3] The average farm increased in size from 133.7 acres in 1880 to 136.5 in 1890. More important was the four-per-cent gain in the amount of improved land. The contribution of the farmer to the national wealth grew by some $4,000,000,000.

Not only did agriculture provide the food supply of

[1] Professional and personal services accounted for 4,074,238; trade and transportation for 1,810,256; and manufacturing, mechanical and mining industries for 3,837,112. *U. S. Compendium of Tenth Census* (1880), pt. ii, 1343.

[2] The exact amount was $2,213,402,564. *U. S. Compendium of Tenth Census*, pt. i, 685.

[3] Bureau of the Census, *Abstract of the Twelfth Census* (1900), 217.

the nation and, to an increasing extent, of Europe, but it formed the basis of some of the country's biggest industries. Thus, in 1880, the flour and grist-mill industry stood first in the United States with a total value of over $505,000,000, and meat packing and slaughtering ranked second with an output of more than $303,-500,000. The milling industry was the outcome of the efforts of a few manufacturers in and near Minneapolis to make a better grade of flour with less waste of grain than had been possible by the old-fashioned method of grinding between an upper and nether millstone. The first step had been taken in 1870 with the invention of the middlings purifier, a machine for removing the thick coat between the bran covering of the wheat kernel and the stock centers.[1]

But the real revolution came with the introduction of a machine for breaking the grain by rollers. The inventor of the process was John Stevens, son of a Welshman who had brought his family to Neenah, Wisconsin, in 1854. At the age of fifteen the boy had gone to work in a flour mill and from the first he had taken an intelligent and critical interest in what was going on about him. Later he was able to buy a share in the mill and became its manager. Having seen a fellow miller getting more efficient results through using rough instead of smooth stones, he began experimenting, keeping his conclusions to himself until in 1880 he produced a machine in which a roller of corrugated chilled iron broke the grain. Attached to it was a valuable device for feeding in the wheat. With this machine Stevens could get five hundred barrels of flour where his competitors at best got two hundred. Moreover, he was able to produce a much higher proportion of "good"

[1] See Allan Nevins, *The Emergence of Modern America* (*A History of American Life*, VIII), 38-39; also W. W. Folwell, *A History of Minnesota* (St. Paul, 1921-1930), III, 68-69.

flour than they did. According to Charles A. Pillsbury, one of the greatest millers of the day,

> The old process aimed to get as much flour as possible at one grinding; the new seeks to get as little flour as possible at the first two or three breakings. . . . The old process sought to avoid middlings as far as possible, because they entailed loss of flour. The new process seeks to produce as much middlings as possible, because out of the middlings comes the high-grade "patent" flour.[1]

The country's largest milling center in 1880 was Minneapolis. Eighteen years before, when its first flour was sent out, the product had been labeled "Muskingum Mills, Troy, Ohio—The Genuine." Nobody then had heard of Minnesota flour, and the millers feared it would be turned back if its origin were known. Presently conditions changed, however, and Minneapolis attained its preëminent position in the milling business, a position assured by the continued adoption of up-to-date processes and of energetic methods of marketing. The stencil with which the first flour made in Minnesota was marked was cut by James J. Hill out of the oil paper he used in his manifold book as a bill clerk on the levee.[2]

A new industry built on a product of the farm was glucose. Started in the 1870's, it had developed so rapidly that by 1881 there were nineteen factories in New York, Ohio, Illinois, Michigan, Iowa and Missouri with an estimated capital of two million dollars. Together they consumed about thirty-five thousand bushels of corn a day and between eleven and twelve million a year, and they employed two thousand one hundred persons.[3] By 1884 it was estimated that the yearly

[1] C. M. Depew, ed., *One Hundred Years of American Commerce* (N. Y., 1895), I, 270.
[2] J. G. Pyle, *The Life of James J. Hill* (Garden City, 1917), I, 42.
[3] *Appletons' Annual Cyclopædia*, n.s., VI (1881), 350.

manufacture and sale of glucose amounted to about ten pounds per capita. It was used chiefly in the making of table syrups, strained honey, confectionery and the cheaper grades of sugar, also as food for bees and in the manufacture of condensed milk and mucilage. With continued expansion the glucose trust was formed in 1897 under the name of the Glucose Sugar Refining Company, including all the plants but one in the country, at a capitalization of over forty million dollars. According to the testimony of H. O. Havemeyer, head of the sugar trust, before the United States Industrial Commission, "the sirup made from glucose has virtually knocked out the consumption of refined molasses in this country." [1]

In the extraordinary increase of the national wealth the farmer felt that he was not getting his share, that too large a percentage went to the agencies which had been built up to serve him: the railroads, the banks, the marketing agencies, the industries based on his raw products. All this economic machinery bewildered and antagonized him. By habit and conviction he was deeply individualistic. He believed that the most satisfactory material results, as well as the finest individual development, came from self-reliance. Yet he saw himself growing more and more dependent upon an economic order which was yielding to a form of irresponsible collectivism. Moreover, he resented the increasing predominance of the cities whence the masters of capital and Big Business directed the course of economic conquest frequently to his disadvantage, and where the people enjoyed social and intellectual advantages denied to himself and his children. [2]

Once, the cycle of growing, harvesting and distribut-

---

[1] U. S. Industrial Commission, *Report* (Wash., 1900-1902), I, 114.
[2] See A. M. Schlesinger, *The Rise of the City* (*A History of American Life*, X), 58-59, 76-80.

ing his crop had been largely in the farmer's own hands. He understood its problems—bad years, inefficient labor, wayward sons—and he had learned in a practical way to deal with them. He had hauled his produce to town where in the open market he traded it in and returned home with the fruit of his labor in calico, sugar, seeds, new implements. It was an intimate, personal process which gave him a sense of adequacy and control. Now all this was over. His market was made elsewhere and with its making he had nothing to do. His prices rose and fell according to the operations of those whom he considered gamblers. By what right did James R. Keene and his associates attempt a corner in wheat in Chicago? Though it failed with great loss to the manipulators, why should they be allowed to juggle what he had produced? How did the farmer benefit when Armour & Company in the same year 1880 cornered his pork, controlling the supply for months to reap huge profits in the fall? [1]

For a similar reason he distrusted the railroads. During rate wars they carried his produce at a loss to themselves, but when they effected an agreement, it usually entailed a loss to him. Moreover, the instability of rates was unsettling to the marketing of his crops. He was coming to look on the railroad as his enemy, not as the friend he had expected it to be in the days when the government aided it with huge grants of land, presumably for his benefit. Particularly did he fear the steady consolidation of the roads into systems by which one man or group of men controlled the transportation and trade of a great area.

Only less was the farmer disturbed by the newly formed industrial combinations which handled many of the necessaries of his life. He saw with anxiety that this process of consolidation was beginning to touch

[1] *Appletons' Annual Cyclopædia*, n.s., V (1880), 126.

the small neighborhood crafts on which he had depended. The grist mill was being put out of business by the great milling centers. The number of carpenter shops, of cooper shops, of blacksmith shops, decreased under his eyes.[1] At the same time he saw the number of middlemen multiply. On them he blamed, in part, the high prices he was obliged to pay for the manufactured articles which he and his family needed. In all this the farmer sensed a concentration of the growing wealth of the community in fewer and fewer hands, and he feared power in wealth even as he feared it in government.

The growing restlessness of farm dwellers deeply troubled him: the ease with which his neighbors sold out, moved west or south, went into new deals and new places, gave up the land for the factory, the country for the town.[2] Something was wrong when a whole countryside was abandoned, as sometimes happened, and rural communities were left to fall apart. The waste involved in the breaking up of traditional ways, the change, the instability of men, disturbed the thoughtful. They had been reared to what Horace Bushnell called

a closely girded habit of economy. Harnessed all together into the producing process, young and old, male and female, from the boy that rode the plow-horse to the grandmother knitting under her spectacles, they had no conception of squandering lightly what they all had been at work, thread by thread and grain by grain, to produce.[3]

Yet such conditions were the inevitable outcome of the economic burdens which every year bore more

[1] *U. S. Compendium of Tenth Census*, pt. ii, 926-927.
[2] On the trend to the city, see Schlesinger, *Rise of the City*, 57, 60-64, 67-72, 76.
[3] Horace Bushnell, "Work and Play," C. D. Warner, ed., *Library of the World's Best Literature* (N. Y., 1896-1898), V, 2921.

heavily on the farmer's shoulders.[1] Because of the enormous expansion of Western agriculture and of stiffer
competition in the world's markets with the grain-
growing regions of Russia, Australia and the Argentine,
farm prices fell disastrously during the eighties.   Much
the same thing held true of Southern cotton which had
now to compete with cotton raised in India and elsewhere.   Corn, which commanded sixty-three cents a
bushel in 1881, sold for twenty-eight in 1890.   Wheat
averaged but seventy-three cents a bushel from 1883 to
1889.   Cotton fell from fifteen cents in the period
1870-1873 to about eight in 1886-1889. Overproduction as an explanation of the farmer's ills was cold comfort. He could not well adjust his production to market
needs as could the Standard Oil Company or the cordage
trust.   On the contrary, he urged that no real overproduction existed when low prices caused farmers to burn
corn for fuel though at the same time thousands of people elsewhere were facing hunger and even starvation.

To carry on his business, the farmer found it increasingly difficult to obtain money at what seemed to him
reasonable rates of interest.   Obliged to borrow in the
spring to put in his crop, he claimed that short-term
credits cost him more than they did other wealth producers such as the railroads and industries. If he had
not been heavily mortgaged, the cost of money while he
was growing his cotton or corn or wheat would have
been less of a burden, but in certain states the weight of
debt was mounting alarmingly. By 1890 the majority
(64.4 per cent) of Kansas farms were mortgaged up to
38 per cent of their value, and their owners were sweat-
ing under interest rates averaging 8.1 per cent. It is
not remarkable that a large increase in tenant farmers
occurred.   Though no other state was quite so deeply

[1] J. D. Hicks, *The Populist Revolt* (Minneapolis, 1931), 55-60.

in debt as Kansas, there were several where the situation was threatening. In Minnesota 46.4 per cent of the farmers carried mortgages at 8.2 per cent; in Iowa 53.8 per cent of the farmers paid an average interest charge of 7.3 per cent.

The *New York Evening Post* ascribed the Western predicament to "a credit system which enables farmers to borrow heavily where tradesmen in like circumstances cannot. Such borrowers take the chances . . . ." [1] Yet conditions not unlike existed in certain parts of the East. Vermont, Massachusetts and New Jersey farmers carried almost as many mortgages as those in the Western states named, but at a lower interest charge, under six per cent. A similar situation prevailed in the cotton-growing South where the crop-lien system constituted the chief mortgage evil. [2] In the words of a song widely sung by distressed Southern farmers,

> My husband came from town last night
>   As sad as man could be,
> His wagon empty, cotton gone,
>   And not a dime had he.
>
> Huzzah—Huzzah
>   'Tis queer I do declare:
> We make the clothes for all the world,
>   But few we have to wear.

Gradually the farmer was driven to the conclusion that it was necessary for him to take things into his own hands and seek to regain control of the essential factors in his problem. To do this he must employ the principle that the railroads and industries were using to such good effect: national consolidation. In a sense, the

[1] Editorial digest of the report on farm mortgages made by the Eleventh Census, *N. Y. Evening Post*, Sept. 6, 1893.
[2] See Schlesinger, *Rise of the City*, 6-8.

makings of such a national union already existed in the
Grange, which had been powerful in the mid-seventies; [1]
but by 1878 this once popular body was beginning to
be replaced in many sections by more radical organizations known as alliances.   The first of these had been
formed in 1875 in Lampasas County, Texas, originally
for the purpose of protecting farmers against the depre-
dations of horse and cattle thieves.   Similar alliances
later started in other parts of the state, and in 1880 these
groups coalesced and were chartered under the name of
the Texas Farmers' State Alliance.   Spreading rapidly
over the state, it united in 1887 with the Farmers'
Union of Louisiana to form the National Farmers' Alliance and Coöperative Union of America.   Into this
new body soon came alliances which had been forming
in ten or more other states of the South and Southwest.[2]

In 1889 a merger was effected with the Agricultural
Wheel and the name changed to Farmers' and Laborers'
Union of America, though popularly the organization
was known as the Southern Alliance.   Begun in 1882
by W. W. Tedford, a farmer and school-teacher, the
Agricultural Wheel had increased rapidly in membership
and in 1886 had launched the National Agricultural
Wheel.[3]   The constitution of the merger was general
and theoretical with no more specific demand than
"equal rights to all and special favors to none," no more
direct pledge than to "suppress personal, local, sectional,
and national prejudices, all unhealthy rivalry and all
selfish ambition"—in which pledge no doubt it was ex-
pressing its opinion as to what had made earlier efforts

[1] Nevins, *Emergence of Modern America*, 169-173, 176-177, 371-
372.
[2] S. J. Buck, *The Granger Movement* (*Harvard Hist. Studies*, XIX),
302-304.
[3] N. B. Ashby, *The Riddle of the Sphinx* (Des Moines, 1890), 439-
440.

of the alliances no more successful than they had been.[1] The leaders, however, had pretty definite notions of what needed to be done to improve farm conditions.

Meanwhile, in the Northwest, there had developed a similar movement. The National Farmers' Alliance, or Northern Alliance as it was generally called, began with a local organization formed in Chicago in April, 1880, by Milton George, editor of the *Western Rural*, an aggressive farm journal.[2] By October the movement had so spread that it was possible to hold a convention in Chicago to which five hundred representatives came from various local alliances, farmers' clubs and granges. The gathering drafted a constitution declaring that its object was to unite the farmers of the United States against "class legislation, and the encroachments of concentrated capital and the tyranny of monopoly; . . . to oppose, in our respective political parties, the election of any candidate to office, State or national, who is not thoroughly in sympathy with the farmers' interests . . . ."[3] Though growing sporadically for a few years, the alliance profited greatly from the agricultural depression of the late eighties and became a power to be reckoned with throughout the whole Northwest.

From the beginning the state alliances accepted co-operation as the one practical method of escaping the middleman whom they charged with taking an unfair percentage of their profits and overcharging for commodities sold over the counter. The Texas Alliance first tried a plan called the contract store. A committee of trusted members in each county made a contract with a chosen merchant by which he agreed to sell at a discount to alliance members on condition that they would

[1] Ashby, *Riddle of the Sphinx*, 441-442.
[2] Hicks, *Populist Revolt*, 98-104.
[3] Ashby, *Riddle of the Sphinx*, 407-408.

buy only from him.[1]   The result, in most cases, was price-cutting warfare against the contract store by those merchants of a community who had built up a farmer trade largely by means of direct barter coupled with credit and cash advances.   The merchants felt it a violation of an established relation.   The consequence too often was that the farmers, tempted by lower prices, deserted the contract store.

In 1886, after a year's trial, the plan was abandoned, and the Texas Alliance advised the farmers within each county to eliminate the middlemen by coöperating in the sale of their products.   Growers were to turn over to alliance cotton yards their entire crop, and sale days were fixed when it was expected city buyers would compete with one another and bid up the price.   But the buyers did not like the new attempt at coöperation any better than the merchants had the contract store.   So few of them attended on sale days that at the end of the season large stores of cotton remained on hand.[2]

This unanticipated outcome proved less discouraging than it might otherwise have been because by this time the Texas Alliance had a new idea, that of selling cotton direct to the mills.   This notion had originated with C. W. Macune, chairman of the executive committee of the state alliance.   A reflective, self-educated man, he had seen enough of conditions as a farm laborer in the Far and Middle West to persuade him that the only hope for profitable farming lay in coöperation.   Macune now went to New England and, after discussing the scheme with mill owners in Fall River and Boston, he returned convinced that his plan was sound, but that in order to succeed it must be carried out on a large scale. He proposed an organization called the Farmers' Al-

[1] Edward Wiest, *Agricultural Organization in the United States* (Univ. of Kentucky, *Studies,* II), 464.
[2] Wiest, *Agricultural Organization,* 465.

liance Exchange of Texas with a capital of $500,000, to be paid in installments. With this money the buildings and equipment necessary for the enterprise were to be provided, together with supplies sufficient to carry the farmer until his crop was ready to be sold.

The cotton merchants who had been accustomed to advancing money to growers, taking more mortgages on the crop, did not abandon business because of the proposed Alliance Exchange. In fact, they made so many contracts with their old customers that it was crippled from the start. The first installment of the $500,000 amounted to but $56,000 in cash and $40,000 in notes. It was not enough properly to finance the plan; and although Macune did his best to rally the farmers and to convince the banks that the future of the Alliance Exchange provided adequate security, he was unable to obtain the loans he needed. The exchange opened its doors in September, 1887; within twenty months it had gone to pieces. Like the earlier coöperative undertakings, it failed because it lacked proper preparation and a sound financial foundation and did too much business on a credit basis.[1] In the opinion of W. S. Morgan, of the Agricultural Wheel, the farmers needed further education in coöperation before the movement could succeed.[2]

The coöperative efforts of other state alliances were very like those of Texas and, when they failed, it usually was for the same reasons. The "Macune business system" spread until in 1890 it had been introduced into eighteen states. Not all these attempts were as short-lived as the parent exchange. That in Georgia operated successfully until 1893.[3]

---

[1] Wiest, *Agricultural Organization*, 466-467; Hicks, *Populist Revolt*, 134-137.

[2] W. S. Morgan, *History of the Wheel and Alliance, and the Impending Revolution* (St. Louis, 1891), 97, 204, 246.

[3] Hicks, *Populist Revolt*, 137-140.

The disappointing results of coöperation turned the thoughts of the organized farmers more and more to political measures as a means of securing relief. A long period of drought, beginning in 1887 and attended by infestations of chinch bugs, brought fresh despair to the farming population and prepared the way for more decisive action.[1] In 1889 representatives of the Northern and Southern alliances met for the purpose of uniting.[2] For a number of reasons, however, the plan came to naught. The Southern Alliance was secret and wanted to remain so; the Northern was open to all. The Southern Alliance wanted a complete merger, the Northern a federation. There was, besides, a difference of opinion as yet as to the extent of political activity which was wise. A surviving sectional antagonism also contributed to a lack of complete understanding. Nevertheless the gathering made the leaders better acquainted with one another and emphasized the common purposes which the two groups were aiming to achieve.

The pressure for political participation grew constantly stronger. Thus in April, 1890, the United States Supreme Court in the Minnesota Rate case decided that state commissions and state legislatures had no unrestricted right to fix rates even for railroads within state borders, for the final determination as to the reasonableness of charges lay with the courts.[3] The decision came while the executive committee of the Minnesota Alliance was in session. It meant "the subjection of the people and the states to the unlimited control of the railroad corporations of this country," declared the committee, and a resolution was adopted to the effect that the alliance would "appeal from this second Dred Scott decision to the people of the nation . . . with a

[1] Hicks, *Populist Revolt*, 30-31.
[2] Hicks, *Populist Revolt*, 113-127.
[3] Chicago, Milwaukee and St. Paul Railway Co. *v.* Minnesota, 134 *U. S. Reports*, 418.

request that they unite with us in an effort to so amend the constitution as to abolish this new slavery." [1]

By the end of the year the Southern Alliance had promulgated a list of measures which it proposed to demand of the existing parties. This program included the free and unlimited coinage of silver, an increase of circulating medium to not less than fifty dollars a person, abolition of the national banks, the establishment of subtreasuries for granting easier credit to farmers and others, legislation against stock-market speculation, a graduated income tax, stricter regulation of railroads or government ownership, and the popular election of United States senators. [2] These demands were, in the main, agreed to by all other agrarian groups, including the Grange, the Northern Alliance and the Colored Alliance. [3]

By leaders of the old parties the organized farmers were regarded as "hayseed socialists" and their list of demands as crack-brained and visionary. No item on their program caused more excited protest than the subtreasury scheme. By means of this agency the farmer would store his nonperishable crop with the government, and receive in return legal-tender certificates up to four fifths of its value, for which he would pay interest at one or two per cent a year. He would negotiate and sell these certificates "whenever the current price suited him, receiving from the person to whom he sold, only the difference between the price agreed upon and the amount already paid by the sub-treasurer." [4] The *St. Paul Pioneer Press* called the scheme a "transcendent

[1] F. M. Drew, "The Present Farmers' Movement," *Polit. Sci. Quar.*, VI, 300.

[2] The so-called Ocala demands, adopted in December, 1890. Hicks, *Populist Revolt*, 430-431.

[3] See table in Drew, "Present Farmers' Movement," 295.

[4] Morgan, *History of the Wheel and Alliance*, 180-181. Morgan was a member of the monetary committee which devised the subtreasury scheme.

absurdity." It would be as practical "to level the Rocky Mountain Range and spread the material all over the Mississippi Valley." The *New York Commercial Advertiser* did not know which proposal was the madder, the subtreasury or government ownership of railroads.[1]

The embattled farmers, stung by the ridicule of the press and of the leaders of the major parties, decided in the elections of 1890 to support only those candidates who would back the alliance demands. The center of the agitation, the political whirlwind of the movement, was Kansas. The Kansas Alliance, organized in 1888, had at first resisted the effort to turn it to political action, but it was soon swept off its feet. One of the historians of the upheaval declares that what struck Kansas in 1890 was not a political campaign but a religious revival.[2] No one expressed this crusading fervor better than Mrs. Mary E. Lease. Born in Ireland and educated in New York, she had gone to Kansas in 1873 when she was nineteen. In 1885 she was admitted to the bar, and in 1890 joined the Farmers' Alliance Lecture Bureau, being more in demand than any other speaker. During the summer and fall she made more than a hundred and sixty speeches to immense audiences. "What you farmers need to do is to raise less corn and more HELL," was her reiterated message. "We wiped out slavery," she shouted,

> and by our tariff laws and national banks began a system of white wage slavery worse than the first. Wall Street owns the country. It is no longer a government of the people, by the people and for the people, but a government of Wall Street, by Wall Street and for Wall Street. The great common people of this country are slaves, and monopoly is the master. The West and

[1] "The Farmers' Alliance," *Public Opinion*, IX, 408 (Aug. 9, 1890).
[2] Elizabeth N. Barr, "The Populist Uprising," W. E. Connelly, ed., *A Standard History of Kansas and Kansans* (Chicago, 1918), II, 1148.

South are bound and prostrate before the manufacturing East. . . . The parties lie to us and political speakers mislead us. . . . We want money, land and transportation. We want the abolition of the National
Banks, and we want the power to make loans direct
from the Government. We want the accursed foreclosure system wiped out. . . . The people are at bay,
let the blood-hounds of money who have dogged us
thus far beware.[1]

Each of the farm states had its leader. Next to Mrs.
Lease perhaps the most picturesque was Ignatius Donnelly of Minnesota, a talented, oratorical and witty man
of Irish stock. Born in Philadelphia, he had gone to
Minnesota in time to suffer the full effects of the Panic
of 1857. Turning from real-estate promotion and the
law, he entered antislavery politics and served three
terms in Congress as a Republican during and after the
war. Later he joined one after another of the revolting
farmer groups: the Grangers, the Greenbackers and, in
1884, the Farmers' Alliance.[2] Schooled in a knowledge
of the farmers' grievances and adept at argument and
denunciation, he was everywhere greeted by vast crowds
who listened to him with conviction.

While Mrs. Lease was firing Kansas and Donnelly
Minnesota, alliance orators were carrying on effective
campaigns elsewhere. In Nebraska a People's Independent party, made up of the Farmers' Alliance, the Grange
and the Knights of Labor, elected a majority of the state
senate and half the lower house in 1890. In Florida,
Georgia and North and South Carolina the alliance captured the Democratic party. Kansas chose five alliance
congressmen and a United States senator, while Minnesota elected one alliance congressman and South Dakota

[1] Barr, "Populist Uprising," 1150-1151.
[2] J. D. Hicks, "Ignatius Donnelly," *Dict. of Am. Biog.*, V, 369-371.
For his inverted utopian novel *Caesar's Column*, see Schlesinger, *Rise of the City*, 262.

a United States senator.[1] It was a rich harvest. Not since 1856 had there been so real a chance to form a new liberal party.

The farmers' grievances were genuine even if the manner of statement was exaggerated and violent, often to the point of absurdity. It was a fact that the machinery of the economic order favored industry, finance and the railroads at the expense of agriculture. The government alone had it in its power to restore a just balance; therefore the farmers felt they must control the government. Resistance to their demands by the old parties showed that this could be done only by forming a new party. When a call was issued to the leading farmers' organizations, the Union and Confederate soldiers and the Knights of Labor to attend a conference at Cincinnati in 1891, one thousand four hundred delegates appeared.[2]

This body organized the People's party and, in the next year, held a mammoth convention at Omaha to select a presidential ticket. Many of the delegates would have been glad to have as their presidential candidate Judge Walter Q. Gresham, an Illinois Republican who had been an outspoken liberal since 1854 when he had been run out of the Whig party because of opposition to the Kansas-Nebraska bill. After the war he had actively opposed the spoils system and the protective tariff, and as a federal circuit judge had shown his independence by removing from the receivership of the Wabash Railroad a man who was believed to be a representative of Jay Gould. Gresham was given an unofficial tender of the Populist nomination; but, being at heart a hard-money man, he declined it. The convention then turned to James B. Weaver, an Iowa lawyer who, like Judge

[1] F. E. Haynes, *Third Party Movements since the Civil War* (Iowa City, 1916), 236-245.

[2] Haynes, *Third Party Movements*, 246-247.

Gresham, had fought in the Civil War. Originally a Republican, Weaver had been an early leader of the Prohibitionists, and in 1877 had joined the Greenback party, serving as its representative in Congress for several terms.[1] In 1880 he had been its presidential candidate. His change to Populism was natural, for the new movement included most of the old Greenbackers. For second place on the ticket the convention chose James G. Field of Virginia.

The platform, written in part by Ignatius Donnelly, contained a flaming denunciation of the abuses of capitalism:

> The fruits of the toil of millions are boldly stolen to build up colossal fortunes for a few, unprecedented in the history of mankind; and the possessors of these, in turn, despise the republic and endanger liberty. From the same prolific womb of governmental injustice we breed the two great classes of tramps and millionaires.[2]

As cures for this condition the party offered free silver, the subtreasury plan of the Farmers' Alliance, a graduated income tax, government ownership of railways, telegraphs and telephones, restriction of "undesirable" immigration, a shorter workday for urban wage-earners and the popular election of senators.

The extent to which the Populists frightened the Republicans and Democrats can be seen from statements included in their platforms.[3] On the money question the Democrats declared: "We hold to the use of both gold and silver as the standard money of the country. . . . We insist upon this policy as especially nec-

---

[1] F. E. Haynes, *James Baird Weaver* (Iowa City, 1919), chaps. vi-xiv.
[2] Edward Stanwood, *A History of the Presidency from 1788 to 1897* (Boston, 1898), 509-513.
[3] Stanwood, *History of Presidency*, 494-504.

The Leaky Connection

essary for the protection of the farmers and laboring classes . . . ." In a similar spirit the Republicans asserted: "The American people, from tradition and interest, favor bimetallism, and the Republican party demands the use of both gold and silver as standard money . . . ." Both parties eagerly claimed for themselves the rôle of champion of the oppressed, opposed unrestricted immigration and pledged their earnest efforts against the exactions of trusts and combinations. Their main interest, however, was the tariff question, which they represented as involving the vital interests of the masses. The nomination of the protectionist, Benjamin Harrison, by the Republicans and of the "free trader," Grover Cleveland, by the Democrats made this the paramount issue in the campaign.

To the Populists, however, the emphasis upon this question represented the usual game of the old parties "to drown the outcries of a plundered people with the uproar of a sham battle over the tariff . . . ." [1] As far as the revolting farmers and wage-earners were concerned, their ties with the major parties were broken. Exultantly they conducted their campaign to the tune of the old song, "Good-bye, My Lover, Good-bye," the chorus running:

Bye, party, bye, lo; bye, party, bye, lo;
Bye, party, bye, lo; good-bye, my party, good-bye. [2]

The outcome of the election demonstrated impressively the extent of the agrarian unrest. The Populists polled over a million popular votes. Moreover, for the first time since 1860, a third party secured electoral votes—22 out of a total of 444. [3] In addition it elected five United States senators, ten congressmen, fifty state

[1] Stanwood, *History of Presidency*, 510.
[2] Hicks, *Populist Revolt*, 169.
[3] Haynes, *James Baird Weaver*, 335-338.

officials and one thousand five hundred county officials and members of the state legislature. Small wonder that Weaver was happy over the result. "Unaided by money," he wrote, "our grand young party has made an enviable record and achieved surprising success at the polls." [1] But the old-party leaders anxiously asked themselves: what of the future?

[1] Haynes, *Third Party Movements*, 270.

CHAPTER IX

THE NATIONAL CONSOLIDATION OF LABOR

PARALLEL with the growth of agrarian organizations went a rapid consolidation of labor. In 1878 the most powerful labor body was that known as the Noble Order of Knights of Labor. The significant feature of the organization, that which distinguished it from the trade unions, was the miscellaneous character of its membership. It admitted anybody who worked without regard to occupation, color, nationality or religion. The order, now nine years old, had hitherto consisted of "local assemblies," sometimes associated together in "district assemblies." [1] By 1878 the district assemblies had become so widespread and so vigorous that a convention of delegates met at Reading, Pennsylvania, to effect a central national organization of the Knights.

The dominating figure in the gathering was the then mayor of Scranton, Terence V. Powderly. The labor life of Powderly was typical of the day. Born of Irish parentage in 1849 at Carbondale, one of twelve children, he had gone to work at the age of thirteen as a switch tender. Later he learned the trade of a machinist. While working in the railway shops at Scranton, he became a prominent member of the strong Machinists' and Blacksmiths' Union, a connection which cost him his job in 1873 and put him on the employers' blacklist. Leaving Scranton, he worked in various

[1] Allan Nevins, *The Emergence of Modern America* (*A History of American Life*, VIII), 392-393.

places in Ohio and western Pennsylvania and finally returned to Scranton. Everywhere he went he identified himself with labor interests, with the result that he was soon marked as a nuisance and dismissed. In turn, he was active in the Machinists' and Blacksmiths' Union, the Industrial Brotherhood of the United States and the Greenback-Labor party. It was as a candidate of the last organization that he was elected mayor of Scranton in 1878.[1]

The keynote of the constitution which the convention adopted was a quotation from Edmund Burke: "When bad men combine, the good must associate, else they will fall, one by one, an unpitied sacrifice in a contemptible struggle." A highly centralized organization was provided for, and a list of fifteen demands drawn up. These were later added to until in 1895 they numbered twenty-three. They give a broad view of the labor aspirations of the period. The aims of the Knights were asserted to be

   I.   To make individual and moral worth, not wealth, the true standard of individual and national greatness.

  II.   To secure to the workers the free enjoyment of the wealth they create; sufficient leisure in which to develop their intellectual, moral and social faculties; all of the benefits, recreations and pleasures of association; in a word, to enable them to share in the gains and honor of advancing civilization.

As specific measures, the Knights pledged themselves to the "establishment of coöperative institutions productive and distributive" and the substitution of arbitration for strikes whenever possible, and demanded the creation of bureaus of labor statistics, the abolition of

[1] J. R. Commons and others, *History of Labour in the United States* (N. Y., 1918), II, 245 *n.*

all laws bearing unequally upon capital and labor, the prohibition of child labor, equal pay for the two sexes, a graduated tax on incomes and inheritances, and other provisions of like import.[1]

As soon as the consolidation of the Knights had been achieved, Powderly as Grand Master Workman threw himself energetically into building up the order. On a meager salary, paying his own traveling expenses, he gave his full time to strengthening and enlarging the sprawling and idealistic undertaking. The order grew rapidly in membership. From about 28,000 in 1880 it numbered nearly 52,000 in 1883 and approximately 104,000 in 1885.[2]

To Powderly coöperation promised the greatest hope for the organized worker. It was, in his opinion, destined to be "the lever of labor's emancipation," a means which would eventually "make every man his own master, every man his own employer."[3] At his urging the national organization in 1883 bought a coal mine at Cannelburg, Indiana, in order to sell coal at reduced prices to the members. A more common plan was for local assemblies, or groups of members subsidized by their assembly, to establish coöperative workshops and, to a less extent, stores. Most of these undertakings were run by the stockholders though, in some instances, the assemblies managed them. A notable example of the latter arrangement was the Solidarity Coöperative Association, set up and conducted by District Assembly 49, New York. The committee in charge, investing the money as it saw fit, financed a cigar factory, a leather shop, a printing shop, a watch-case factory, a building

[1] G. E. McNeill, ed., *The Labor Movement: the Problem of To-day* (Boston, 1887), chap. xix; Independent Order of the Knights of Labor, *Constitution of the General Assembly Adopted at Columbus, Ohio, February 14, 1895* (n.p., n.d.), 3-6.

[2] Leo Wolman, *The Growth of American Trade Unions, 1880-1923* (Natl. Bur. of Econ. Research, *Publs.*, no. 6), 32.

[3] McNeill, ed., *Labor Movement*, 411.

association and a plumbing shop as well as certain other enterprises.[1]

The movement reached its peak in 1886, though it had not wholly spent itself by the close of 1887. At least one hundred and thirty-five coöperative ventures were set going, the largest number in mining, cooperage and shoe manufacturing, industries in which starvation wages prevailed.[2] Most of these enterprises were conducted on a small scale. As a "lever of labor's emancipation" coöperation never materialized; but as a means of enabling some ambitious and energetic wage-earners to become independent, it proved fairly successful. Too often, however, the success assumed a form harmful to the very cause which coöperation was intended to serve, for the well-managed undertakings sooner or later became joint-stock companies.

The causes which brought disaster to most of the coöperative undertakings were the same as those which ruined the farmers' similar enterprises: inefficient management, internal squabbling, inadequate capital, and discriminations instigated by competitors.[3] The coal mine at Cannelburg, the order's sole experiment of a centralized kind, met the common fate. After twenty thousand dollars had been spent on improving the property and one thousand dollars' worth of coal had been dug, the mine was obliged to lie idle for nine months until the railroad company saw fit to connect it with the main track. Other obstacles quite as unexpected appeared. The available funds being exhausted, the order succumbed to the pressure and sold out. Only three or four years after it had begun, the Knights' adventure in coöperation came to an ignominious end.

In its political program the order was somewhat more

[1] E. W. Bemis, *Co-operation in the Middle States* (Johns Hopkins Univ., *Studies*, VI), 162.

[2] Commons and others, *History of Labour*, II, 433.

[3] Commons and others, *History of Labour*, II, 437-438.

successful. Powderly was instrumental in securing the establishment of labor bureaus in a number of states and also in inducing Congress to pass the law forbidding the importation of labor under contract.[1] The Knights had at first been reluctant to oppose unrestricted immigration, but presently they changed their minds. Was it fair, they asked, that articles made abroad should be imported only by paying a duty while a foreign workman came in free? If the employers were to be protected, why not the wage-earners? Drafting their own bill on the subject, the Knights had it introduced into Congress. The House passed it in June, 1884, and the Senate in February of the following year.[2]

The hard times, beginning with the Panic of 1884, produced great labor unrest. Fresh recruits swelled the ranks of the Knights of Labor until the membership in 1886 reached seven hundred thousand.[3] The rapid expansion brought into the order many men impatient of the conservative methods which Powderly stood for. Their demands for immediate action forced the leadership increasingly to countenance the use of the weapons of industrial warfare: the boycott and the strike. During 1885 the boycott reached epidemic proportions, affecting all parts of the country. No less than one hundred and ninety-six were conducted, nearly seven times as many as in 1884.[4] A notable instance was the boycott against the Dueber Watch Case Company. The company had discharged all its employees who were connected with the Knights and refused to discuss the matter with any representatives of the order. There-

---

[1] See earlier, 14.

[2] U. S. Immigration Commission, *Reports* (Wash., 1911), XXXIX, 29-50.

[3] Commons and others, *History of Labour*, II, 381.

[4] The figure for 1885 does not include 41 anti-Chinese boycotts on the Pacific Coast. Nearly all the boycotts began with, or were taken up by, the Knights of Labor. Commons, *History of Labour*, II, 365-366.

upon the order's official organ, the *Journal of United Labor,* instructed the members not to buy watches with Dueber cases or patronize jewelry stores which sold them. The pressure proved effective, and the company soon reversed its former position.

Strikes occurred with increasing violence and frequency. The most extended series in which the Knights were directly involved took place on the Gould railway system. The first began in March, 1885, when some four thousand workmen of the Missouri Pacific in the states of Missouri, Texas and Kansas struck for a restoration of wages which had been cut without warning. The walkout was short-lived, being ended by the efforts of the governors of Kansas and Missouri. The shopmen received more than they had asked: not only was the former wage scale restored, but one-and-a-half pay for overtime was granted. The company further agreed not to change rates thereafter without thirty days' notice. This settlement was due largely to the sympathy of the public. Reducing wages at a time when there was believed to be no decline in the company's earnings outraged the Southwest. The rail officials, quickly realizing this, had the good sense to yield.[1] Six months later a second strike, caused by discrimination against workers belonging to the Knights of Labor, terminated triumphantly for the men.[2]

The third and greatest of the disorders ended in their utter rout.[3] It began in March, 1886, when a foreman, a prominent Knight, was laid off without notice in the car shops of the Texas & Pacific at Marshall, Texas, for alleged incompetence. This action, the strikers claimed, violated the settlement of the preceding year. The federal commissioner of labor, discussing the strike in his

[1] U. S. Commissioner of Labor, *Third Annual Report* (1887), 30-33.
[2] Selig Perlman, *A History of Trade Unionism in the United States* (N. Y., 1922), 86-87.
[3] Commons and others, *History of Labour,* II, 383-384.

third annual report, held that this claim was not well founded since the agreement referred to dealt only with wage rates. Moreover, the Texas & Pacific was now no longer in the Gould system, but in the hands of receivers who were free to run the road according to their best judgment. Martin Irons, who directed the walkout, saw in the receivership, however, merely a legal device revealing Gould's grim determination to destroy the power of the Knights at any cost. In a manifesto he declared this view and added that the strike was designed to defeat "these contemptible and blood-sucking corporations and their governmental allies . . . ." [1]

Irons called on the shopmen of the entire Gould system to quit work, and some nine thousand obeyed. The disturbance affected more than five thousand miles of railway in Missouri, Kansas, Nebraska, Arkansas and Indian Territory. The men not only quit work, but undertook to stop all freight traffic on the roads. They invaded yards and shops and, when attempts were made to take out a train, promptly "killed" the engine by removing some indispensable part. Within two weeks practically all the locomotives at every strike center were dead, and no freight moved over the vast territory affected. Passenger trains carrying mail were not molested, however, the strikers apparently fearing to provoke federal interference. In the opinion of an acute observer, "The strike was a struggle for power. The Knights . . . thought that they were irresistible. They had 'downed Jay Gould' once, and they were going to do it again. In order to win their victory, they were determined to choke the railroad company, and, if need were, the community also." [2]

For a time hatred of Jay Gould was sufficient to in-

[1] *St. Louis Republican,* March 11, 1886.
[2] F. W. Taussig, "The South-Western Strike of 1886," *Quar. Journ. of Economics,* I, 184-222.

sure popular sympathy for the fighters regardless of the merits of the case. But when business came to a standstill for lack of supplies, factories closed for want of coal, houses were cold and tables short of eggs and butter, the public began to demand that order be restored. Once again the governors of Missouri and Kansas sought to settle the trouble, but the Knights, calling their offers interference, declined to negotiate. Thereupon the governors of four states ordered the companies to run their trains and forbade all persons to interfere. Attempts to intimidate crews and cripple rolling stock ensued, but the people along the lines, now thoroughly aroused, transferred their sympathy from the strikers to the railroad. On March 28 the strike was temporarily halted by Grand Master Powderly, who wished to submit the dispute to arbitration, but no agreement could be reached with Gould. Early in April hostilities resumed with a bitterness and a violence far greater than before. But the men never regained the old backing of the public and in May surrendered unconditionally.

These railroad strikes, together with the participation of the Knights in the many other labor disputes which occurred in the turbulent years 1885 and 1886, destroyed much of the public confidence in the order. Powderly himself, in a secret circular issued to the assemblies early in 1886, admitted ruefully,

> While I, as the chosen mouthpiece of the Order, am proclaiming to the world that the Knights of Labor do not advocate nor countenance strikes until every other means has failed, the wires from a thousand cities and towns are bearing the news of as many strikes by Knights of Labor, in which arbitration and conciliation were never hinted at. . . . In some cases these strikes were entered upon against the advice of the General Executive Board. It is claimed by our members that arbitration is one-sided . . . but the voluntary con-

cessions made to us within the past three months prove most conclusively that the just claims of labor will be listened to if we go forward in the way we started.[1]

Side by side with the Knights, a second great national labor body had been forging to the front, an organization which from its birth in 1881 had been the chief competitor of the Knights. Known originally as the Federation of Organized Trades and Labor Unions of the United States of America and Canada, the body changed its name in 1886 to the American Federation of Labor. Conflict between the two groups was inevitable. The American Federation of Labor, believing that only the members of a given craft or trade could properly protect and develop its interests, guaranteed the autonomy of each trade union belonging to the Federation; and its activities were directed toward improving the condition only of those unions which joined. The Knights of Labor, on the other hand, were organized on the principle of "one big union," and were usually hostile to trade unions, holding that they sacrificed the general interests of labor to the selfish principles of temporary advantage.[2] Basically the conflict was one between the practical and the idealistic, the hard-headed common sense of Samuel Gompers, the American Federation's foremost leader, and the all-embracing humanitarianism of Terence V. Powderly.

Their conflicting philosophies reflected, in some considerable part, their differing personal backgrounds. Powderly had found the direction of his ideas in the loose, emotional thinking of the Machinists' and Blacksmiths' Union and of the Greenback party; Gompers, in the closely knit organization of the British trade

[1] *Phila. Evening Item*, March 27, 1886. The circular is published here in full.
[2] L. L. Lorwin, *The American Federation of Labor* (Brookings Inst., Publs., no. 50), 16-19, 113-114.

union. Born in London in 1850, his father a cigar maker, he had chosen at the age of ten to learn his father's trade rather than shoemaking because the former was organized.[1] In 1863 the Gompers family had migrated to New York. There, in spite of his long twelve-hour day, the boy found time to attend Cooper Union and, for twenty years thereafter, listened to its lectures and worked in its night study classes.

Always a strong sense of reality guided him. When he was only eighteen his union struck against the introduction of molds, a labor-saving device. The strikers lost, and saw untrained immigrants taking their places, turning out a larger output than they had ever been able to do. "From that time," he later said, "I began to realize the futility of opposing progress."[2] As an interested spectator and sometimes actor in the strikes and demonstrations bred by the long depression of the seventies, he noted how radical leaders took advantage of labor discontent to preach their gospels of economic salvation. The more thoroughly he studied the philosophies of socialism and communism, the more convinced he became that the solidarity of workers in craft unions was the only sure road to betterment of conditions. Moreover, leadership in the labor movement, he believed, "could be safely entrusted only to those into whose hearts and minds had been woven the experiences of earning their bread by daily labor."[3]

Gompers's success in reorganizing the Cigar Makers' Union and giving it a nation-wide membership marks the real beginning of militant, persistent unionism in America. His union became the model for all others. When a sufficient number had copied it, they joined together in the national federation in 1881 under his

[1] Samuel Gompers, *Seventy Years of Life and Labor* (N. Y., 1925), I, 17-18.

[2] Gompers, *Seventy Years of Life and Labor*, I, 47.

[3] Gompers, *Seventy Years of Life and Labor*, I, 97.

leadership.   The new organization was at first set on achievement through legislation.   Its chief objectives were compulsory education laws, the prohibition of child labor, sanitary and safety regulations for factories, uniform apprentice laws, a national eight-hour law, the prohibition of contract convict labor and of the truck system of wage payment, the repeal of conspiracy laws, a national bureau of labor statistics and the protection of American industry against cheap foreign labor.[1] After a few years, however, it subordinated its legislative program to economic action, regarding the strike as the wage-earner's chief weapon and the trade agreement, by which collective bargaining was to be accepted, as the ultimate goal of unionism.

In 1884 the Federation called upon its affiliated bodies to direct their energies toward the establishment of an eight-hour day by May 1, 1886.[2] The long day was one of the oldest grievances of American labor. The first call for eight hours seems to have been in Maine where a slogan, "Eight hours for work, eight hours for sleep, and eight hours for God and the brethren," was sounded as early as 1844; but it had come to nothing.[3] Even such fiery and persistent friends of labor as Horace Greeley and William Lloyd Garrison had talked of ten hours.[4] After the Civil War the eight-hour demand was included in most labor programs, and Eight Hour Leagues sprang up in various states to promote the cause.[5] Though some states took favorable action, the laws always left loopholes by which employers could escape their obligations.   Nevertheless conditions in the

---

[1] Gompers, *Seventy Years of Life and Labor*, I, 225.

[2] Commons and others, *History of Labour*, II, 376-377.

[3] Illinois Bureau of Labor Statistics, *Fourth Biennial Report* (1886), 466.

[4] See C. R. Fish, *The Rise of the Common Man* (*A History of American Life*, VI), 272-274.

[5] Nevins, *Emergence of Modern America*, 71.

course of half a century had in some respects improved. Thus, in 1830, four out of five wage-earners had worked more than ten hours a day; in 1880 only about one in four.[1] The eight-hour day, however, was virtually nonexistent.

The Federation had allowed two years in which to educate the public as to the need of the shorter day. Reluctant employers it expected to whip into line through the strike. Its most important ally should have been the Knights of Labor, but after considerable hesitation Powderly refused to coöperate. He was reluctant to resort to the strike until all other means were exhausted; besides, he did not think that the people most concerned were sufficiently educated. It may be, too, that he saw more clearly than Gompers that most industries at that day were too badly managed to stand a change to shorter hours. Gompers himself wrote thirty-nine years later that in 1886 there were "hardly twelve industries in the United States sufficiently organized to establish an eight-hour day," but that he considered the campaign valuable as an "educational influence." [2]

The approach to employers was carefully planned, conferences were sought, and many employers promised to coöperate. While most of them were doubtless actuated by fear of the consequences of refusal, others, more enlightened, believed that a shorter day would make the workers more productive.[3] Labor was so convinced of this that it had a slogan:

Whether you work by the hour or work by the day,
Decreasing the hours increases the pay.

[1] D. A. Wells, *Recent Economic Changes* (N. Y., 1889), 415.
[2] Gompers, *Seventy Years of Life and Labor*, I, 291.
[3] See later, 171. Of writers on economics, George Gunton, *Wealth and Progress* (N. Y., 1887), chaps. iii-iv, supported this contention; Wells, *Recent Economic Changes*, 439-444, argued against it.

The main argument for the reform, however, was to provide work for the jobless, of whom a million were to be found in the nation. Apart from the direct benefits so accruing, it was urged that the employment of this great number "would necessarily increase the number of consumers, and thereby enlarge the market for commodities to that extent." [1] While the intelligence of the country generally supported the cause, there were also violent critics—newspapers like the *Illinois State Register* which declared the eight-hour movement a "consummate piece of humbuggery . . . too silly to merit the attention of a body of lunatics . . . ." [2]

Preparation for the general strike was left largely in the hands of the local labor organizations. Workmen throughout the country were urged to lay aside a certain sum of money each week, invest it in the necessities of life before May 1, 1886, and thus be in a position to defy defeat. By this time the goal of the movement had changed to a demand for shorter hours, not necessarily an eight-hour day. When May 1 arrived, 150,000 secured a reduced workday (eight or nine hours) without striking, and 190,000 struck, of whom only 42,000 were successful. [3] The advantage of many of these gains, however, was lessened by the practice of employers of paying smaller wages for fewer hours. Moreover, *Bradstreet's,* June 12, six weeks after the strike, reported a withdrawal of one third of the concessions, with a prospect of more to come. This result was in part due to the public hostility to labor excited by the Haymarket riot in Chicago. [4]

[1] Gunton, *Wealth and Progress,* 254-256.

[2] E. L. Bogart and C. M. Thompson, *The Industrial State, 1870-1893* (C. W. Alvord, ed., *The Centennial History of Illinois,* IV, Springfield, 1920), 163 *n.*

[3] Commons and others, *History of Labour,* II, 384-385.

[4] Gompers's opinion, U. S. Industrial Commission, *Report* (Wash., 1900-1902), VII, 623.

Chicago, with eighty thousand wage-earners participating in the strike, had been the storm center of the eight-hour movement. There the tension between capital and labor was rapidly reaching the breaking point. Not only were aggressive employers determined to break the growing power of the unions, but the labor movement in Chicago was shot through with all kinds of European radicalism. In hysterical rhetoric the *Illinois State Register* described one labor demonstration as consisting of "Communistic Germans, Bohemians and Poles, representing the lumber-yards, coopers, bakers, the cigar shops, the breweries, and the International Workingmen's Association . . . the Nihilistic character of the procession was shown by the red badges and red flags which were thickly displayed through it." [1]

Among the leading industrialists of the city was Cyrus H. McCormick, jr., head of the harvester works. In February he had locked out his fourteen hundred employees when they tried to enforce the principles of unionism. "I told them," he said, "that the right to hire any man, white or black, union or nonunion, Protestant or Catholic, was something I would not surrender." [2] He declined to consider either compromise or arbitration. When "scabs" replaced the locked-out workers, disorder became rife, guards were taken into the factory and the police were continually called on to break up threatening meetings. McCormick decided, however, to concede the eight-hour day demanded by organized labor. The decision was announced on May 3 and a half-holiday was granted to celebrate it. As the workers came out of the factory they were greeted

[1] Bogart and Thompson, *Industrial State*, 168. See also the *Arbeiter-Zeitung*, Nov. 28, 1884, quoted by Commons and others, *History of Labour*, II, 389-390.

[2] Bogart and Thompson, *Industrial State*, 166. W. T. Hutchinson, *Cyrus Hall McCormick: Harvest, 1856-1884* (N. Y., 1935), 615-617, sheds light on the family background of the younger McCormick's attitude toward labor.

with hoots of contempt and derision by the union men assembled near by. Not far away, in a vacant lot, striking lumbermen were holding a meeting which August Spies, editor of the radical *Arbeiter Zeitung*, was addressing.[1] The two groups joined forces. The owner summoned the police and, in the fighting that followed, several workingmen were killed and a score or so wounded.[2]

That night five thousand copies of a circular, printed in English and German, were scattered over the city. "Revenge! Revenge! Workmen to arms!" it shrieked:

> Men of labor, this afternoon the bloodhounds of your oppressors murdered six of your brothers at McCormick's! Why did they murder them? Because they dared to be dissatisfied with the lot which your oppressors have assigned to them. They demanded bread, and they gave them lead for an answer.[3]

Meetings of protest were at once called by the strikers, the most important one for the evening of May 4 near Haymarket Square. Three leading anarchists addressed the gathering, which numbered perhaps one thousand five hundred. Mayor Carter Harrison attended and, finding it orderly, went home. The crowd had begun to break up when a squad of police appeared with Inspector John Bonfield at their head. As they reached the crowd, ordering it to disperse, there occurred a terrific explosion. It was a bomb thrown from no one knew where into the ranks of the police, killing one and wounding many more. Instantly an indiscriminate firing opened on both sides. When it was over, sixty-eight policemen were so injured that seven died and

---

[1] C. E. Russell, *These Shifting Scenes* (N. Y., 1914), 85.
[2] Morris Hillquit, *History of Socialism in the United States* (N. Y., 1903), 245.
[3] Bogart and Thompson, *Industrial State*, 169-170.

many were crippled for life, while of the crowd four were killed and about fifty wounded.[1]

What followed that awful night's work is an illuminating demonstration of what a city and its forces of law and order are capable when in the grip of fear, suspicion and a lust for revenge. The almost universal, and probably true, conviction was that the bomb came from the hand of a member of one of the small bands of anarchists which for months had been urging upon strikers the necessity of direct action. But such apostles of violence were few. Charles Edward Russell, who as a reporter covered the Haymarket riot and in 1907 made a detailed investigation of the affair, declared that Chicago in 1886 possessed "a very small group, comprising perhaps fourteen in all, of physical force anarchists, depraved and desperate men of the type that assassinated Sadi Carnot and the king of Italy."[2] Even more sinister to conservatives than the anarchist philosophy was the fact that its adherents were tolerated, included even, by many unions which, while decrying the doctrine of direct action, were willing to use the threat of it to wring concessions from the employing class. Business men sympathetic with the eight-hour demand saw in this alliance with violence proof that what labor really sought was an overturn of the industrial order.

"Those who threw the explosives that resulted so disastrously," declared the *Chicago Inter Ocean*, May 5, "aimed to destroy the law. They have made the issue and they should be hunted to the ends of the earth." On the Sunday following the outbreak the ministers of the city dealt with the affair under such titles as "Anarchy," "Dead Policemen," "Protection against Anarchy" and "Our Foreign Population."[3] The press

---

[1] Hillquit, *History of Socialism*, 246-247.
[2] Russell, *Shifting Scenes*, 106.
[3] *Chicago Inter Ocean*, May 10, 1886.

did not report a single pulpit as advising the use of
Christian moderation in dealing with the offenders.   In
other parts of the country public opinion was quite
as febrile.   The *Indianapolis News*, May 5, held that
the "Chicago police would have been justified in whole-
sale slaughter."   The *Louisville Courier-Journal* of the
same date impatiently demanded that the "blatant
cattle" be "immediately strung up."   The *Philadelphia
Times*, May 6, gave Chicago definite orders "to kick the
anarchists out."   Even the usually even-tempered
Springfield Republican, May 8, declared, "It is no time
for half measures."

Meanwhile, the police, egged on by popular sentiment and blind with rage at the slaughter in their ranks,
set out to find the guilty parties.   "For days," remarks
Charles Edward Russell, "the police stations were filled
with suspected persons, rigorously examined in the
method of the third degree; persons for the most part
that had no knowledge of the bomb nor of the meeting,
nor of anything connected with either, and could not
have." [1]   In the end, the authorities settled on eight
well-known anarchists, men conspicuous for their advo-
cacy of social revolution.   These were Albert Parsons,
editor of the *Alarm;* August Spies, Michael Schwab and
Adolph Fischer of the *Arbeiter-Zeitung;* Samuel Fielden,
George Engels, Oscar W. Neebe and Louis Lingg.[2]   All
but Parsons and Neebe were of foreign birth.   On June
21 the eight were brought to trial and, after many
weeks of almost frenzied public attention, all were

[1] Russell, *Shifting Scenes*, 88.
[2] Rudolph Schnaubelt and William Seliger were also arrested; but
Schnaubelt, released by the police for reasons not clear, escaped from the
country, and Seliger was granted immunity for turning state's evidence.
In the judgment of those observers closest to the affair as well as of later
students, Lingg had manufactured the bomb and Schnaubelt threw it.
Through the European anarchist press, however, Schnaubelt repeatedly
denied any connection with the deed.   Bogart and Thompson, *Industrial
State*, 172 *n.*; Hillquit, *History of Socialism*, 247.

found guilty. Seven were sentenced to death and the other, Neebe, to fifteen years' imprisonment. No one of the eight was proved to have had any hand in making or throwing the bomb: the men were condemned because of their revolutionary opinions. As Joseph E. Gary, the presiding judge, later declared, the defendants "had generally by speech and print advised large classes of the people . . . to commit murder, and . . . in pursuance of that advice, and influenced by that advice, somebody not known did throw the bomb . . . ." [1] Yet Judge Gary's opinion was not more than an assumption, for the fact was not established by court evidence.

The death sentences aroused strong opposition in and out of Chicago. Leonard Swett, one of Chicago's ablest lawyers, held the verdict legally wrong. Lyman Trumbull, friend of Abraham Lincoln, wrote Governor Richard Oglesby that he knew of no other state trial in history where eight men were tried together for their lives on an indictment containing sixty-nine counts. He declared that not an enlightened nation on the globe would permit it. From the East William Dean Howells wrote of the condemned men, "I have never believed them guilty of murder, or of anything but their opinions, and I do not think they were justly convicted." [2] In many parts of the country meetings were held urging clemency. The Knights of Labor at their general assembly in 1886 took similar action, and so did the Chicago Central Labor Union. These appeals were harshly criticized by the press of the country, which was almost unanimous in approving the verdict.

The case was carried to the state supreme court and the verdict sustained. The hanging was fixed for No-

[1] J. E. Gary, "The Chicago Anarchists of 1886," *Century Mag.*, n.s., XXIII (1892-1893), 835.
[2] W. D. Howells, *Life in Letters of William Dean Howells* (Mildred Howells, ed., Garden City, 1928), I, 393.

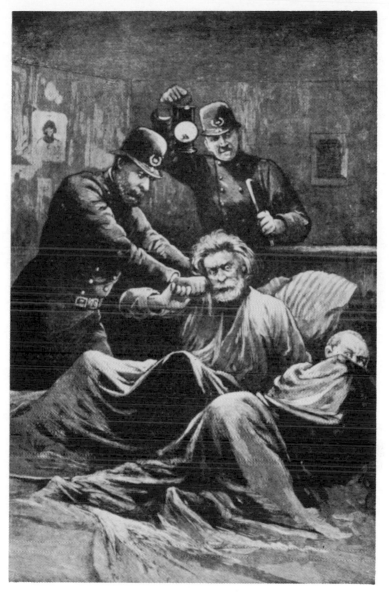

Capturing Anarchists

vember 11, 1887. On the day before, the sentences of
Fielden and Schwab were commuted to life imprisonment. Lingg escaped the penalty by blowing out his
brains with a bomb believed to have been given him by
his sweetheart who had visited him in his cell.[1] The
four remaining men were hanged. "The time will
come," declared Spies as the noose was placed about
his neck, "when our silence in the grave will be more
eloquent than our speeches."[2]

Six years later Governor John P. Altgeld, a few
weeks after his inauguration, pardoned the men who
had been sentenced to life terms. He accompanied the
act with a thoroughgoing analysis of the evidence and a
scathing arraignment of the unfair and partial methods
of the judge.[3] "If I do it," he had told Clarence Dar-
row, "I will be a dead man politically."[4] He was right.
The act, prompted by an uncompromising love of justice, brought down on his head a flood of vituperation
such as few men in public life have ever received. Advertised by the nation's press as a friend of "anarchy,"
he faced political oblivion.

The year 1886, which brought so many setbacks to
the labor movement, led Terence V. Powderly to make
futile efforts to stay the process of disintegration which
had begun in the Knights of Labor. His most difficult
task was to combat the widespread belief that the order
reeked with radicalism and anarchism. In the period of
rapid expansion anarchists and socialists had been admitted to membership and many of them had cunningly
used the order as a recruiting ground for their doctrines.
Some of them, Powderly believed, had been "hired by

[1] Russell, *Shifting Scenes*, 102.
[2] Hillquit, *History of Socialism*, 252.
[3] W. R. Browne, *Altgeld of Illinois* (N. Y., 1924), 95-105; J. P.
Altgeld, *Reasons for Pardoning Fielden, Neebe and Schwab* (Chicago,
1893).
[4] Bogart and Thompson, *Industrial State*, 187 *n*.

monopolists to become members . . . so that public opinion might be turned against the order." On one occasion the attorney of a manufacturers' association frankly told him, "We have paid Anarchists to become members of your assemblies that they might stir up the devil and bring discredit upon your whole movement." [1]

In place of the discredited methods the general assembly now endeavored to stress education "on the great questions of labor." Not only was militancy to be discarded, but also politics. It proved as difficult, however, to keep the local assemblies out of political struggles as it had been to keep them out of strikes. Though their national officers warned them "so surely as we run into politics we shall be destroyed," few remembered the warning when a fight occurred for some law which they favored. Both their wide sympathies and their itch for political action made the Knights of Labor a natural ally of the Farmers' Alliances.[2] In the Knights' opinion, the two sets of interests were alike: the interests of those who labored. In 1891 the Knights were strongly represented at the Cincinnati convention which formed the People's party, and in the campaign of 1892 they also took an active part. By this time, however, the organization was only the shadow of its former self. Its membership had fallen from 700,000 in 1886 to less than 260,000 in 1888 and to 100,000 in 1890, with the downward tendency unchecked.[3]

While the Knights were declining, the American Federation of Labor was increasing its hold on the labor movement and strengthening its position in American life. At a meeting in Columbus, Ohio, in December, 1886, the organization took stock and decided it needed a thorough overhauling, a headquarters, full-time offi-

---

[1] T. V. Powderly, *Thirty Years of Labor* (Columbus, 1889), 540.
[2] Commons and others, *History of Labour*, II, 423.
[3] Commons and others, *History of Labour*, II, 482.

cers and salaried organizers.[1]   Samuel Gompers was elected president at a salary of one thousand dollars a year, occupying as his first office a room eight by ten, its desk a kitchen table, its chair a box and its filing cases tomato cans.   Under his vigorous direction the Federation eschewed politics, avoided the pitfalls offered by radical doctrines and stressed trade-union methods.

In 1888 the Federation decided to launch forth on a new general strike for the eight-hour day, to begin on May 1, 1890.   But the plan was later changed for one by which a single well-organized union, that of the carpenters, should make the first effort, supported with financial contributions from members of the Federation.[2]   The strike proved moderately successful.   An attempt in 1891 to repeat this feat, with the miners, fell through, however, because their union, rent with internal dissension, failed at the last moment to act as agreed.   The number of national unions affiliated with the Federation steadily increased, and from 1886 to 1898 the membership rose from about 140,000 to 278,000.[3]

The eighties and nineties proved a crucial period in the history of the American labor movement.   Two great experiments in the nation-wide organization of wage-earners had been tried and tested: one involving the amalgamation of all workers, and the other the federation of those already combined in separate crafts. The events of these years decreed the greater acceptability of the federative type of structure.   This decision involved, further, an emphasis on organizing skilled labor rather than all grades of labor.   Unskilled workers, representing the bulk of the wage-earners, remained outside the fold of the unions.

[1] Lorwin, *American Federation of Labor*, 21-23.

[2] Perlman, *History of Trade Unionism*, 131-133.

[3] Commons and others, *History of Labour*, II, 410 *n.*; Lorwin, *American Federation of Labor*, 484.

CHAPTER X

EFFORTS FOR INDUSTRIAL PEACE

WHILE public attention was fastened on industrial disturbances and portents of what seemed an impending class struggle, other forces were quietly at work in an effort to bridge the widening gulf between capital and labor. From the mid-eighties employers' associations came into increasing prominence.[1] Though most of them were formed to combat working-class pretensions, many of them endeavored to render practical the ideal of collective bargaining which the labor movement advocated. In their form of organization the employers' associations profited greatly from the experience of the trade unions; almost every important feature was copied.[2] Like the unions, the employers' associations sought to control the action of their members in respect to the inauguration or settlement of labor disputes. They also had their defense funds and stood ready to aid financially any member involved in a lockout or other cessation of work. Moreover, just as the unions found it desirable to maintain salaried agents or "walking delegates," so the employers' groups had their commissioners with analogous duties.

The first employers' organization on a national scale was the Stove Founders' National Defense Association, dating from 1886. Its avowed purpose was "the unification of its members for protection and defense against unjust, unlawful and unwarranted demands of labor."

[1] J. R. Commons and others, *History of Labour in the United States* (N. Y., 1918), II, 414-416.
[2] W. F. Willoughby, "Employers' Associations for Dealing with Labor in the United States," *Quar. Journ. of Economics*, XX, 144.

The labor organization aimed at was the strong and aggressive Iron Molders' Union, numbering some thirteen thousand members.[1] Though the Defense Association was successful in its contests with the molders, these struggles proved expensive and demoralizing. In the end, the two bodies decided to attempt to work out a method of peaceful settlement. At a joint conference held in 1891 they agreed to abandon strikes and lockouts and to compose all differences amicably upon a basis which they outlined. Conferences were held each year and the agreements made seem to have been honorably observed by both sides.[2] So successful was the plan that foundries manufacturing other articles than stoves decided to organize along similar lines. In 1898 came the National Founders' Association, formed avowedly "with the distinct understanding and the knowledge that a labor organization existed, had a right to exist; that men had a right to join each other for their mutual benefits."[3]

Along with such efforts to work out practical machinery for peaceably settling disputes went constructive attempts by enlightened employers to remove sources of difficulty before trouble arose. Hours, wages and conditions of work were at the bottom of most of such differences. Could they not be corrected before trouble broke out? Ought not, and could not, employers lead, instead of follow, in improving the life of their employees? One serious handicap from which labor suffered was the paying of wages by the month. To remedy this, the Knights of Labor listed among their

---

[1] Leo Wolman, *The Growth of American Trade Unions, 1880-1923* (Natl. Bur. of Econ. Research, *Publs.*, no. 6), 32.

[2] Willoughby, "Employers' Associations for Dealing with Labor," 114; F. T. Carlton, *The History and Problems of Organized Labor* (Boston, 1911), 246-249.

[3] C. E. Bonnett, *Employers' Associations in the United States* (N. Y., 1922), 68.

demands a law compelling corporations to pay employees weekly.

After Andrew Carnegie in 1889 settled a strike for higher wages by introducing a sliding scale, he set out to find what further changes in the method of payment were desirable. To his questioning one man answered,

> I have a good woman for wife who manages well. We go into Pittsburgh every fourth Saturday afternoon and buy our supplies wholesale for the next month and save one third. Not many of your men can do this. Shopkeepers here charge so much. . . . If you paid your men every two weeks, instead of monthly, it would be as good for the careful men as a raise in wages of ten per cent or more.[1]

Carnegie not only acted upon the suggestion, but he helped the men start a coöperative store in order to combat the high price of necessities. The mill paid the rent of the building; the men themselves bought the stock and managed the concern. Carnegie believed that not the least benefit of the plan was that it "taught the men that business had its difficulties." Dissatisfaction over the price of coal was cured by an agreement by which the company sold coal to its employees at the net cost, which was about half of what the regular dealers had charged.[2]

The hazardous character of railway employment presented a special labor problem because the workers faced the constant possibility of accidents which might leave their families helpless and without means of support. In the hope of coping with this difficulty the Baltimore & Ohio Company made a thorough study of what had been accomplished by English societies formed for the purpose. As a result it established in 1880 a Relief As-

---

[1] Andrew Carnegie, *Autobiography* (N. Y., 1920), 250.
[2] Carnegie, *Autobiography*, 250.

sociation which has continued in existence ever since. The company agreed to pay the operating and administrative expenses. From a fund accumulated by regular contributions of the Relief Association members, provision was made for injured or sick employees and, in case of death, for their families.

In 1882 a savings feature was added in the nature of both a mutual savings bank and a building association. Two years later the company followed these undertakings with a pension plan which, with certain modifications, is still in existence. The pensions were charged to monthly operating expenses. No pension should exceed fifty per cent of a man's average monthly earnings and none be less than $22.50 a month.[1] Before the end of the century a number of other leading roads had adopted features of the comprehensive Baltimore & Ohio scheme. In no case, however, did the variant plans cover the needs so thoroughly and generously.

Though, as we have seen, the capitalist class generally resisted the demand for an eight-hour day, certain large employers saw in shorter hours an assurance of higher efficiency and bigger output. "Cap" Jones, it will be recalled, found in the eight-hour day one reason for the ability of the Carnegie steel plant at Braddock to produce many more tons than any of its British competitors. "Flesh and blood cannot stand twelve hours' continuous work," he had said.[2]

Other employers were slowly beginning to see that not only humanitarian considerations but also enlightened self-interest justified a shorter workday. Thus

[1] According to information supplied by the Public Relations Department of the Baltimore & Ohio Railroad, the Relief Association had paid out nearly fifty and a half million dollars to Baltimore & Ohio employees up to December, 1934. At that time there were seventeen and a half million of deposits in the savings department and about eight and a half million on loan to employees. More than twenty million dollars has been paid by the road since the beginning for pensions.

[2] H. N. Casson, *The Romance of Steel* (N. Y., 1907), 28.

George McMurtry, head of a galvanized-iron mill on the Kiskiminetas River, forty miles northeast of Pittsburgh, tried the experiment of reducing hours from ten to eight. Watching the men, he had become convinced that they "pumped themselves out in eight hours." Hours beyond eight were "tired hours," also dangerous hours, for in them most of the accidents happened and work was apt to be spoiled. He discovered that with eight-hour shifts the men got more out of their machines than by laboring two hours more. As McMurtry put it, "They worked to the tune of 'Yankee Doodle,' not to that of 'Old Hundred.'" [1]

The shorter shift, however, did not apply to the furnace men, those who worked intensely for twenty or thirty minutes and then rested for an equal period while the furnace was made ready for the next "heat." One reason was opposition on the part of the Amalgamated Iron, Steel and Tin Workers. They believed that under the eight-hour plan their earnings would be less since at that time it was difficult to make five heats in the shorter day and they did not want to be hurried in producing what was called a reasonable output. They asserted, further, that they had more freedom under the twelve-hour shift than they would have under the eight-hour because of the frequent rest periods which they could use as they wished. Still another reason, which the report of the proceedings of 1894 emphasized, was the fear that the eight-hour arrangement would bring in new labor and increase competition for jobs. [2]

Along with experiments with the shorter workday went ventures in what was called profit sharing. This was an attempt by the employer to restore the feeling of association in a common cause which had charac-

---

[1] Ida M. Tarbell, *New Ideals in Business* (N. Y., 1914), 172-173.
[2] J. S. Robinson, *The Amalgamated Association of Iron, Steel and Tin Workers* (Johns Hopkins Univ., *Studies*, XXXVIII, no. 2), 106-107.

terized the relations of master and men in simpler industrial times. To many exponents of the doctrine, profit sharing seemed a necessary step by capital to combat both socialism and producers' coöperation.[1] It was designed to give the employee a reason beyond his daily wage for rendering an honest day's work and, at the same time, to make him regard himself as a part of the establishment, willing to stay by and interest himself in economies and more efficient production. What was sought was a stable and contented labor body.

Interest in the subject had been stimulated by experiments in many European countries. Thirty-one French firms adopted some form of profit sharing in the 1880's, raising the whole number reported in France in 1890 to seventy-one.[2] In the British Empire during the same period the plan was undertaken by fifty-one concerns.[3] In the United States before 1878 profit sharing had been tried by but two establishments: the Peace Dale Rhode Island Manufacturing Company and the Riverside Press of Cambridge, Massachusetts.[4] But stirred by the unrest of labor and influenced by European example, other employers began to explore its possibilities. By 1893 a hundred or more concerns had gone over to one or another form of profit sharing.[5]

One of the most carefully prepared undertakings was that of the N. O. Nelson Manufacturing Company. Nelson, a Norwegian by birth, was engaged in manufac-

[1] N. P. Gilman, *Socialism and the American Spirit* (Boston, 1893), 295-298.

[2] The returns were made sometimes in cash, sometimes in investments in a provident fund. Frequently they were indefinite in amount, being adjusted according to the earnings of the company. N. P. Gilman, *A Dividend to Labor* (Boston, 1899), 366-368.

[3] Usually the bonus was paid in cash. In a few cases it was paid partly in cash and partly in stock in the concern or in a provident fund supported by the company. Gilman, *Dividend to Labor*, 374-376.

[4] N. P. Gilman, *Profit Sharing between Employer and Employee* (Boston, 1889), 296-300, 321-322.

[5] Gilman, *Socialism and the American Spirit*, 303.

turing plumbing and building supplies in St. Louis at the time the great railroad strike on the Gould system tied up business in 1886. Being called upon to serve as conciliator and arbitrator in one of the disputes, he began to study the basic causes of industrial discord and determined to work out in his own business a plan which would meet what he considered the legitimate grievances of labor. Before making any move he investigated the experiments in profit sharing which had been tried abroad. In 1886 he inaugurated his own plan. The business was to pay the customary wages, earn a six-per-cent dividend and take care of a sinking fund and other obligations. The profits remaining were to be divided among the employees in proportion to their wages, the payments to be made either in cash or stock. The employees from the start seem to have regarded themselves as actual partners in the enterprise: the notion that capital and labor were necessarily enemies vanished. Though the annual dividend paid to labor varied, it never fell below ten, and some years rose as high as thirty, per cent paid in stock.[1]

Many years later Nelson set down what he regarded as the secret of the success of the plan. "We have not been ambitious to become great or rich," he declared, "but we have sought to make business a means to independence and social life." [2] Certain other profit-sharing schemes had failed, he said, for reasons that might have been cured: the plans were arbitrary and coupled with hampering restrictions; or too quick results were expected; or the primary motive was "better business, not more equal division."

An equally notable venture in profit sharing was that undertaken by Procter and Gamble, the soap manufacturers in Cincinnati. As they frankly informed their

---

[1] Gilman, *Profit Sharing*, 305-308.
[2] Tarbell, *New Ideals in Business*, 232-233.

employees, the purpose was to increase "diligence, carefulness and thoughtful coöperation" in order to enlarge earnings—earnings in which, of course, the employees would share. The sum divided was to bear the same relation to the total profits as the amount of wages, including the partners' salaries, bore to the total cost of carrying on the business. Only those who had been three months or more with the firm were to participate. The semiannual day of distribution was set aside as a holiday.

In May, 1890, on the sixth dividend day, it was reported that profits of sixty thousand dollars had been distributed in the three preceding years, equal to about sixteen per cent of the wages paid. The "diligence, carefulness and thoughtful coöperation" which the firm sought had not, however, been fully secured. Certain changes were therefore made in the plan: the employees were divided into four classes, and dividends were to follow merit. But the revised regulations did not work out as well as the company desired. Just before and after dividend days enthusiasm was great; the diligence was all that could be asked. But gradually this wore off, to return only as the next celebration approached. Instead of being satisfied with a moderate degree of achievement the firm in 1903 put into effect an entirely new scheme, called "trust-receipt dividends for employees through stock ownership." [1] The years of trial and error culminated in a highly successful plan.

Not infrequently the company that adopted profit sharing also interested itself in improving the conditions under which its workingmen lived. In 1890 Nelson removed his manufacturing plant from St. Louis to southern Illinois, believing that his profit-sharing plan would fare better there than in a large city. Purchasing a tract of land near Edwardsville, he founded upon

[1] Tarbell, *New Ideals in Business*, 222-257.

it the village of Leclaire which he laid out as a model community. With the firm's help it was made possible for every employee to build and own his own home. The town's population was not confined to employees, however. If an outsider wanted to live there, the company would build him a home also, allowing him, as it did its employees, to pay in monthly installments. His income and the size of his family were taken into consideration in fixing the monthly payments. There was practically no upkeep in Leclaire. It was not an incorporated town, and the inhabitants looked after themselves, caring for the streets, the lighting, the water, the ball grounds, the kindergarten, etc.[1] For many years it was the boast of the residents that they had no policeman, no pauperism and an extraordinarily low death rate.[2]

The most ambitious of the made-to-order towns was that founded in 1880 by the Pullman Car Company. This concern, desiring to secure greater room for growth than Chicago afforded and to give its labor force better homes, bought some four thousand acres in the town of Hyde Park ten miles south of Chicago. There it had the best landscape architects in the country lay out an industrial community, provided with the most scientific drainage, sewerage and water supply. The houses, built of brick, attractive in style and possessing up-to-date conveniences, were suited to a variety of purses. Two rooms rented for four dollars a month; separate dwellings from fourteen to one hundred dollars. Garbage was carried away every day and the streets were swept and watered. Among the special features of Pullman, as the town was called, were a single large market house, an arcade onto which all the shops opened, a modern hotel, a gymnasium, a playhouse and an amphitheater

[1] Tarbell, *New Ideals in Business*, 145.
[2] Gilman, *Dividend to Labor*, 323-333.

A street

The arcade and public square

Pullman, Illinois

for games. The company provided the inhabitants with a physician and medicines. So healthy was Pullman that in the first three years the death rate was said to be less than a third the average for an American town.

The undertaking attracted wide attention. In the fall of 1884 representatives from the labor bureaus of thirteen states, along with Carroll D. Wright, United States commissioner of labor, spent three days at Pullman studying the community. Their report was, on the whole, favorable. Though they found rentals a little higher than in Chicago, the people enjoyed broad avenues, prompt collection of garbage, and other advantages which they would not have had in Chicago.[1] The most serious criticism was that the residents had little or nothing to say about the conduct of community affairs. Thoughtful students of the labor problem doubted whether the American workman would be willing to live permanently in a town where he was under strict guardianship, where he could not own property and where he had nothing to say about the government.

Still another experiment in improving the living conditions of employees was that undertaken by the iron-master George McMurtry. Finding that his plant was outgrowing the land available in its vicinity, he bought a farm of six hundred and forty acres a few miles away and in 1890 built both a model factory and a model town. His plans had been formed after careful study of Essen in Germany, Creusot in France and the co-operative villages in Belgium. In laying out Vandergrift, as he named the town, he employed the best known specialists. When the streets were finished, trees planted, water, sewerage and electricity in, lots were offered to the mill men on terms which they could easily

---

[1] Massachusetts Bureau of Statistics of Labor, *Annual Report for 1885*, pt. i; Gilman, *Dividend to Labor*, 239-244; R. T. Ely, "Pullman: A Social Study," *Harper's Mag.*, LXX (1885), 452-466.

meet. The construction of homes was financed through a building and loan company. Vandergrift was organized as a borough with a burgess and a council consisting usually of mill workers. They controlled also the school and health boards.[1] The fact that labor owned its homes and had a full voice in the government explains why the history of Vandergrift proved so different from that of Pullman.[2]

Quite as important, though far different in character, was the effort to better the relations of employer and employee through the introduction of rational principles of shop management. Though large-scale production had come to dominate American industry, it was generally carried on with a scorn of science on the part of the employer, a devotion to hit-and-miss methods on the part of labor. To submit practice to observation and tests was ridiculed in the average machine shop by the management and fought by the men. Even the mechanical engineer was too often an empiricist, building his engine on hunches. "Now, boys, we have got her done, let's start her up and see why she doesn't work" was the jocular introduction which one of the most successful engineers of the day gave to new machines of his designing.[3]

The man who inaugurated a bold departure from this rule-of-thumb system was Frederick W. Taylor who in 1878, at the age of twenty, entered the employ of the Midvale Steel Company at Philadelphia. Because of weak eyes he had been obliged to give up Harvard for which he had prepared at Exeter after two years of travel and study in Europe. Unable to continue his

[1] In 1914, when the author visited Vandergrift, it had 4500 people, most of them mill employees owning their own homes. The building and loan association had never lost money except in one case. Tarbell, *New Ideals in Business*, 146-155.

[2] See later, 233-235.

[3] F. B. Copley, *Frederick W. Taylor, Father of Scientific Management* (N. Y., 1923), I, 101.

academic career, he chose to become a mechanic, beginning at the bottom. It was a case of good brains counting, for young Taylor rose rapidly in the concern. In turn he was common laborer, gang boss, foreman of the machine shop, master mechanic, chief draftsman and eventually engineer.[1]

As foreman he was confronted with the characteristic attitude of the workmen towards their job. It was to stretch it as far as possible, not to do their best. To Taylor this seemed not only uneconomic but, what was more fundamental in his mind, stultifying to manhood. He decided to see that the men got from their machines a full day's work. But what was a full day's work? What could a particular machine do? Nobody knew. In order to find out he analyzed the job into its several parts and, through studying them, he began to pick out wastes of time and motion. The wastes were by no means all due to the men; they were due also to their machines, their tools, the shop conditions, the ways of management. Everything must be changed, he saw, if he was to get the full day's work he sought.

What Taylor was working toward was the most efficient way to perform each operation from the simplest to the most complex. A chorus of doubts and jeers from above and below greeted this unheard-of attempt to apply scientific methods to labor. Science was something for professors in laboratories: what had it to do with the way men worked? It certainly seemed bizarre to apply it to the shoveling of ashes and slag; but Taylor did it by demonstrating that shoveling could be reduced to a series of motions and those motions taught to a man to his own and his employer's profit.

It was one thing, however, to discover the best way of performing a task and another and more difficult one to persuade the workers to adopt the formula. The

[1] Copley, *Frederick W. Taylor*, I, 116.

systematic soldiering of employees sprang in part from their almost universal belief that the world had only so much work to do and that, if a man did more than the amount considered "right" by his shop mates, he was depriving others of the means of employment. Furthermore, the men had learned from experience that, if they did twice as much as they were doing, their rate of pay was not advanced. They were not allowed to earn according to capacity. The system put a premium on inefficiency. To correct this condition Taylor insisted that each employee be paid according to output. A first-class man should be a "high-priced man," he contended. In the end he was able to demonstrate that high wages in a scientifically managed shop meant lower labor costs.[1]

Taylor's attack on existing forms of management was no less severe than that on the practices of the workmen. He saw from the start that the chief obstacle to a full day's work lay in management, its failure to plan and properly to regulate production. Machines lay idle because care had not been taken to keep them busy. Men stretched out a job because they had no assurance that when it was finished another would be ready. Taylor stood for the principle that production should never run ahead of or behind a carefully reckoned demand. But when he set about to reduce the operations of management to scientific terms he met an opposition stiffer than he had from the workmen. Chiefly, those in authority had to learn that the essence of scientific management lay in a coöperation with the employees that was "intimate and friendly." In Taylor's opinion, work of any account, in order to be done rightly, must be done through true coöperation rather than through the individual effort of any one man.

[1] F. W. Taylor, "A Piece-Rate System," *Supplement to Economic Studies*, I, no. 2, 89-129.

Rapid progress was attained in arriving at this attitude. Under the new conditions the shop managers laid out ahead the day's work for each man at his machine; to him they went with their instructions; to them he went for explanations and suggestions. Office and shop intermingled, realizing a mutual dependence as never before. Both sides came to feel, more or less as Taylor himself, that nothing of moment was ever accomplished save by teamwork.

Out of Taylor's experiments in the Midvale plant from 1878 to 1881 grew the science of management. Probably no other plant in the country would have allowed him the same freedom for trying out his ideas. He was fortunate in having as head of the business William Sellers, a prolific inventor and a man who, though not always agreeing with Taylor, fully appreciated the importance of what he was trying to achieve.[1] Most employers remained unconvinced even after the success of Taylor's methods was demonstrated. In increased production they saw the likelihood of overproduction and hence lowered prices. Similarly labor leaders objected. Make too much, they said, and the work will not go round. Taylor argued otherwise. "There is hardly any worse crime to my mind," he declared,

> than that of deliberately restricting output. . . . The world's history shows that just as fast as you bring the good things that are needed by man into the world, man takes and uses them. That one fact, the immense increase in the productivity of man, marks the difference between civilized and uncivilized countries . . . it is due to that increase of productivity that the working people of today, with all the talk about their misery and their horrible treatment, . . . have better

[1] Copley, *Frederick W. Taylor*, I, 106-115.

food, better clothing, and on the whole more comforts than kings had 250 years ago.[1]

All these attempts to improve industrial relations attracted wide attention and, when considered sufficiently important, were recorded in the publications of the state and federal labor bureaus. One of the demands of organized labor had been the establishment of statistical bureaus which should report regularly on conditions of employment. Massachusetts had set up such a bureau in 1869; by 1878 three other commonwealths had them in operation. Before 1898 a total of twenty-seven, including all the leading industrial states, took this action.[2] Meanwhile, in 1884, the government at Washington followed suit by creating a federal bureau of labor with a commissioner at its head. His duty was to make an annual statistical report on the hours and wages of labor, also to take up, as his judgment dictated or as Congress or the executive directed, any matter concerning labor which needed investigation before action should be taken. In general, he was instructed to collect and disseminate reliable information touching on labor conditions.

Happily for the future of the new bureau the first commissioner of labor was Carroll D. Wright, as capable a man as the country possessed for such an undertaking. He had keenly interested himself in labor problems from the time when, as a member of the Massachusetts state senate in 1872-1873, he had brought about the passage of a law compelling suburban railroads to run trains at hours convenient for workingmen. In particular, he

[1] F. W. Taylor, "The Principles of Scientific Management," *Addresses and Discussions at the Conference on Scientific Management Held October 12, 13, 14, Nineteen Hundred and Eleven* (Hanover, N. H., 1912), 25-26.

[2] J. D. Richardson, comp., *A Compilation of the Messages and Papers of the Presidents* (Wash., 1896-1899), X, 446.

was a student of labor statistics and in 1880 acted as a special agent to investigate the factory system for the federal census. He was busy with statistical work for his state when he was called to Washington to his new office.

As federal commissioner of labor his annual reports made an immediate impression as did also his reports of findings in special cases. Legislative bodies, harassed by labor and an emotional public to pass laws forbidding this or regulating that, found in the commissioner's reports solid information on which to base action. For example, he took up the demand of both the Knights and the American Federation of Labor to abolish convict labor. What was the factual basis of their charge that the practice injured outside employment in the same trades? The answer was an exhaustive study of the system in vogue in each prison and in each state, accompanied by an historical review of the handling of convict labor in other countries.

So far as the United States was concerned, the results showed that the product of all the prisons was but 0.54 per cent of the total mechanical products of the country. Nevertheless, at certain points, convict labor was of a quantity and quality to displace free labor. Thus in 1885, the last year of the investigation, 67.8 per cent of the barrels, tierces and kegs sold in Chicago had been made by convicts. While the prison contractors' business had grown 360 per cent between 1875 and 1885, private cooperage increased but 31 per cent. It was a feebler industry relatively than eleven years before. The report further pointed out:

> But the proprietor has not been the only nor the greater sufferer in this struggle. Under the natural and inevitable operation of the contract system, prices have continually declined, and the citizen, in his fruitless

effort to compete with the contractor, has visited every reduction in price upon the journeyman cooper in the form of a reduction in wages.[1]

Though the report revealed relatively few instances of harmful competition with free labor, nevertheless the moral effect of the supposed competition and the possibility of further real competition caused most of the states to adopt legislation to restrict or abolish productive industry by convicts.[2] From 1885 to the close of the century there occurred a general slump in prison employments. This development interfered seriously with the plans of penologists who saw in self-support an essential means of rehabilitating the inmates, and in time led to a replacement of the contract system with the public-account and state-use systems.[3]

Meanwhile, in his third report, that of 1888, Commissioner Wright had given a temperate and well-considered review of the railway strikes in the Southwest in 1885-1886. This afforded further evidence of the value of the labor bureau to the nation. It was not surprising, therefore, that Congress in June, 1888, elevated the bureau to a department. Continuing as head, Wright in the next few years investigated and reported on such important matters as compulsory insurance, building and loan associations, the housing of working people and industrial education.

If President Cleveland could have had his way, the labor arm of the government would have played an even more vital part in the industrial situation. "The present condition of the relations between labor and capital is far from satisfactory," he informed Congress on April 22, 1886. In his opinion the proper means for settling

[1] U. S. Commissioner of Labor, *Second Annual Report* (1886), 375.
[2] H. E. Barnes, *The Repression of Crime* (N. Y., 1926), 273-276.
[3] See A. M. Schlesinger, *The Rise of the City* (*A History of American Life*, X), 363.

these difficulties was voluntary arbitration, not by "arbitrators chosen in the heat of conflicting claims," but by a "stable body" acting as a part of the bureau of labor. The bureau should be given power to investigate "all disputes as they occur, whether submitted for arbitration or not, so that information may always be at hand to aid legislation on the subject when necessary and desirable."[1]

Congress was not willing to follow Cleveland's suggestion in full. It did, however, pass a law in 1888 for arbitrating differences between interstate railways and their employees on condition that both parties should consent and neither be bound by the outcome. The arbitrators were to be specially chosen for each dispute according to a plan which the law set forth. Ten years later Congress strengthened the provision by specifying that, once a dispute was submitted to arbitration, the decision should be binding.[2] The states also turned to arbitration. In 1886 and 1887 Massachusetts, New York, Iowa and Kansas provided for voluntary arbitration and nonenforceable decisions. By 1898 at least eleven other states had followed their example.

However inadequate these multifarious efforts to promote industrial accord may seem to a later generation, the record discloses a varied and resourceful attack on the problem as well as a growing consciousness by society that the relations between the contending forces should be composed by means other than those of tooth and claw. In transmitting his arbitration message to Congress, Cleveland did not hesitate to say, "The discontent of the employed is due in a large degree to the grasping and heedless exactions of employers and the alleged discrimination in favor of capital as an object of governmental attention. It must also be conceded

---

[1] Richardson, comp., *Messages and Papers*, VIII, 395-397.
[2] Carlton, *History and Problems of Organized Labor*, 233-235.

that the laboring men are not always careful to avoid causeless and unjustifiable disturbance." [1] In a sense, neither party to the controversy was in a proper frame of mind to embark upon schemes based upon mutual trust and respect. Nevertheless some of the experiments that were tried proved of enduring value. Others, which failed to reckon with all the essential factors in the problem, resulted in breeding new difficulties. In both respects, however, the experience of this generation provided material for a wiser handling of the problem by those who were to come later upon the scene.

[1] Richardson, comp., *Messages and Papers*, VIII, 395.

CHAPTER XI

THE STRUGGLE OVER THE TARIFF

ALTHOUGH the tariff question was an old one in American history, it entered a new phase in the eighties. The duties prevailing in 1878 were practically the same as those imposed during the Civil War. Regarded originally as emergency war measures, they had remained on the statute book in the years of peace with little change except for occasional increases of particular schedules.[1] To meet an outcry from the Western agrarians Congress in 1872 had effected a slight general reduction, but a revenue deficit caused by the Panic of 1873 had brought a restoration of the rates in 1875.

In and out of the government a strong effort to put the tariff on a revenue basis had manifested itself. Many of the ablest men of the time took part: Carl Schurz; "Sunset" (S.S.) Cox of Ohio, whose nickname came from his proposal to Congress to tax sunshine since it competed with the coal producers of Pennsylvania; Joseph S. Moore of New York, known from his journalistic pseudonym as the "Parsee Merchant"; and Professor William G. Sumner of Yale, David A. Wells and Horace White, the economists. Their efforts had done something to prevent Congress from plunging into more extreme measures of protection. Presently they were to gain a stalwart ally in Grover Cleveland.

Four groups of industrialists led in the campaign for a higher tariff: the wool growers, sponsored by a trio of Ohioans known in Congress as the "wool trinity";

[1] Allan Nevins, *The Emergence of Modern America* (*A History of American Life*, VIII), 167.

the wool manufacturers who operated through the National Association of Wool Manufacturers, headed by John L. Hayes; the sugar growers and refiners; and, most important of all, the American Iron and Steel Association. This last body exerted its influence chiefly through the Industrial League, founded in 1867 to represent all protected industries. Powerful in the League from its beginning was a Pennsylvania iron-master, Joseph Wharton, head of the nickel trust. In a speech at Pittsburgh in 1880 Wharton bluntly served notice on the major parties. "It is meet that we should declare to the country," he said,

> that we will support no party and no candidate who cannot be depended upon . . . to protect and defend home labor. It is fitting for us to call "hands off" to those who are itching to tear our tariff laws to shreds; . . . to call upon the representatives of all other American industries to stand by us as we will stand by them in resisting all changes in the tariff laws and all tariff-making by treaty until these laws can be carefully and prudently revised by a Congress or a commission known to be devoted to the interests of the nation.[1]

Sentiment for tariff reduction gained fresh impetus from the accumulation of a large revenue surplus. This excess of government receipts over expenditures meant that the people were paying needless taxes and also that money desirable for business development was being kept out of circulation. The root of the difficulty lay in the tariff. President Arthur took notice of the situation in his message of December 6, 1881, declaring that "the people may justly demand some relief from their present onerous burden." [2] Though stressing the de-

[1] Ida M. Tarbell, *The Tariff in Our Times* (N. Y., 1911), 96-97.
[2] J. D. Richardson, comp., *A Compilation of the Messages and Papers of the Presidents* (Wash., 1896-1899), VIII, 48-49.

sirability of diminishing internal taxes, he also proposed the appointment of a commission which should recommend a revision of the tariff.

In May, 1882, Congress acted on Arthur's suggestion, authorizing a commission of "experts" who should submit to Congress proposals "upon a scale of justice to all interests." [1] All nine appointed were protectionists by conviction, and four of them were connected with the great protected industries: iron and steel, sugar, wool growing and wool manufacturing.   John L. Hayes, secretary of the National Association of Wool Manufacturers, served as chairman.   The commission spent the summer and fall taking testimony.   The hearings began in July at Long Branch, New Jersey, an easy and comfortable place of access for the business men of New York, Philadelphia and other Eastern centers.   After a month the commission moved on to Boston where the New England industrialists were interviewed.   It next proceeded westward as far as Des Moines, southward to St. Louis, and then eastward to Atlanta and Savannah.[2] Some six hundred witnesses were heard in all.   Among the different industries presenting reasons for protection were makers of neckwear, quinine, bicycles, oil cloth, chemicals, crockery, glass, lumber, salt, as well as all conceivable products from iron and copper, oils, wool and cotton.   Thus the hearings defined both the geographical spread and the nature of American industry.

No better method for gauging the industrial mentality of the period could have been devised.   As a rule, the witnesses were so absorbed in the protection of their own businesses that they failed or refused to consider consumer and related interests.   Joseph Wharton, for

[1] G. F. Howe, *Chester A. Arthur* (Allan Nevins, ed., *American Political Leaders*; N. Y., 1934), 220.

[2] It had planned to go to the Pacific Coast but decided that there was not enough time.   It gave up the Gulf states because of a "dangerous epidemic."   U. S. Tariff Commission, *Report* (Wash., 1882), I, 2-3.

example, was apparently convinced that the high profits of his nickel monopoly could not be hampering to anybody else, nor did he believe that they might in the long run weaken his own market. When American makers of German silver asserted that the high price Wharton could and did charge for nickel was making it impossible for them to compete with foreign manufacturers, and when they pointed out that already the Meriden Britannia Company had established a factory in Canada in order to hold the foreign markets it had developed, Wharton's answer was, "There is no country in the world that is comparable to this country as a market for manufactured goods." [1]

The report of the commission, however, attested that it did have a fairly clear idea of such effects and relations. It argued that the existing high tariff not only hurt consumers but, by encouraging "rash and unskilled speculators" and destroying "the sense of stability required for extended undertakings," frequently undermined the very interests which it was supposed to benefit. The commission held that the extraordinary improvement in machinery and processes during the preceding twenty years should enable manufacturers to compete with foreign rivals under a "substantial reduction of existing duties." It recommended an average cut of from twenty to twenty-five per cent, and announced its conviction that "No rates of defensive duties, except for the establishment of new industries, which more than equalize the conditions of labor and capital with those of foreign competitors can be justified." [2]

In his message to Congress of December 4, 1882, Arthur gave his support to the commission's findings. "The present tariff system is in many respects unjust," he declared.

[1] U. S. Tariff Commission, *Report*, I, 204.
[2] U. S. Tariff Commission, *Report*, I, 5-6.

. . . I recommend an enlargement of the free list . . . , a simplification of the complex and inconsistent schedule of duties upon certain manufactures, particularly those of cotton, iron and steel, and a substantial reduction of the duties upon those articles and upon sugar, molasses, silk, wool, and woolen goods.[1]

But when Congress set about to make a bill which would accord with the recommendations of the President and of the commission, the combined industries began an assault on the proposed reductions unlike anything Washington had ever known. For example, John L. Hayes, chairman of the Tariff Commission, now laid aside his function and, as agent of the woolen manufacturers, undertook a campaign to get higher rates for them than he as commissioner had consented to.[2] The outcome was an almost complete rout of the attempt to scale down duties. Not only did the act finally adopted fall far short of the cuts recommended, but the reductions lacked both consistency and harmony.[3] They represented what each industry could secure by threats of political revenge. The measure was generally recognized as a victory for the organized business interests. The successful operations of this "third house of Congress," moreover, had the effect of saddling industrial lobbies on the national legislature whenever in the future it might take up the matter of tariff changes. For this and other reasons Senator John Sherman of Ohio, himself a protectionist, declared in his *Recollections* that the "tariff act of 1883 laid the foundation of all the tariff complications since that time." [4]

[1] Richardson, comp., *Messages and Papers*, VIII, 135-136.
[2] Tarbell, *Tariff in Our Times*, 113.
[3] F. W. Taussig, *The Tariff History of the United States* (7th edn., N. Y., 1923), chap. iv.
[4] John Sherman, *Recollections of Forty Years in the House, Senate and Cabinet* (Chicago, 1895), II, 855.

The most powerful of the four big intrenched industries was iron and steel. Instead of the twenty-per-cent average reduction which the Tariff Commission had recommended, it came out with 4.54 per cent—a demonstration that its political power was in keeping with its economic importance. The relation of the tariff on iron and steel to such a combination as Andrew Carnegie had created by 1890 is clear. It had prevented that foreign competition, with the consequent lower prices to the consumer, which duties computed strictly on the basis of costs of production in a well-managed mill would have allowed. The tariff, in other words, was a big factor in Carnegie's forty-per-cent dividends. At the same time it had enabled him to undersell his rivals steadily while making his forty per cent. Yet there can be no doubt that, given a reasonable tariff or no tariff at all, a man of his ability, energy and resourcefulness would have quickly risen to the top in the industry.

While the tariff helped to make Carnegie one of the biggest money-makers in the industry, it did not give him a monopoly, nor at this time was an iron and steel monopoly in sight. What disturbed the public was the part the tariff was playing in pushing certain other large industries along the road to monopoly. President Cleveland, entering office on March 4, 1885, gave thought to the same matter. He was also deeply concerned by the continued piling up of a huge surplus in the treasury. His own party was divided in its views, however. Indeed, Samuel J. Randall of Pennsylvania, an influential Democrat in the House, had supported the tariff of 1883. A year later a Democratic House measure, proposing a twenty-per-cent horizontal cut of most duties, had failed of passage because of a coalition of forty-one Randall Democrats with the Republican minority.[1] In

[1] Taussig, *Tariff History*, 251-253.

the first two years of Cleveland's term Randall's followers continued to obstruct action by the Democratic House.

To emphasize the need and the reasons for lower duties President Cleveland finally did an unprecedented thing: he devoted his message to Congress on December 6, 1887, entirely to the tariff question.[1] Pointing to the great surplus annually accumulating in the treasury, he called it "indefensible extortion," a device for "preventing investment in productive enterprise, threatening financial disturbance, and inviting schemes of public plunder." The remedy lay in reducing the tariff. To the argument that high protection insured high wages, he replied that, even if it were just to tax fifty million people in order that the 2,623,089 in protected industries might receive better compensation, it was deceiving those so favored since each must pay "a very large increase in the price of nearly all sorts of manufactures, which, in almost countless forms, he needs for the use of himself and his family." The tariff, he said, put money into one pocket of the workman and took it out of the other. As for the farmer it took money out of his pocket and put little or none back in.

He further pointed to a definite relation of protection to the combinations "frequently called trusts." "The necessity of combination to maintain the price of any commodity to the tariff point," he asserted, "furnishes proof that someone is willing to accept lower prices for such commodity and that such prices are remunerative . . . ." As we have seen, however, the determining factor in the Standard Oil Company, up to that time the most effective monopolistic combination, was a control of transportation through rebates and drawbacks; the tariff was not an element in its success. On the other hand, the protective system had much to do with the

[1] Richardson, comp., *Messages and Papers*, VIII, 580-591.

making of the sugar trust, the American Cotton Oil Company, the American Pipe Manufacturing Company, the whisky trust and the Pittsburgh Plate Glass Company.

No message of a President of the United States since the Emancipation Proclamation had awakened an enthusiasm so general as this appeal of President Cleveland to Congress to consider the tariff "in a spirit higher than partisanship." Its chief effect, however, as events were to show, was to solidify the high protectionists' interests as they never had been before. The bill which the House ways-and-means committee now framed produced one of the ablest, as well as the longest, discussions of the tariff ever heard in Congress.[1] To the protectionist argument that the tariff benefited labor, Democratic spokesmen replied with figures, provided by statistical experts, showing that ninety-four per cent of the wages of the community were not affected by the tariff and that the earners of these wages were paying higher prices for many of the necessities of life because of the tariff.

The Mills bill, as the first response to Cleveland's famous message was called, passed the Democratic House in July, 1888, and went to the Republican Senate where William B. Allison of Iowa took charge of it, aided by the senator from Rhode Island, Nelson W. Aldrich. The Mills bill smelled too strongly of "free trade" to suit them and therefore they set about making an entirely new bill, taking article after article off the free list where the House had placed them, hoisting rates that had been lowered, in short, doing their utmost to give to the organized manufacturers the protection they demanded.[2]

Before the Allison bill came to a vote the presidential

---

[1] Tarbell, *Tariff in Our Times*, 152, 159-164.

[2] Taussig, *Tariff History*, 254-255; E. P. Oberholtzer, *A History of the United States since the Civil War* (N. Y., 1917, in progress), IV, 487-491.

campaign of 1888 took place.   The protectionists were
victorious, electing Benjamin Harrison of Indiana.   In
his first message the new President recommended a
revision of the tariff which would not "impair the just
and reasonable protection of our home industries." [1]
Probably no one in American political history ever had
so complete and untarnished a faith in the doctrine of
high protection as William McKinley of Ohio, the new
chairman of the House ways-and-means committee.   He
had been in Congress almost continuously since 1876
and his chief interest had always been the tariff.   He
esteemed it as the true secret of American wealth and
progress, never doubted that it alone gave high wages,
nor allowed himself to consider that these wages went
to only a comparatively small group of workingmen.
There was something devout, as well as childlike, in
McKinley's devotion to the dogma.

The Allison bill of the Senate was taken by McKinley
as the basis of the new legislation.   The tariff act of
1890, popularly called the McKinley bill, was pushed
through after long and wearisome debates and received
the President's signature in October.   It was a signal
triumph for the protectionists, registering the highest
scale of duties yet enacted, some of them practically prohibitive.[2]   Among other things it arranged to give to a
feeble industry, tin plate, a chance to prove it could
establish itself if the people paid sufficiently high for the
experiment.   In addition, the act embodied two new
principles in tariff legislation.

The first was the provision for paying a bounty to
the producers of domestic sugar.   Four conflicting points
of view had long been active as regards the sugar
schedule.[3]   Advocates of a tariff for revenue only wished

[1] Richardson, comp., *Messages and Papers*, IX, 39.
[2] Taussig, *Tariff History*, chap. v.
[3] Tarbell, *Tariff in Our Times*, 195-199, 201-203.

to fix the duties according to the needs of the treasury, shifting them up and down as the government required more or less money.   Those seeking protection for domestic beet and cane sugar contended for a steady high duty which would foster their infant.   Though sugar growers had been protected for many years, they produced only about an eighth of the amount consumed. A third group comprised those who saw that an increasing foreign market was essential to take care of the surplus products of the farmers and of certain manufacturers.   They wanted to take advantage of the trading value in the sugar duties to secure favorable openings for American exports.   The leader of this group among the high protectionists was James G. Blaine, Harrison's secretary of state, who argued that the duties on raw sugar could be used in barter with Cuba and other sugar-producing countries for the benefit of the American farmers who, he saw clearly, were more and more oppressed by the high duties on manufactured articles essential to their existence.[1]

As for the fourth group, the sugar refiners, they insisted that all inedible raw sugar should be on the free list.   On high-grade raw sugar and on all half-refined sugar that could be eaten—"poor man's sugars," as they were called—they favored taxes so heavy that the imported article would be made too dear to eat.   In the same spirit they urged prohibitive duties on the refined sugars of other countries.   There was a great outcry against granting the sugar trust its demands for free raw sugar and a high duty on the refined product; but, in the end, the McKinley act effected a compromise by putting raw sugar on the free list, providing a bounty for the domestic beet, cane and sorghum raisers and con-

[1] Edward Stanwood, *James Gillespie Blaine* (*American Statesmen*, ser. 2; Boston, 1905), 327-331.

ceding the sugar refiners the continuance of a high rate on refined sugar.

The second fundamental change was the reciprocity provision. It represented an attempt to face the facts, an admission that protection as it was practised sacrificed the farmer to the manufacturer. While the tariff bill was under consideration, Blaine protested to McKinley against the proposal to remove hides from the free list where they had long been. "It is a slap in the face of the South Americans, with whom we are trying to enlarge our trade," he declared. "It will benefit the farmer by adding five to eight per cent to the price of his children's shoes. It will yield a profit to the butcher only, the last man that needs it. . . . Such movements as this for protection will protect the Republican party only into speedy retirement." [1] The protest proved effective, but Blaine was not yet satisfied. His concern for foreign trade made him hammer at the tariff makers until finally they agreed to a clause which empowered the President to impose certain duties on sugar, molasses, tea, coffee and hides—all free in the McKinley bill— whenever the countries exporting them to American shores levied duties that he deemed "unjust or unreasonable" on products of the United States.

The reciprocity clause marked an important innovation in tariff policy. To men like Blaine, concerned with extending the frontiers of trade, it promised a new era in American commercial expansion. The dyed-in-the-wool protectionist, however, felt that the most enlightened feature of the new law was the tin-plate duty. This provision was a victory for McKinley personally. Ten years earlier he had been persuaded by W. C. Cronemeyer, a Pittsburgh steel-plate manufacturer, that the United States could make all the tin plate it needed if the

[1] Tarbell, *Tariff in Our Times*, 204.

industry were properly protected.[1] McKinley had never wavered after his conversion, but for many years he had been unable to interest Congress in the subject. The importers, a strong group, many of them protectionists, fought the duty as involving destruction of an established business. In framing the new tariff bill, however, McKinley induced the House to fix a duty of 2.2 cents a pound on tin plate instead of the one cent provided by the act of 1883. But in the Senate J. C. Spooner of Wisconsin, who called it an extra tax on the farmer, expressed grave doubts as to the possibility of establishing the industry in a reasonable time. At his instigation the Senate added an amendment specifying that after October 1, 1897, all tin plate should be admitted free unless the domestic production for some year before that date should have equaled a third of the importations during any one year in the interval. The sequel showed that McKinley's faith was justified.[2]

One of the chief opponents of the higher duty on tin plate was the Standard Oil Company which used an enormous amount in the cans in which oil was exported. For many years it had secured a drawback from the government. In other words, when the tin plate it imported had been made into cans and exported, the duty it had paid was returned.[3] Cronemeyer and McKinley thought that the Standard ought to use home-made tin plate and pay the higher price, but the Standard did not agree and managed to secure a retention of the privilege in the bill as adopted.

The McKinley tariff stirred the organized farmers of the South and West to impassioned protest and called

[1] W. C. Cronemeyer, "The Development of the Tin-Plate Industry," *Western Pa. Hist. Mag.*, XIII, 34-35.
[2] C. S. Olcott, *The Life of William McKinley* (Boston, 1916), I, 170-173.
[3] Tarbell, *Tariff in Our Times*, 278-279.

forth bitter comments from the independent press.   In words of the *Chicago Times,*

> The trick tariff committee . . . express deep sympathy for the struggling farmer.   They tell him that the principal reason why he suffers is because he is subjected to ruinous competition with the pauper tillers of the soil of other lands. . . . But when we come to look at the facts what do we find they have done? . . . The McKinley Committee propose to relieve the farmer by increasing the duties so far that they may partly exclude $45,000,000 worth out of $356,000,-000 worth of imported agricultural products, leaving the other $311,000,000 worth to come in and compete on precisely the same terms as at present.   And to make up for this lean streak of goodness the Committee propose to add at least $105,000,000 to the burden of taxes on the kinds of articles the farmers have to buy.   Oh, how these high tariff economists do love the suffering farmer.[1]

The new act did not prevent the steady decline in the country's business.   Its failure to do this along with the rising prices of certain everyday articles—not only tin plate, but also coal, lumber and many foods—was adroitly used by the Democrats.   With the slogan of tariff reform they secured a majority in the House in the fall of 1890, and in 1892 carried both houses of Congress and the presidency.   Their platform, in a plank written by Henry Watterson, editor of the *Louisville Courier-Journal,* pledged Grover Cleveland and the party to a tariff for revenue only.   Cleveland's practical mind told him that a sudden application of such a scheme would create a destructive confusion in industry.   In his letter of acceptance he therefore declared, "We wage no exterminating war against any American interests.   We believe a readjustment can be accom-

[1] *Chicago Times,* April 19, 1890.

plished, in accordance with the principles we profess, without disaster or demolition." [1]

The bill which the Democrats had ready by the meeting of Congress in December, 1893, had been prepared in advance by the House ways-and-means committee of which William Lyne Wilson of West Virginia was chairman. It placed on the free list such basic raw materials as wool, coal, iron ore, hemp and flax, and certain of the farmers' necessities such as agricultural machinery, salt, binding twine and cotton bagging. It cut, but not drastically, duties on refined sugar and many manufactured articles, including the product of what Wilson called the "bogus industry" of tin plate. [2] The chief addition the House made to the Wilson bill was an income tax adopted as a sop to the Populist members.

The bill passed the lower branch on February 1, 1894, and went to the Senate for consideration. There the Democrats commanded only a narrow working majority and there, too, the industrial interests of the nation had a stronger proportionate representation. Through the all-pervasive influence of Senator A. P. Gorman of Maryland, assisted by Senator C. S. Brice of Ohio, the protectionists proceeded to modify the measure not only as to details but also as to principles. [3]

One of the bitterest assailants of the House bill was H. O. Havemeyer, president of the sugar trust. As a result of the favorable rates on sugar which the McKinley tariff had provided, the profits of his concern in three years had been close to twenty-five million dollars. "As long as the McKinley Bill is there," declared Havemeyer, "we will exact that profit." [4] Under the operation of the law sugar stocks had advanced eighty-five

[1] Tarbell, *Tariff in Our Times*, 213-215.
[2] Tarbell, *Tariff in Our Times*, 218.
[3] Taussig, *Tariff History*, 289.
[4] Tarbell, *Tariff in Our Times*, 223.

points.   Much was said during and after the session of
1890 of the influence exerted by the sugar trust on certain senators.   An investigation brought to light that
the trust had made campaign contributions to both
political parties in the presidential election of 1892.
Havemeyer justified the action.   "The American Sugar
Refining Company has no politics of any kind," he told
the committee.   "Only the politics of business?" he was
asked.   "Only the politics of business," he replied.[1]

Along with scandals over campaign contributions
went one as unsavory: the charge that United States
senators had been speculating in sugar stocks while that
schedule was under consideration.   The accusation was
investigated and several of the most eminent men of the
time, including John Sherman and George F. Hoar, were
questioned.   Senators M. S. Quay of Pennsylvania and
J. R. McPherson of New Jersey frankly admitted that
they had done so.[2]   "I do not feel," asserted the former,
"that there is anything in my connection with the Senate
to interfere with my buying or selling the stock when I
please; and I propose to do so."

Under Gorman's leadership the Senate emasculated
the Wilson bill.   In all, six hundred and thirty-four
amendments were made.   The most important articles,
including sugar, were removed from the free list, refined sugar was given a more favorable rate than under
the McKinley tariff, and protective duties were generally
advanced.   Of the new rate on refined sugar the *Nation*
said:

> It would have been quite as . . . good policy, to have
> enacted that the Standard Oil Trust should receive
> $30,000,000 out of the public treasury during the next
> six months as a reward of merit, and two and one-
> eighth cents per gallon for all the oil they might here-

[1] Tarbell, *Tariff in Our Times*, 226.
[2] Tarbell, *Tariff in Our Times*, 227; Taussig, *Tariff History*, 314.

after sell in this country, as to do what is done for the sugar trust.[1]

The House was indignant but, in the end, felt obliged to accept the Senate bill. Cleveland, assailing the Senate's action as "party perfidy and party dishonor," allowed the measure to become a law without his signature on August 27, 1894.[2] The Wilson-Gorman act, as it was called, did little or nothing to stabilize business. For different reasons it was challenged by both Democrats and Republicans from the hour it became a law. Presently its provision for an income tax was to be invalidated by the Supreme Court. The tariff was certain to be remade at the first opportunity offered to either party. Yet the passage of the act of 1894 was a symbol the significance of which the historian cannot fail to recognize. The betrayal of the cause of tariff reform in the house of its friends indicated plainly that protectionism represented the dominant conviction of the industrial forces which controlled the effective action of the national government. The consolidation of the nation's internal economic life had bred the doctrine of economic nationalism in the country's international relations.

[1] Tarbell, *Tariff in Our Times*, 225.
[2] *Congressional Record*, XXVI, pt. viii, 7712; editorial, *Public Opinion*, XVII, 511 (Aug. 30, 1894).

CHAPTER XII

THE DRIVE ON MONOPOLY

CRITICISM of the protective system as a breeder of trusts and combinations reflected the growing sensitiveness of the public to the strong centralizing trend in the economic world. Popular dislike based on the unscrupulous business practices of the "hydraheaded monsters" was intensified by increasing evidences of their clandestine activities in state and national politics. The Standard Oil Company was brought into offensive notoriety in 1886 through the election of H. B. Payne as Democratic senator from Ohio.[1] It was believed that his son Oliver H. Payne, treasurer of the Standard, had spent one hundred thousand dollars to secure this result. The Republican lower house of the next legislature ordered an investigation and examined fifty-five witnesses. The committee of the federal Senate on elections declined, however, to act on the evidence. Are we to conclude, asked Senator W. P. Frye of Maine, that the Standard Oil Company, "a power which makes itself felt in every inch of territory in this whole Republic, a power which controls business, railroads, men and things shall also control here . . . ?"[2]

The appearance of powerful lobbies—the "third house of Congress"—whenever tariff measures were up for consideration confirmed popular fears as to the iniquitous influence of Big Business in legislation. W. L. Wilson, confronted with the wreck of his tariff-reform

[1] Ida M. Tarbell, *The History of the Standard Oil Company* (N. Y., 1904), II, 112-119.
[2] *Congressional Record*, XVII, pt. vii, 7323.

bill of 1894, asked, "Is this to be a government by a self-taxing people or a government of taxation by trust and monopolies? The question is now, whether this is a government by the American people for the American people, or a government of the sugar trust for the benefit of the sugar trust." [1]

Such misgivings and apprehensions fed on the secrecy which surrounded the organization and practices of the great business consolidations. State and federal governments concluded that the first step in controlling the trusts, if control were necessary, was to lay bare their structure and plan of operation. In February, 1888, a senate committee of New York began an investigation of the Standard Oil Company. "This is the original trust," it declared. "Its success has been the incentive to the formation of all other trusts or combinations. It is the type of a system which has spread like a disease through the commercial system of this country." [2]

In July the committee on manufactures of the national House of Representatives reported the results of an inquiry which it had made into the Standard Oil and sugar trusts. It informed the House that both combinations were formed on the same plan. Corporations, organized under the laws of different states and subject to state control, had surrendered their stock to trustees named in the agreement which created the trust. In exchange for the stock turned over to them the trustees had issued trust certificates. In accepting these certificates the individual corporation did not lose its identity. It kept up a separate establishment and ostensibly carried on an independent business.

"This form of combination," the committee held, "was obviously devised for the purpose of relieving the trusts and trustees from the charge of any breach of the

[1] Ida M. Tarbell, *The Tariff in Our Times* (N. Y., 1911), 235.
[2] Tarbell, *History of Standard Oil Company*, II, 131.

conspiracy laws of the various States, or of being a combination to regulate or control the price or production
of any commodity . . . ." For this reason, continued
the committee, the trustees insist

> that the corporations themselves . . . remain with
> their organization intact and distinct, and not in com-
> bination with each other; that the stockholders, who
> owned only the stock, and by well-settled legal rules
> had no legal title in the property of the corporations,
> . . . sold their stock in the corporations and accepted
> in payment trust certificates, and that the trustees . . .
> hold only the stock of corporations, and have no legal
> title to any of the property of the corporations, and
> neither buy nor sell anything nor combine with any
> one to fix prices or regulate production of any com-
> modity.[1]

The resentment of certain states at this evident attempt to evade their control was like the resentment they
had shown against railroads which had defied the terms
of their charters. The state of New York felt so
strongly on the subject that in 1889 it brought suit
against the North River Sugar Refining Company, one
of the members of the sugar trust. The upshot was that
the North River Sugar Refining Company lost its charter. The court in making its decision affirmed that, so
far as New York was concerned, there could be "no
partnerships of separate and independent corporations,
whether directly or indirectly, through the medium of
the trust," but that "manufacturing corporations must
be and remain several, as they were created, or one under
the statute." [2]

[1] Report submitted by Henry Bacon from the committee on manufactures, 50 Cong., 1 sess., *House Rep.*, IX, no. 3112, ii.
[2] People *v.* The North River Sugar Refining Company (1890), 121
N. Y., 582, quoted by W. Z. Ripley, ed., *Trusts, Pools and Corporations* (Boston, 1905), 247.

The sugar trust, uncertain of what might happen to its members in other states, decided to adopt a different form of centralization, one less vulnerable to legal attack. For the avowed purpose "of protecting property and promoting the interests of its certificate holders," it arranged that certificates could be placed in the Central Trust Company of New York. Nobody knew what would happen to them there. The *Nation*, discussing this maneuver, defined trust certificates as "aliquot parts of a mass of amalgamated stocks of certain incorporated companies, whose shares are bunched together and locked up in a safe." [1] The next step was the incorporation, under the lax laws of New Jersey, of the fifty-million-dollar American Sugar Refining Company, which in January, 1891, took over the entire business of the sugar trust. [2] Except for the change in legal structure the business continued to be carried on as before. Under the new organization the management was further unified since there was now but one board of directors and one set of officers.

Controlling about eighty-five per cent of the total sugar output, the American Sugar Refining Company was able to raise prices at will. Representatives of the concern could offer no satisfactory reason why the price of sugar should rise in face of the economies claimed except that the company exercised a monopolistic control. From the beginning it adopted the policy of issuing no public statements. The only information it vouchsafed appeared in the annual reports required by the state of Massachusetts, and these were simply balance sheets which revealed little of its inside workings. According to H. O. Havemeyer, president of the company, even stockholders were not given information unless they demanded it as a body.

[1] *Nation* (N. Y.), LI, 85 (July 31, 1890).
[2] John Moody, *The Truth about the Trusts* (N. Y., 1904), 61-67.

AND HE ASKS FOR MORE!

In the same year that the New York court invalidated the charter of the North River Sugar Refining Company, the state of Ohio brought action against the Standard Oil Company of Ohio, one of the units of the Standard Oil trust. The origin of this suit lay in one of those accidents which sometimes influence human affairs. The state attorney-general, David K. Watson, was looking over some new publications at a bookshop in Columbus when he found among them a little volume entitled *Trusts*, written by a New York lawyer, W. W. Cook. Buying the book, he read in it for the first time the trust agreement which the House committee of Congress had brought to light. Watson realized that, if the document was to be depended upon, the Standard Oil Company of Ohio was violating its charter and it was his duty to prosecute.[1] In May, 1890, having ascertained the authenticity of the agreement, he filed a petition in the state supreme court, charging the company with breaking the law when it transferred, as it had done, 34,993 shares out of its 35,000 to the trustees of the Standard Oil trust, thus allowing these trustees to direct its affairs. Because of this relinquishment of the duties laid upon it by its charter he asked that the company be "adjudged to have forfeited and surrendered its corporate rights, privileges, powers and franchises" and that it be dissolved.[2]

Rarely had the business world of that day been so shocked, the complacent political world of Ohio so outraged. It was the general conviction that somebody or something was behind Watson's action. Few could believe that he had taken this amazing step in the discharge of what he conceived to be his duty. In reply to the petition the company did not deny the existence of the

[1] Tarbell, *History of Standard Oil Company*, II, 142-143.
[2] G. H. Montague, *The Rise and Progress of the Standard Oil Company* (N. Y., 1903), 110-111.

trust agreement, but maintained that nevertheless the company as such had nothing to do with the Standard Oil trust. The agreement, it said, was signed by individual stockholders, not by the company in its corporate capacity. This was the essential point of the defense; but the argument was also put forth that, if the court should hold the action of the stockholders in becoming parties to the agreement in their individual capacity to be a corporate act of the Standard Oil Company of Ohio, even then the charter should not be forfeited since the law debarred from its operation an act committed more than five years before a petition was filed.[1]

When the suit came to trial after alleged offers of bribes and other efforts to stop Watson had failed, the Standard's leading counsel, Joseph H. Choate, pleaded for the concern's life because of the "absolute innocence and absolute merit for everything we have done within the scope of the matters brought before the court . . . ."[2] The court was unconvinced. The decision, delivered in March, 1892, held that the object of the agreement was "to establish a virtual monopoly" and hence that it was "contrary to the policy of our state and void." The court did not take the charter from the company as the New York court had from the North River Sugar Refining Company, but it declared illegal the act of entering into the trust agreement, the transfer of the stock, and the power of permitting the trustees to control its affairs. The company was also ordered to pay the costs of the action.[3] In a broad assertion of public policy the court added:

> Much has been said in favor of the object of the Standard Oil Trust and what it has accomplished. It

[1] Tarbell, *History of Standard Oil Company*, II, 144-145; Montague, *Standard Oil Company*, 111-113.
[2] Tarbell, *History of Standard Oil Company*, II, 145-149.
[3] Tarbell, *History of Standard Oil Company*, II, 150.

may be true that it has improved the quality and cheapened the cost of petroleum and its products to the consumer. But such is not one of the usual or general results of a monopoly, and it is the policy of the law to regard not what may, but what usually happens. Experience shows that it is not wise to trust human cupidity where it has the opportunity to aggrandize itself at the expense of others. . . . A society in which a few men are the employers and a great body are merely employees or servants is not the most desirable in a republic; and it should be as much the policy of the laws to multiply the numbers engaged in independent pursuits, or in the profits of production, as to cheapen the price to the consumer.[1]

The force of the decision was to put an end to the trust as a form of business combination. Nine days later the Standard Oil trustees called a meeting to terminate the trust agreement. As S. C. T. Dodd, the lawyer who had framed the agreement in the first place, told the gathering, "this agreement was not entered into as a corporate agreement, and as this decision gives it an effect quite different from the intent of the parties who entered into it, it seems better to end it." [2] It was provided that the trust certificates should be turned back and, in exchange, the holders should receive their proportionate share in each of the twenty companies which then comprised the trust. As a matter of fact, the same nine men, under the name of "liquidating trustees," continued to conduct the business of the twenty concerns as they had been doing.

This state of affairs lasted for five years when another attorney-general of Ohio, Frank S. Monnett, brought contempt proceedings against the Standard Oil

[1] Ripley, ed., *Trusts, Pools and Corporations*, 249. A similar decision was made by the Nebraska supreme court in State *v.* Nebraska Distilling Co. (29 *Nebraska*, 700), decided in 1890.

[2] Tarbell, *History of Standard Oil Company*, II, 152-153.

Company of Ohio for evading the court order of 1892. There followed a long and stormy wrangle which finally convinced the trust that its only peace, if not safety, lay in incorporating as the sugar trust had done in 1891. This reorganization took place in 1899 under the laws of New Jersey. The new corporation was in form a continuation of the old Standard Oil Company of New Jersey, with an amended charter and a capital increased from one million dollars to one hundred and ten million dollars. It was authorized to own the stock of any of the different corporations connected with the Standard interests and to buy from all persons who owned such stock whenever they desired to sell.[1] As a holding company the Standard stood ready to proceed to new conquests.

Other business groups, realizing the vulnerability of the trust form of organization, also chose the path of incorporation as single great companies. This was, for example, the course pursued by the manufacturers of steel wire. In 1874 Joseph F. Glidden of De Kalb, Illinois, had taken out a patent for a barbed-wire fencing, the marketing of which was undertaken by Ellwood & Company of the same city. There had been earlier attempts to invent wire fencing with sharp points, one called the "spur wheel," another the "thorny fence," but both the spur and the thorn slipped on the wire. Glidden made the barbs rigid by twisting them between wires. So great was the demand for the new product that the leading wire manufacturers of the country, Washburn & Moen of Worcester, Massachusetts, from whom Ellwood & Company bought their wire, sent out an agent to find the reason for the big orders. The result was that the two concerns formed a partnership, the

---

[1] U. S. Industrial Commission, *Report* (Wash., 1900-1902), I, 11, 1228; Tarbell, *History of Standard Oil Company*, II, 257-265.

manufacturing being done at Worcester while Ellwood supplied the Western market.[1]

From the first they had trouble over patents. Glidden's device was challenged by a fellow townsman, Jacob Haish, who had actually made and sold a barbed wire from his shop probably as early as Glidden though he applied for a patent some eight months later. A fierce trade war was carried on, and the uncertainty over rights brought outsiders into the field. Among these outsiders was John W. Gates—"Bet-You-a-Million" Gates— who had been a salesman of Ellwood & Company. Setting up his own factory in St. Louis, he promptly became involved in legal difficulties with Ellwood. But Gates tired out his opponent by removing his plant from one side of the river to the other to avoid the service of injunctions, and in 1885 they reached an agreement by which he secured a license to manufacture.[2]

He then turned to the task of "putting together," as he phrased it, the various wire interests. This led to the formation in 1892 of the Consolidated Steel and Wire Company with a capital of four million dollars, incorporated in Illinois. It was the first combination framed by Judge Elbert H. Gary, a Chicago lawyer, who had made himself an authority on corporation law.[3] The prevailing bad times gave Gates an excuse for pushing the consolidation further, and the outcome in 1898 was the organization of the American Steel & Wire Company of New Jersey with a capitalization of ninety million dollars, embracing most of the wire and nail manufacturers of the country. It was the first big combination in steel specialties.

[1] A. G. Warren, *Barbed Wire: Who Invented It?* (reprinted from *Iron Age*, CXVII, June 24, 1926), 3-6.

[2] O. A. Owen, "Bet-You-a-Million Gates," *Sat. Eve. Post*, CXCVIII, 6-7 (Nov. 7, 1925) ; Max Lerner, "John Warne Gates," *Dict. of Am. Biog.*, VII, 188-189.

[3] Ida M. Tarbell, *The Life of Elbert H. Gary* (N. Y., 1925), 77.

On its heels came the tin-plate amalgamation. The McKinley tariff, it will be recalled, had given tin plate a duty of 2.2 cents a pound, subject to withdrawal by the President of the United States after six years if it had not justified itself. The interests which for many years had been agitating for a high duty at once started a drive, notably in Ohio, Indiana and western Pennsylvania, to induce capital to build mills. Loyal protectionists, ignorant of manufacturing of any kind, mostly small-town bankers and prosperous farmers, rushed into the breach: it was a chance to prove the doctrine as well as to make money. Among the most enterprising was Daniel G. Reid, a banker of Richmond, Indiana. Joining with a railroad division superintendent, William B. Leeds, one afternoon in 1891 he secured three hundred thousand dollars in stock subscriptions for starting a tin-plate mill. They built their plant and then discovered, as scores of others were doing, that money and a duty were not all that was needed: there must also be skilled and experienced workers, of whom few were to be had in America. Forced to scrap their first mill, they hunted out men who knew how both to construct a proper plant and to manufacture the product.

While they learned by experience, many others were less fortunate. They shut down or sold out. Nevertheless business grew even through the depression, for iron and steel interests, fearing to lose the preferential tariff, financed and refinanced the most promising ventures.[1] To put the industry on a firmer basis Reid and certain manufacturers near Chicago turned in 1898 for help to Judge W. H. Moore who, with his brother J. H. Moore, had floated the Diamond Match Company in 1889. In an incredibly short time Moore secured options from a

---

[1] United States of America *v.* United States Steel Corporation and Others, *Transcript of Record in the District Court of the United States for the District of New Jersey* (n.p., n.d.), I, 436.

majority of the tin-plate makers.   Carnegie, who detested speculation in all its forms, might denounce the
promoters as "stock jobbers," "destroyers of values" and
"Chicago adventurers"; [1] but for some manufacturers it
was a chance to unload properties which they feared
could never be made to pay.   Ninety per cent of them
insisted, as a condition of transfer, that they be paid in
cash, a decision which many of them later regretted
when the combine proved a success. [2]

Two hundred and sixty-five mills went into the
newly formed American Tin Plate Company which was
headed by Reid as president. [3]   In 1900, when for the
first time the federal census of manufactures included
the tin-plate industry, the value of its total product
stood at nearly thirty-two million dollars, its wages at a
little under two million dollars.   No large industry had
ever been established in the country in so short a time,
nor one with a larger list of casualties to investors and
would-be manufacturers.

Another huge merger in 1898, this time in the iron
and steel industry, involved an integration of the factors
essential to the making of these metals and all their
products.   It was a creation of the legal skill of Judge
Gary who had been active in bringing about the tin-
plate combination.   Gary had been counsel for the
Illinois Steel Company and for some years one of its
directors.   The company had had to encounter severe
competition, especially from the Carnegie Company
which owned an abundance of raw material, controlled
transportation and operated furnaces and mills of the
latest type.   He advised the Illinois Steel Company to
become self-sufficient and then go after foreign trade.

[1] B. J. Hendrick, *The Life of Andrew Carnegie* (Garden City, 1932),
II, 81-88.
[2] United States of America *v.* United States Steel Corporation, I, 478.
[3] Moody, *Truth about the Trusts*, 157-158; Ripley, ed., *Trusts,
Pools and Corporations*, 289-321.

The suggestion found favor and he set about to effect an aggregation of the resources necessary to carry out the plan.[1] By September, 1898, the Illinois Steel Company had been combined with a considerable number of iron, coal, railroad, steamship and manufacturing concerns and J. Pierpont Morgan backed the formation of the Federal Steel Company at a capitalization of one hundred million dollars.[2]

One advantage which the great business amalgamations had enjoyed was the widely varying systems of state incorporation laws. What Massachusetts, for example, would not tolerate, certain other commonwealths, notably New Jersey, Delaware and West Virginia, would befriend and protect. Moreover, state comity required that all corporations be allowed to engage in interstate commerce throughout the length and breadth of the land. The situation called for supplementary legislation by Congress. The disclosures of the major trust investigations, as well as the variety of information obtained through suits brought by different states, at last stirred that body to action.

As early as 1888 J. H. Reagan of Texas, who had been so active in securing the creation of the interstate-commerce commission, submitted an antitrust bill. It was one of fourteen similar measures placed before the House.[3] The same year Senator John Sherman of Ohio, deeply concerned about the effect the trust situation might have on tariff legislation, introduced in the upper branch a bill "to declare unlawful trusts and combinations in the restraint of trade and production." For the moment the bill went unnoticed, but when Congress

[1] Tarbell, *Elbert H. Gary*, 91.

[2] For the subsequent merging of the Federal Steel Company with other companies into the United States Steel Corporation (1901), see H. U. Faulkner, *The Quest for Social Justice* (*A History of American Life*, XI), 29-32.

[3] H. R. Seager, "The Recent Trust Decisions," *Polit. Sci. Quar.*, XXVI, 582.

opened in December, 1889, and Sherman reintroduced it, Congress proceeded to give the matter serious attention.

The chief objection to Sherman's measure seems to have been that the majority considered it unconstitutional. His arguments make it quite clear, however, that he was not wedded to any particular form. He had, he said, no intention of interfering with control of combinations by the states: "each state can and does prevent and control combinations within the limit of the state." He pointed out, however, that the state courts "are limited in their jurisdiction to the state, and, in our complex system of government, are admitted to be unable to deal with the great evil that now threatens us." [1]

Opposition was also raised to the bill on the ground that it interfered with "lawful trade, with the customary business of life"—an objection which had frequently been heard in the discussion of the interstate-commerce bill a few years before. Sherman was strong in his denial. "It aims only at unlawful combinations," he declared. "It does not in the least affect combinations in aid of production where there is free and fair competition." He held that "the right of every man to work, labor, and produce in any lawful vocation, and to transport his production on equal terms and conditions and under like circumstances," lay "at the foundation of the equality of all rights and privileges." [2]

Sherman's bill was referred to the finance committee and there put in the hands of Senator George F. Hoar of Massachusetts to rewrite. Early in 1890 the new bill was ready. For some six months it received the attention of the Senate and the House and finally on July 2, 1890, President Harrison signed it. This measure is

[1] John Sherman, *Recollections of Forty Years in the House, Senate and Cabinet* (Chicago, 1895), II, 1072.
[2] Sherman, *Recollections of Forty Years*, II, 1073.

always spoken of as the Sherman act, "for no other reason that I can think of," says Senator Hoar in his autobiography, "except that Mr. Sherman had nothing to do with framing it whatever." [1]

The first section of the statute pronounced illegal "every contract, combination in the form of trust or otherwise, or conspiracy in restraint of trade or commerce among the several states, or with foreign nations." The second section turned from restraint of trade to monopoly, declaring it to be a misdemeanor to "monopolize, or attempt to monopolize, or combine or conspire with any other person or persons to monopolize, any part of the trade or commerce among the several states or with foreign nations." [2] It was a much more drastic statute than the interstate-commerce law inasmuch as it inflicted penalties of fine and imprisonment—one or both—for violations.

Harrison's attorney-general immediately started action against the whisky combination which, a few months before the bill was signed, had abandoned the trust agreement and formed a corporation under the laws of Illinois with a capital of thirty-five million dollars. After the usual procedure all the property in the hands of the trust had been transferred to the new creation and the old trust certificates exchanged for stock. [3] A careful study of the testimony that had already been produced in investigations by Congress and New York state would seem to prove beyond any doubt that the whisky combine had attempted to monopolize and had conspired with other persons to monopolize the business. But the indictment was quashed by a district-

[1] G. F. Hoar, *Autobiography of Seventy Years* (N. Y., 1903), II, 363. "My own opinion," declared another senator, "is that Senator Edmunds had more to do with framing it than any other Senator." S. M. Cullom, *Fifty Years of Public Service* (Chicago, 1911), 254.

[2] *U. S. Statutes at Large*, XXVI, 209-210; Seager, "Recent Trust Decisions," 583.

[3] A. J. Eddy, *The Law of Combinations* (Chicago, 1901), I, 632.

court judge on the ground that it was "clearly insufficient according to the elementary rules of criminal pleading."[1] This amounted to saying that the attorney-general had not produced the factual evidence available or, in other words, that he had not properly prepared his case.

The troubles of the whisky combine were not over, for in 1895 the attorney-general of Illinois brought suit against the company, alleging that it was, in fact, a continuation of the old trust and that it exercised a monopoly. The state supreme court in 1896 decided that it was "organized for the purpose of getting control of the manufacture and sale of all distillery products, so as to stifle competition, and be able to dictate the amount to be manufactured, and the prices at which the same should be sold, and thus to create, or tend to create, a virtual monopoly . . . ."[2] The corporation was ousted, but on petition to the federal circuit court a receiver was appointed. Subsequently the shareholders were permitted to buy back their company by giving up their rights as stockholders in the old company.[3]

Harrison's attorney-general also started suit in a few other cases. One, against the cash-register combination, was allowed to lapse in the Cleveland administration. Another, against the E. C. Knight Company, a Philadelphia sugar refinery, possesses special interest as it was the first under the law to reach the federal Supreme Court. The occasion for the action was the purchase in 1892 by the American Sugar Refining Company of four Pennsylvania refineries, its only remaining competitors of importance. This purchase practically completed its monopoly, leaving only two per cent of the sugar refined and sold in the United States in the hands of com-

[1] Seager, "Recent Trust Decisions," 585.
[2] Eddy, *Law of Combinations*, I, 580-581.
[3] Ripley, ed., *Trusts, Pools and Corporations* (rev. edn., Boston, 1916), 45.

panies outside the combine.[1]   The attorney-general
brought suit not against the American Sugar Refining
Company but against the units which it had bought.
The government charged that the contracts of sale constituted a combination in restraint of trade and aimed
at monopoly.

But the Supreme Court, agreeing with the lower federal courts, held in 1894 that the purchase of the property, though it might perfect a monopoly and so produce restraint of trade, was not in itself an illegal act.
"What the law struck at," asserted the majority decision, "was combinations, contracts, and conspiracies to
monopolize trade and commerce among the several
states or with foreign nations . . . ." Since "the contracts and acts of the defendants related exclusively to
the acquisition of the Philadelphia refineries and the
business of sugar refining in Pennsylvania," they "bore
no direct relation to commerce between the states or
with foreign nations." [2]

Another case brought by the Harrison administration
involved two significant points: did the antitrust law
apply to railroads; and did it intend to declare illegal
all contracts in restraint of trade whether "reasonable"
or "unreasonable"?   In the Trans-Missouri Freight Association case the government attacked an agreement of
a large number of interstate railways fixing rates on
what had been competitive freight traffic south and west
of the Missouri River.   It was not until 1897 that the
case reached the Supreme Court.   The majority opinion
maintained that the law did apply to railroads and
further declared that "the language of the act included
every contract, combination in the form of trust or

[1] Ripley, ed., *Trusts, Pools and Corporations* (rev. edn.), 506-507,
531.
[2] Ripley, ed., *Trusts, Pools and Corporations* (rev. edn.), 515.

otherwise, or conspiracy in restraint of trade or commerce . . . ." [1]

In spite of the Sherman antitrust law and the efforts to find out what could and could not be done under it, in spite of the activities of certain states in exercising authority over the corporations they had created, industrial combinations continued to thrive and multiply. Fifteen had been organized between 1880 and 1890; twenty-five came into being in the five years, 1891 to 1895.[2] Hope for relief awaited a less legalistic attitude on the part of the court and an administration at Washington determined to put Big Business in its place.[3]

[1] 166 *U. S. Reports*, 290. It was a five-to-four decision. Mr. Justice E. D. White, one of the minority, who insisted on the distinction between "reasonable" and "unreasonable" restraints of trade, at last persuaded the court to his way of thinking in the Standard Oil and American Tobacco cases in 1911. See Faulkner, *Quest for Social Justice*, 119.

[2] Moody, *Truth about the Trusts*, 453-475.

[3] See Faulkner, *Quest for Social Justice*, 117-120.

CHAPTER XIII

THE COMING OF THE PANIC OF 1893

THE opening of the last decade of the century found an increase in the wealth of the United States over that in 1880 of nearly twenty-one billion dollars.[1] Unfortunately this did not indicate an even pace of economic advance. Agriculture had fallen back relatively. Instead of producing about twenty-six per cent of the national wealth, as in 1880, it was down to nearly twenty-one per cent. On the other hand, manufacturing, transportation, urban real estate, wealth abroad, all registered substantial gains.[2] It was clear that the essential elements of the national economic structure were changing shape and size and that these changes were going on without regard to the stresses and strains on the structure as a whole. Each considered only its own form, its own gain. Those who watched the process realized that a sudden shock might topple over the edifice, bring on a severe panic and depression.

A premonitory shock came in 1890 with the failure of the Baring Brothers of London, a banking house which handled many American securities.[3] It forced curtailments and reorganizations on business concerns the world over, so far-reaching were the Baring interests. In the United States the sudden dumping of a great number of American securities on the market pre-

[1] R. R. Doane, *The Measurement of American Wealth* (N. Y., 1933), 11.

[2] Doane, *Measurement of American Wealth*, 13, 44. See also A. M. Schlesinger, *The Rise of the City* (*A History of American Life*, X), 76-77.

[3] J. F. Rhodes, *History of the United States from Hayes to McKinley, 1877-1896* (N. Y., 1919), 368-369.

cipitated a short-lived stock panic. Among the firms threatened with disaster was the George Westinghouse Electric & Manufacturing Company in Pittsburgh.

Westinghouse needed a half-million dollars for his business, but when he tried to borrow the sum from local bankers, they told him that they could not give him a free hand in using the money; they had to know what he was going to do with it. Ignorant though they were of the electrical industry, they thought he spent too much on experimentation, was too liberal in buying patents. When Westinghouse refused the terms, the bankers declined to accommodate him. This assertion of a right to exercise control over a man's business was a growing function of the banking of the day. It was deeply resented by many borrowers as threatening to give the financiers too large a place in the business world. In a sense, however, it was only an expansion of the part country bankers had long played for good or evil, counseling the farmer about his methods, refusing loans when he was overoptimistic or spendthrift, and sometimes foreclosing for no other reason than that they might gather in the property.

Westinghouse now turned to New York, where the banking house of August Belmont formed a financial syndicate and reorganized the concern. Westinghouse fully justified Belmont's confidence. The total outstanding liability of more than $10,000,000 with annual interest charges exceeding $180,000 was reduced to $9,000,000, all in stock, "thanks to a voluntary sacrifice on the part of the stockholders and the willingness of the bankers and creditors concerned to take preferred shares in an enterprise of which the success must depend almost wholly on one man." [1] Westinghouse, however, was more fortunate than many others who,

[1] F. E. Leupp, *George Westinghouse; His Life and Achievements* (Boston, 1918), 161.

caught by the Baring failure, found themselves without money or credit with which to enable them to carry on their businesses.

Iron and steel suffered sorely from the bad economic conditions which, for divers reasons, began to plague the country. Early in 1890 the price of rolled-steel products started to fall. Steel billets which had sold in Pittsburgh around thirty-five dollars a gross ton at the beginning of the year declined to twenty-five at the end and to twenty-two early in 1892.[1] Iron and steel men began saying that wages would have to be cut. This was the conclusion of H. C. Frick, general manager of the Carnegie Company, as in the spring of 1892 he faced the expiration of the three-year contract with the members of the Amalgamated Association of Steel and Iron Workers employed in the Carnegie plant at Homestead, near Pittsburgh. The contract followed a model which Andrew Carnegie had approved: a sliding wage-scale, going up without limit as prices rose, and falling as they fell though never below a minimum of twenty-five dollars a ton for steel billets.[2]

In place of the old contract Frick offered one which lowered the minimum pay to twenty-two dollars, with a reduction in tonnage rates whenever new machinery and improvements substantially enlarged output. He also changed the date for ending contracts from June 30 to December 31. The existing date, coming as it did in full season, gave labor an advantage in bargaining; the end of the year would shift the advantage to the management. In the matter of wages the men contended for a twenty-four-dollar minimum, and Frick raised his offer to twenty-three dollars but refused

[1] W. Z. Ripley, ed., *Trusts, Pools and Corporations* (Boston, 1905), 79.

[2] Andrew Carnegie, *Autobiography* (Boston, 1920), 246-247.

more.[1]   He also refused further conference with the Amalgamated.

June was a month of growing bitterness among the laborers and citizens of Homestead.   When finally Frick was hung in effigy, he closed the plant and deputy sheriffs were sworn in to guard the property.   The men ordered them out of town, saying that they themselves would guard the plant.   There is reason to suppose they would have done so.   It was their all; the jobs were theirs, they felt, a contention in which they had always been upheld by Andrew Carnegie.

But Frick recognized no vested right of labor in industry.   At midnight on July 5 he sent up the Monongahela River to Homestead two barge loads of Pinkerton detectives armed with Winchester rifles.   When they attempted to take possession of the mills, the strikers, intrenched behind piles of steel billets, met them with volleys of fire, picking off the members of the invading force as rapidly as they showed their heads. The detectives made repeated efforts to land, but the defenders had the advantage of numbers, position and weapons.   On the second day of the battle the workers endeavored to destroy the barges with brass cannon, planted behind breastworks of railroad ties.   This attempt failing, they sprayed the barges with oil and poured barrel after barrel of it into the river above the mooring place in order to set the boats afire.   After seven detectives had been killed and twenty or more wounded, the Pinkerton force surrendered.   They were guaranteed safe conduct out of the community on condition that they give up their arms and ammunition. Notwithstanding this promise the maddened mob fell upon them with fists, stones and clubs.   From the sixth to the twenty-seventh of July eleven workmen and

[1] J. H. Bridge, *The Inside History of the Carnegie Steel Company* (N. Y., 1903), 206-208.

spectators were also killed and many others wounded.[1] The reëstablishment of order proved too much for the sheriff and his deputies. On the twelfth the governor of Pennsylvania sent in a force of militia, the town was placed under martial law, and the plant was reopened with a small force of nonunion workmen.

Hardly had order been restored before a new element of terror was injected. On July 21 Frick was shot and stabbed in his office, though not fatally.[2] The natural supposition was that the strikers were responsible, but it was soon proved that they had no connection with the assailant, who was an anarchist named Alexander Berkman, a Russian by birth. It was believed that he had been inspired to the deed by his anarchist mate, or wife so-called, Emma Goldman, also a native Russian. At the time she claimed to be innocent of any complicity though she expressed pride in Berkman's courage and his loyalty to their common cause.[3] Many years later she told the full story. When news of the lockout at Homestead first reached Emma Goldman and Berkman, then keeping a restaurant in Worcester, Massachusetts, they immediately closed their business and went to Pittsburgh. There, sheltered by two or three comrades, they prepared, as was the anarchist custom in times of serious labor trouble, a manifesto. After this they returned East. It was the later war between the Pinkerton detectives and the workers which prompted Berkman to make his attack on Frick. The only person who knew of his intention was Miss Goldman. They

[1] *Appletons' Annual Cyclopædia*, n.s., XVII (1892), 626-627. Other sources for the Homestead strike are Secretary of Internal Affairs of the Commonwealth of Pennsylvania, *Annual Report for 1892*, pt. iii; C. D. Wright, *The Industrial Evolution of the United States* (N. Y., 1897), chap xxv; Bridge, *Inside History of Carnegie Company*, 209-223; and contemporary newspapers.

[2] Bridge, *Inside History of Carnegie Company*, chap. xv.

[3] J. G. Speed, "Anarchists in New York," *Harper's Wkly.*, XXXVI, 798-799 (Aug. 20, 1892).

had only money enough for one of them to make the trip. The greatest regret in Emma Goldman's life evidently was that she was unable to accompany him, "all for the lack of a paltry $50.00." [1] Berkman was sentenced to twenty-one years in the penitentiary for assault with intent to kill. [2]

The Homestead affair was carried to the courts by both sides. On July 19 some of the leaders of the workmen were arrested on a charge of murder. On August 3 retaliatory suits were begun against the Carnegie officials, the Pinkerton agency and five of its men on a similar charge. Frick was arrested as soon as he recovered sufficiently to be about. Later a charge of high treason was brought against the Homestead advisory committee which had conducted the strike. The grand jury returned true bills in the treason cases, and also in the charges of murder, conspiracy, and aggravated rioting against the Carnegie officials and the Pinkerton detectives. Eventually all the cases were allowed to drop. [3] Meanwhile, very gradually, the Homestead plant returned to steady operation. It was late in November before the strike was declared off. At that time not more than eight hundred of the old employees had been reinstated.

For Andrew Carnegie, retired and busy at his castle in Scotland, but in contact with the management as befitted one who owned over half the company's capital stock of twenty-five million dollars, the upheaval was

[1] Emma Goldman, *Living My Life* (N. Y., 1931), I, chaps. viii-ix. Berkman later came to regard such deeds as "harmful to the spread" of anarchist doctrines. See his *Now and After* (N. Y., 1929), 177.

[2] He was released after thirteen years' imprisonment. Frick died in December, 1919, and by a strange coincidence Berkman and Emma Goldman were deported to Soviet Russia the same month by the United States government. George Harvey, *Henry Clay Frick, the Man* (N. Y., 1928), 144-145. See also P. W. Slosson, *The Great Crusade and After* (*A History of American Life*, XII), 88.

[3] *Appletons' Annual Cyclopædia*, n.s., XVII, 627; Bridge, *Inside History of Carnegie Company*, 243.

a devastating experience. To William E. Gladstone, who in September wrote him a sympathetic note, he replied:

> This is the trial of my life (death's hand excepted). Such a foolish step—contrary to my ideas, repugnant to every feeling of my nature. Our firm offered all it could offer, even generous terms. Our other men had gratefully accepted them. They went as far as I could have wished, but the false step was made in trying to run the Homestead Works with new men. It is a test to which workingmen should not be subjected. It is expecting too much of poor men to stand by and see their work taken by others. . . . The pain I suffer increases daily. The Works are not worth one drop of human blood. I wish they had sunk.[1]

Reviewing the incident in his autobiography he expressed the opinion that "disputes about wages do not account for one half the disagreements between capital and labor. There is lack of due appreciation and of kind treatment of employees upon the part of the employers."[2]

Though it is difficult to see anything but loss for the contestants in this ghastly affair, there were certain gains for public opinion, notably a deepening conviction that society had a right to demand machinery for adjusting labor disputes. What had happened at Homestead might under the existing disorganization of industry happen in any locality where large numbers of men toiled in great manufacturing plants. In Congress the disturbance caused agitated discussion. Senator J. M. Palmer of Illinois voiced a widespread view of one practice of the employing class:

[1] B. J. Hendrick, *The Life of Andrew Carnegie* (Garden City, 1932), I, 410-411. For a somewhat different representation of Carnegie's attitude, with supporting documents, see Bridge, *Inside History of Carnegie Company*, 203-206.

[2] Carnegie, *Autobiography*, 253.

The army raised and commanded by the Pinkertons is as distinctly known in this country as is the regular army of the United States. . . . The commander in chief of this army, like the barons of the Middle Ages, has a force to be increased at pleasure for the service of those who would pay him or them. . . . They have been employed in New York, and have shed the blood of citizens of that State. They . . . have shed the blood of citizens of Illinois.[1]

Subsequently the Senate undertook an investigation of the use of Pinkerton detectives in labor disputes.[2] Palmer was no less emphatic in asserting that the men at Homestead had earned the right to live there and to have employment as long as their work was satisfactory. These large manufacturing establishments, he declared, "must hereafter be understood to be public establishments in the modified sense, . . . and the owners of these properties must hereafter be regarded as holding their property subject to the correlative rights of those without whose services the property would be utterly valueless."[3] This was a doctrine, however, in which he had little support.

The Baring crisis and the declining prices in the steel industry proved danger signals of a much greater economic catastrophe. The long depression of agriculture in the West and South had steadily curtailed the purchasing power of a large section of the population, thus contracting the domestic market for manufactures. The continued economic instability abroad after 1890 also lessened the demand for American products and, at the same time, caused further withdrawals of foreign gold invested in American enterprises. Another disturbing influence in the business world was the new silver policy

[1] *Appletons' Annual Cyclopædia*, n.s., XVII, 209.
[2] *Appletons' Annual Cyclopædia*, n.s., XVII, 627.
[3] *Appletons' Annual Cyclopædia*, n.s., XVII, 210.

adopted by Congress in 1890, which threatened to force the country off the gold standard.[1] Behind all such factors lay the vast amount of speculation in railways and especially in industrial corporations, which had been going on at an accelerating tempo.

By the opening of 1893 there was great uneasiness in the stock market because of signs, particularly in railroads, of overstrained credit. The first startling event was the failure of the Philadelphia and Reading, a railroad which had been in the hands of receivers several times in the previous decade—a victim, as one shrewd financial observer said, of a management alternating between "visionaries and plunderers."[2] The Drexel-Morgan Company had carried out the most recent reorganization. In the course of doing so it had leased both the New York Central and the Lehigh Valley, guaranteeing dividends on their stock, and in addition had bought up many roads and coal companies, evidently planning to build up an anthracite monopoly with which to feed the new system. The announcement of this combine on February 11, 1892, caused the biggest day's business which the New York stock exchange had ever known.

So far as outsiders could see, everything was going well with the Reading. In January, 1893, the management issued a report assuring the public, nervous over general conditions, that it had ample capital to meet the year's obligations. Shortly thereafter it paid a five-percent dividend on its preferred income bonds.[3] Then, apparently without warning and certainly to the bewilderment of many astute financial observers, the

---

[1] See later, 244. For contemporary explanations of the Panic, see Felix Flügel and H. U. Faulkner, eds., *Readings in the Economic and Social History of the United States* (N. Y., 1929), 710-717.

[2] *N. Y. Evening Post*, Sept. 5, 1893.

[3] *Commercial and Financial Chronicle* (N. Y.), LVI, 754 (May 6, 1893).

Reading went into the hands of a receiver. The announcement caused great alarm in the stock market, the sales of the day (February 25) being even greater than those of just a year before when the combination was launched.[1]

The blow to the financial world was in part cushioned, however, by the Stock Exchange Clearing House. This institution, less than a year old, had been organized in May, 1892, to do for the exchange what the Clearing House Association had been doing for forty years for New York bankers. The Reading bankruptcy was one of many proofs of the advantage enjoyed in a crisis by small business concerns. It was loaded with tremendous liabilities which it could meet only by selling at high prices all the coal which its great territory consumed. When business slowed down and demand and prices both fell, the bottom dropped out of the scheme. Small competitors with low expenses undersold the Reading and even thrived while it starved.

The blasting shock to public confidence came in May, 1893, with the failure of the rope trust, the National Cordage Company. The company was unsound in its structure, but few of those who speculated in its stock had taken pains to inform themselves about the character of the securities. They were interested only in their market performance and that had been highly successful. It had long been the practice of the management to borrow money on its stocks of binder twine to tide over the winter and spring. Early in 1893 the trust had over five million dollars' worth on hand and no worries about the future. Then came the Reading failure and the bankers notified the concern that they could not take care of the usual loans. In order to secure the necessary working capital the company made a new issue of preferred stock. This alarmed the mar-

[1] *Appletons' Annual Cyclopædia*, n.s., XVIII (1893), 297.

ket, producing a panic in National Cordage stock and causing all its creditors to jump on it. The president of the trust assured the Industrial Commission in 1900 that "the failure was entirely due to the inability to get credit, which had never been curtailed before in our history, and the uneasiness due to the general distrust in regard to the silver question and the failure of the Reading Railroad Company." [1] The receivers into whose hands the company passed found other things amiss, however. They reported the accounts of the trust, of its officers and subsidiaries, so confused that it was impossible to make head or tail of the business— "a fine thing for the speculators but a poor reliance for investors." [2]

The failure of the rope trust marked the beginning of the general collapse. Banks, corporations, mortgage companies, fell on every hand. New York banks refused to rediscount notes offered by interior institutions, and this tightening of credit led to a suspension of banks and business houses throughout the West and South. Terrible sacrifices of supposedly valuable properties were made. Thus a Boston mortgage concern was obliged to sell for nine thousand dollars a mortgage which it regarded worth two hundred and twenty thousand. In July the Erie Railroad failed, in August the Northern Pacific, in October the Union Pacific, and in December the Atchison and the New York & New England.[3] No part of the country escaped the blows of the

---

[1] U. S. Industrial Commission, *Report* (Wash., 1900-1902), XIII, 130-131.

[2] *N. Y. Evening Post*, May 6, 1893.

[3] "Retrospect of 1893," *Commercial and Financial Chronicle*, LVIII, 9-19 (Jan. 6, 1894). A general complaint of brokers and investors in railroad securities was that the information furnished the public was so meager that no intelligent appraisal could be made of their value. See a study called *The Anatomy of a Railroad* (N. Y., 1895), published by Thomas Woodlock of the *Wall Street Journal*. His conclusion as to the Erie was that its fixed charges were too heavy to be earned even in average years.

economic disaster. Industries refused by their bankers the money to meet pay rolls save at excessive premiums resorted to all sorts of expedients, often issuing scrip. In Pittsburgh one large industry which continued to pay in cash was the Westinghouse Electric & Manufacturing Company. The money was in small denominations—dollars, half dollars, quarters—taken in at the gate of the Chicago World's Fair and sent weekly to Westinghouse because of his services in lighting the grounds.[1]

While the Westinghouse concern, which, it will be recalled, had been saved from bankruptcy in 1890 by reorganization, was weathering the storm, its chief competitor in the electric field was in deep trouble. This company, the General Electric, was a consolidation only a year old, made up of two of the most famous electric concerns in the United States: the Thomson-Houston Electric Company and the Edison General Electric Company of New York. Since its formation in 1883 the Thomson-Houston Company had enjoyed a spectacular growth, enlarging its capital from some ninety thousand dollars to over ten million. The Edison Company, organized by Henry Villard in 1889 with a capital of twelve million dollars, represented all the activities and interests of Edison's incandescent-lamp development.[2] In 1891 the Edison directors had suggested a combination of the two concerns. To Charles A. Coffin, founder of the Thomson-Houston Company, it offered a welcome opportunity to end much of the costly patent warfare which the firm had had to carry on. In April, 1892, the consolidation was completed: a fifty-million-dollar capitalization under the name, the General Electric Company. It was a title which named

---

[1] Leupp, *George Westinghouse*, 169-170.
[2] Henry Villard, *Memoirs* (Boston, 1904), II, 326.

no man, not Edison, Thomson, Sprague, Van Depoele, Brush or any other.

Coffin was chosen president of the new General Electric which in its first report, June, 1893, announced twelve hundred and seventy-seven central stations using its apparatus. But before the end of the year the concern was in dire financial straits. It had been the practice of both the companies comprising the General Electric to indorse the notes of young utility companies willing to buy electric equipment if they could get credit. As security for these indorsements they accepted bonds and stocks of the concerns. When the Panic of 1893 came, Coffin found himself with securities normally worth something like sixteen million dollars but which had now greatly shrunk in value. Being badly in need of money, he sacrificed the holdings for four million dollars to a syndicate known as the Street Railway and Illuminating Properties.[1] Rehabilitation of these small bankrupt concerns became one of the difficult financial problems of the next few years. Though the Panic had jeopardized the life of the General Electric, the orders on its books taken in 1892 actually produced a profit in both 1893 and 1894. Not until 1895 and 1896 did the output drop. Revival quickly began, however, and the year 1898 showed the largest volume the company had ever handled.[2]

The hard times beginning in 1890 formed a prolific breeding ground for labor troubles. When the continued fall in prices reacted on the wage scales, organized labor was aroused to strong and often violent resistance. The year 1894 saw nearly seven hundred and fifty thousand wage-earners involved in industrial

[1] General Electric Company, *Second Annual Report* (Jan. 31, 1894), 5-8.
[2] General Electric Company, *Seventh Annual Report* (Jan. 31, 1899), 7.

warfare, an even larger number than in 1886.[1] Moreover, unlike the earlier year, the workers now fought
on the defensive.   One of the most destructive and
significant disturbances was the Pullman strike.   The
Pullman Palace Car Company had suffered from the
beginning of the depression.   A labor force of over five
thousand eight hundred at the beginning of 1893 fell
to two thousand before the year was out, and wages
were cut twenty-five per cent.   In order to build up
business George Pullman, head of the concern, began
taking orders at a loss.[2] By this means he returned
some two thousand two hundred to the pay roll.

In May, 1894, the men asked for a restoration of
their wage scale.   The works were busy; the company
was paying dividends; but their pay had not been restored, nor had their rents in the town of Pullman been
reduced.   Their request, made through an employees'
committee, was refused, Pullman explaining that the
company was losing money in order to keep the plant
going.   As for the complaint that the rents charged at
Pullman were higher than the employees could afford
and should be lowered since wages were cut, he contended "that none of the reasons urged as justifying
wage reduction by it as an employer can be considered
by the company as a landlord." [3] The day after the
interview three of the committee were discharged on the
plea of no work.   They belonged to a local union of the
American Railway Union, a body organized by Eugene
V. Debs at Chicago in 1893 for the purpose of embracing all railway workers born of white parents in "one
great brotherhood."

[1] J. R. Commons, *History of Labour in the United States* (N. Y.,
1918), 501.

[2] Pullman claimed that he built in 1893 three hundred passenger cars
each at $300 less than cost.   Cattle cars and refrigerator cars were built
at a corresponding loss.

[3] U. S. Strike Commission, *Report on the Chicago Strike* (53 Cong.,
3 sess., *Senate Exec. Doc.*, no. 7), xxxv-xxxvi.

When the Pullman local learned of the dismissals it called a strike on May 11. The company promptly laid off its entire labor force and closed the works; Pullman announced great relief at the removal from his shoulders of the responsibility for the bread and butter of over four thousand men and their families.[1] The men, however, were allowed to remain in their homes. This was the situation when in June a convention of the American Railway Union in Chicago proposed arbitration to the Pullman Company. The company refused to consider any communications from the body and thereupon the convention voted that after June 26 the members should handle no Pullman cars on any railroad until the Pullman Company should consent to arbitration. Members might handle trains of which Pullman cars were not a part and it was particularly asked that such cars be separated from mail trains.[2]

The strike was thus transferred to the national field. Its principals became the railways under contract to move Pullman cars and their employees who refused to move them. As Eugene V. Debs, president of the American Railway Union, saw it, "The contest is now on between the railway corporations united solidly on the one hand and the labor forces on the other." Accepting this issue, the *Chicago Herald* declared on July 4, "The necessity is on the railroads to defeat the strike. . . . If the strike should be successful the owners of the railroad property . . . would have to surrender its future control to the . . . labor agitators and strike conspirators who have formed the Debs railroad union." In the East the *New York World* joined in calling the action of the strikers a "war against the government and against society . . . iniquitously directed

---

[1] "The Pullman Boycott," *Nation*, LIX, 5-6 (July 5, 1894).
[2] W. R. Browne, *Altgeld of Illinois* (N. Y., 1924), 117-120.

by leaders more largely concerned to exploit themselves than to do justice or to enforce the right." [1]

Though such newspapers undoubtedly represented the dominant opinion of the country, the refusal of the Pullman Company to arbitrate nevertheless caused much dissatisfaction. The common council of Chicago called for a peaceful settlement. Mayor H. S. Pingree of Detroit, a large employer, went himself to Pullman with Mayor J. P. Hopkins of Chicago, carrying a sheaf of telegrams from the mayors of some fifty cities to beg the Pullman Company to reconsider.[2] Mark Hanna who for years had employed big bodies of labor, handling them much as Andrew Carnegie did by a combination of generosity, force and paternalism, raged at George Pullman in the Union Club of Cleveland. He was a "damned idiot" not to "arbitrate, arbitrate and arbitrate." When somebody answered that Pullman had done fine things for his men, giving them a model town, Hanna exploded: "Oh, hell! Model—! Go and live in Pullman and find out how much Pullman gets sellin' city water and gas ten per cent higher to those poor fools!" [3]

The extension of the strike by the American Railway Union involved some twenty-four railways centering in Chicago, operating about forty-one thousand miles and capitalized at over two billion dollars. These roads as a group were represented by an organization formed in the troubled days of 1886, called the General Managers' Association. Its business was the "consideration of problems of management arising from the operation of railroads terminating or centering at Chicago." [4] In

---

[1] *N. Y. World*, July 2, 1894.

[2] U. S. Strike Commission, *Report*, xxxix.

[3] "His words," adds Hanna's biographer, "sped out and came into Chicago; in 1896 there was a difficulty in collecting money for the Republican campaign fund from Mr. Pullman's office." Thomas Beer, *Hanna* (N. Y., 1929), 132-133.

[4] U. S. Strike Commission, *Report*, xxviii-xxxi.

the opinion of the federal commission later appointed to investigate the strike, the association had no standing in law: "It cannot incorporate, because railroad charters do not authorize roads to form corporations or associations to fix rates for services and wages, nor to force their acceptance, nor to battle with strikers." It denominated the association "an illustration of the persistent and shrewdly devised plans of corporations to overreach their limitations and to usurp indirectly powers and rights not contemplated in their charters and not obtainable from the people or their legislators."

It was this organization which faced the American Railway Union and refused to deal with its representatives—an action which the federal commission called "arrogant and absurd when we consider its standing before the law, its assumptions, and its past and obviously contemplated future action." [1] Feeling that no alternative remained, the switchmen on June 26 refused to attach Pullman cars to trains. When they were discharged the train crews quit in a body. By the first of July nearly every road west and northwest of Ohio was tied up.[2] Thus in less than a week a large part of the nation's business had been effectually stopped by the refusal of an unincorporated organization, claiming to represent forty thousand miles of transportation, to arbitrate a labor grievance in a manufacturing company.

The railways called loudly on the federal government to protect them in running trains. The strikers contended that the government should not interfere with strikes and, when a resolution was introduced into Congress forbidding such interference, they asked Senator C. K. Davis of Minnesota to support it. "You might as well ask me to vote to dissolve this government," he

---

[1] U. S. Strike Commission, *Report*, xxxi.
[2] Editorial, *Public Opinion*, XVII, 305 (July 5, 1894).

replied.[1] Governor Altgeld of Illinois, confident that he had the situation well in hand, declined to call on Washington for assistance.[2] Unfortunately the federal government had no machinery for compelling arbitration. It had only armed force and it was fairly certain that the use of force to set the trains in motion would provoke resistance. The body of strikers was still in the main orderly, but the makings of a mob were at hand: hoodlums, embittered men vainly seeking work, hoboes and criminals. There was, besides, a sprinkling of direct-actionists asking nothing better than to set a match.

The first force employed by the government was unfortunate, consisting of some thirty-six hundred special deputies sworn in by the United States marshal in Chicago. According to the federal investigating commission, these men were selected by and appointed at the request of the General Managers' Association; they were armed and paid by the railroads and, while exercising governmental authority, were under the direct control of the railroads, not of any public official. Thus, as a first step, the federal government gave over its local police power directly to the railroads, allowing them to recruit (chiefly through detective agencies) a considerable body of reckless and irresponsible men and to arm and send them out in the guise of United States officers to do whatever the railroads required.[3]

With the activities of the special deputies rioting began. Many believed it was started by the railroads themselves, seeking to break the control of the situation which the strikers had established. The charge, how-

---

[1] Editorial, *Nation* (N. Y.), LIX, 19 (July 12, 1894).

[2] See Schlesinger, *Rise of the City*, 415.

[3] In an official report the Chicago superintendent of police referred to these deputies as "thugs, thieves and ex-convicts," a characterization amply supported by the testimony of many witnesses before the United States Strike Commission.

ever, can neither be satisfactorily proved nor disproved. In view of all the conditions rioting was, in any case, inevitable. It took the form of frenzied mobs burning cars, looting railroad property, imperiling all law and order. As a result, federal troops entered the city on July 3. President Cleveland found warrant for this unprecedented action in the constitutional obligation to safeguard the mails and protect interstate commerce.[1] On July 6 state troops made their appearance.

At the time that special deputy marshals were authorized by Washington, Attorney-General Richard Olney had appointed a special counsel for the government. The man chosen was a Chicago attorney, Edwin Walker, whom Cleveland described in his account of the strike as "able and prominent." However, Walker was at that time, and had been for over twenty years, the legal representative of important roads leading out of Chicago. On July 2 he secured from the federal circuit court a blanket injunction forbidding Debs, his fellow strike leaders and "all other persons whomsoever" to interfere in any manner, direct or indirect, with the operation of the rail lines.[2] Eight days later Debs and three others were indicted for obstructing the mails and interstate commerce. Released on bail, they were re-arrested a week later and indicted for contempt in disobeying the injunction. This time they did not give bail with the result, as Debs said, that the men "became demoralized, and that ended the strike."[3] By July 20 all federal troops had been withdrawn. Eleven days later the Pullman Company issued its annual report. It had done a business of about $9,500,000 during the year and had accumulated a surplus of some $2,500,-000, less by $1,700,000 than the year before because

[1] Robert McElroy, *Grover Cleveland* (N. Y., 1923), II, 150-156.
[2] McElroy, *Cleveland*, II, 146-149.
[3] U. S. Strike Commission, *Report*, 143.

of the strike, the report said. It was employing twenty-six hundred and forty men, of whom but three hundred had been newly engaged.

The case of Eugene Debs was carried to the Supreme Court where Mr. Justice D. J. Brewer, delivering the unanimous opinion of the court, answered in the affirmative two questions: "Are the relations of the general Government to interstate commerce and the transportation of mails such as to authorize a direct interference to prevent a forcible obstruction thereof? Second, if authority exists . . . has a court of equity jurisdiction to issue an injunction in aid of the performance of such duty?" [1] Debs's sentence of six months in prison, and that of his associates of three months, were therefore upheld. Thus began the struggle over "government by injunction" which furnished an important plank in the Democratic platform of 1896 and long agitated the ranks of organized labor.[2]

The government, while it was sustained by the Supreme Court and overwhelmingly by public opinion in its determination at all costs to prevent interference with interstate transportation and the moving of mails, failed entirely to take advantage of the opportunity to secure arbitration tribunals to which it could compel the submission of similar disturbances. It remained without means of dealing effectively with elements such as had been primarily responsible for the catastrophe: those who had refused to submit the dispute to arbitration.

Had the Pullman upheaval been the only evidence of social unrest, popular sentiment would not have been so deeply stirred. In every industrial center hordes of men were out of work, and in the West and South the

[1] *In re Debs*, 158 *U. S. Reports*, 564.
[2] See H. U. Faulkner, *The Quest for Social Justice* (*A History of American Life*, XI), 63-65.

farmers lifted up their voices in the general chorus of despair and exasperation. The economic and social order builded by the capitalists in the 1870's and 1880's was being weighed in the balance and found wanting. Among the few million unemployed the spirit of discontent spread like a contagion. Presently they began to form "armies" to make personal presentation of their grievances to the government at Washington.

The most conspicuous of these armies was the one led by Jacob S. Coxey of Massillon, Ohio. A quiet, unassuming man of forty, he had worked for ten years in the iron mills of his native state of Pennsylvania before going to Ohio where he became a farmer, quarryman and horse breeder. So successful had he been that by 1894 he was reputed to be worth two hundred thousand dollars.[1] Despite his profitable business career Coxey was a congenital reformer. Like scores of others in depressions, he had his own plan for ending unemployment: the government should set the jobless to work constructing highways and other public improvements and pay them with irredeemable legal-tender notes.[2] Failing to arouse an interest in his plan in Congress he decided to lead a "petition in boots" in its behalf. "The aim and object of this march to Washington," declared Coxey while the army was *en route*, "has been to awaken . . . the whole people to . . . their duty in impressing upon Congress the necessity for giving immediate relief to the four million of unemployed people and their immediate families, consisting of twelve million to fifteen million more."[3]

Coxey started out with a band of one hundred and twenty-two men which, by April 30 when he reached Washington, had grown to over four hundred. The

[1] Henry Vincent, *The Story of the Commonweal* (Chicago, 1894), 49.
[2] Vincent, *Commonweal*, 51-53.
[3] Speech at Williamsport, Md., April 18, 1894, quoted in Vincent, *Commonweal*, 53-54.

Browne   Jones   Coxey

Three Leaders of Protest Armies

police allowed them to parade, but kept them out of the Capitol grounds, finally arresting Coxey when he broke through their lines and attempted to make a speech on the Capitol steps.[1] "Up these steps," he said in a written protest which he had ready, "the lobbyists of trusts and corporations have passed unchallenged on their way to committee rooms, access to which we, the representatives of the toiling wealth producers, have been denied."[2] It was a pertinent observation, for Washington at the moment was alive with lobbyists fighting the Wilson bill. The tariff-reform press seized the opportunity Coxey gave it to compare the two invading armies. As one editor put it, "The 'Industrial Army' composed of manufacturers besieging the government with their clamor for higher duties and higher profits has prepared the way for the 'Industrial Army' composed mostly of vagabonds marching upon Washington and demanding that the government feed them."[3]

After this experience at the hands of the police Coxey's army presently disbanded and scattered, but by this time at least seventeen other armies were headed for the capital. The largest of these was Kelly's Industrial Army, numbering some fifteen hundred, which the state and local authorities in California had loaded into trains of box cars and headed eastward.[4] Its leader, a thirty-two-year-old printer named Charles T. Kelly, had been elected by the unemployed as "general." At Council Bluffs, Iowa, the railroad dumped the men and took away the cars. On the outskirts of the town they

[1] D. L. McMurry, *Coxey's Army* (Boston, 1929), 113-118.

[2] McMurry, *Coxey's Army*, 120.

[3] Editorial, *Harper's Wkly.*, XXXVIII, 434 (May 12, 1894).

[4] McMurry, *Coxey's Army*, chaps. viii-ix. Nineteen-year-old Jack London was a member of Kelly's army. He kept a diary of the journey from San Francisco until he left the army at Hannibal, Mo. See J. E. Briggs, ed., "A Jack London Diary," *Palimpsest*, VII (1926), 129-158.

camped a week in the mud, fed by a great body of sympathizing townspeople and laborers. In vain they waited for the railroad to furnish transportation, and finally the army took to the road afoot. Through all this pathetic journey Kelly kept order in his force, but not all of the divisions were manageable.

The Montana contingent of the Industrial Army, made up of nearly six hundred and fifty miners, mountaineers and hoboes, when refused a lift by one of the line managers of the Northern Pacific, proceeded to capture a train and run it for themselves. They were followed by a trainload of deputies, and at Billings a fight ensued in which the deputies were worsted with the help of the people of the town. Eventually a band of federal troops surrounded the train at night and the men surrendered without a fight.[1]

Through May and June remnants of the various armies straggled into Washington. They appeared too late, however, and were too few in number, to make the impression on Congress that their cause deserved. Of the hundred thousand men whom Coxey had predicted, never more than a thousand were in the capital at a given time. Congress ignored them; the local authorities harried and harassed them. While some tried to jest at the new "American pilgrims bound on a merely fantastic and adventurous journey,"[2] thoughtful persons realized that a germ of deadly earnestness underlay the movement. "The Coxeyites, ridiculed by the classes, have the sympathy of the masses," declared an English observer. "Organized labor, and labor not organized, has cheered the armies on their way."[3] There could be no doubt, to use the language of an-

---

[1] McMurry, Coxey's Army, 199-205.
[2] "The Progress of the World," Am. Rev. of Revs., IX (1894), 650.
[3] W. T. Stead, "Coxeyism," Am. Rev. of Revs., X (1894), 52.

other contemporary, that the movement despite its farcical ending was "a symptom. Symptoms . . . mean always internal disturbance, they mean the possibility of diseases that may threaten the vitals." [1]

[1] M. J. Savage, "The Present Conflict for a Larger Life," *Arena*, X (1894), 303.

CHAPTER XIV

THE CONTROVERSY OVER SILVER

THE economic collapse of the early nineties fastened public attention anew on the monetary question. According to spokesmen of the depressed classes the breakdown was due primarily to a shortage of circulating medium. According to business and financial leaders it was the result of silver inflation. The government's vaults were stuffed with silver and, under the terms of the Sherman silver-purchase act passed in July, 1890, the treasury was obliged to buy each month 4,500,000 ounces of bullion against which it was to issue legal-tender notes redeemable in either gold or silver.[1] Previous to this, since 1878, it had been purchasing $2,000,000 worth of silver bullion a month under the requirements of the Bland-Allison act.[2] This amount was coined into silver dollars and, as a rule, silver certificates issued for them; the dollars themselves were stored. The result by 1893 was that the treasury had in its keeping about 380,000,000 silver dollars and over 157,000,000 ounces in bullion. All together, about 4900 tons of silver were in the treasury vaults.[3]

As the accumulation grew its value decreased in the eyes of the world. The silver certificates and Sherman notes were not accepted by foreign countries as money: exchange had to be paid in gold. Even Mexico and

[1] *U. S. Statutes at Large,* XXVI, 289-290.

[2] See Allan Nevins, *The Emergence of Modern America (A History of American Life,* VIII), 372. The practical effect of the Sherman act was that nearly twice as much silver was acquired annually by the government as under the law of 1878.

[3] "The Silver in the Treasury Vaults," *Harper's Wkly.,* XXXVII, 670 (July 15, 1893).

the South American countries, all on a silver basis, required payment of debts in gold. As a result gold began to leave the country, nearly $60,000,000 being exported in the first five months of 1893.[1] Moreover, the business classes at home felt increasingly uncertain as to the solvency of the government, and people everywhere rushed to get their Sherman notes redeemed in gold.

The drain fell directly upon the treasury. Though the government possessed the legal authority to redeem the Sherman notes in silver, it did not dare do so because of the weakened state of public confidence. According to the law then in force the treasury was obliged to suspend the issue of gold certificates when the gold reserve fell below $100,000,000. This happened in April, 1893. At once President Cleveland announced that he and his cabinet were determined to maintain the parity between gold and silver and to discharge all the financial obligations of the government. In August he called Congress in special session to repeal the silver-purchase act. A pitched battle resulted, for the members from the West and South demanded more, not less, silver. "Free silver" was the dream not only of the farmers and laborers, but also of the silver-mine owners in the Far West who opposed any curtailment of the big and steady market for their ore which the government had been providing. When the repeal came to a vote in the House at the end of August it had a majority of one hundred and thirty-one. But the upper chamber was in a more recalcitrant mood. Not until November 11 did the bill pass and receive the President's signature.[2]

Politically it proved a costly victory, convincing the silverites that Cleveland was a tool of Big Business and

[1] F. W. Taussig, *The Silver Situation in the United States* (*Questions of the Day*, no. 74; 2d edn., N. Y., 1896), 134.

[2] Cleveland also faced the heartbreaking task of replenishing the $100,000,000 gold reserve. This he finally accomplished by a series of

Wall Street. With every month after the repeal, agitation against the government's monetary policy spread. Organizations were formed, speeches made, books and pamphlets written. In 1894 appeared the most skillful piece of printed propaganda on the silver side: *Coin's Financial School,* written by William H. Harvey. The author, a Virginian about forty years of age, had tried his hand at ranching and silver prospecting in the Far West and, after making money, had lost it all in the Panic of 1893.[1] In free silver he saw a panacea both for his own and his country's ills.

The book began by picturing the distracted state of the country: "the cry of distress is heard on every hand; business is paralyzed; . . . riots and strikes prevail throughout the land."[2] In order to clarify the popular mind as to the source of the troubles, Coin, the hero of the tale, opened a school of finance in Chicago to which he invited the nation's leading financiers, business men, newspaper editors and professors of political economy, indicating them by name. They asked questions and presented arguments against free silver, each of which Coin invariably refuted. The little book contained many caricatures, crudely illustrating the points which Coin set forth. The people, especially those in the West and South, could not but be influenced when they saw a picture of Western farmers feeding loads of hay to a cow while Eastern bankers and stockjobbers milked her, or pathetic personifications of monometallism in the form of men with one eye or one arm or one leg. By May, 1895, three hundred thousand copies had been sold at

bond issues, the last in January, 1896. One of these, in February, 1895, aroused bitter criticism on the score that it yielded excessive profits for the Morgan-Belmont syndicate which handled it. See J. F. Rhodes, *History of the United States from Hayes to McKinley, 1877-1896* (N. Y., 1919), 429-438.

[1] F. E. Haynes, *Third Party Movements since the Civil War* (Iowa City, 1916), 295.

[2] W. H. Harvey, *Coin's Financial School* (Chicago, 1894), 3.

twenty-five cents apiece. Though there was a flood of literature answering Harvey, it had little influence on those who acclaimed him as their prophet.

Popular anger was further inflamed in 1895 by a Supreme Court decision declaring the income-tax provision of the Wilson-Gorman tariff unconstitutional.[1] In 1870 the court had unanimously upheld the validity of the income tax levied during the Civil War. Now this decision was reversed by a final vote of five to four. In arguing the case against the tax Joseph H. Choate had denounced the law in question as "communistic in its purposes and tendencies . . . ." Mr. Justice S. J. Field in his opinion voiced a similar view. "The present assault on capital," he asserted, "is but the beginning. It will be but the stepping stone to others . . . more sweeping until our political conditions will become a war of the poor against the rich . . . ."[2] To the protesting groups the decision offered clear proof that the government was being run by and for the wealthy to the utter misery and despair of the poor.

The Populists, who in 1892 had secured a firm footing in Congress and captured many states of the South and West, actively pressed the issue of free silver. Their vote in the elections of 1894 disclosed a gain of forty-two per cent. In that year they elected six United States senators, seven congressmen and four hundred and sixty-five members of state legislatures.[3] They faced the presidential election of 1896 strong, determined, aflame with zeal for the common man. The campaign had become something more than a campaign for free silver. It was a fight against the "money power" in all its manifestations. "There are but two sides in

---

[1] Pollock *v.* Farmers' Loan and Trust Co., 157 *U. S. Reports,* 429; 158 *U. S. Reports,* 601.

[2] C. A. Beard, *Contemporary American History* (N. Y., 1914), 154-155.

[3] Haynes, *Third Party Movements,* 281.

the conflict that is being waged in this country today,"
declared one of their manifestoes,

> On the one side are the allied hosts of monopolies, the
> money power, great trusts and railroad corporations,
> who seek the enactment of laws to benefit them and
> impoverish the people. On the other side are the farm-
> ers, laborers, merchants and all others who produce
> wealth and bear the burdens of taxation. The one
> represents the wealthy and powerful classes who want
> the control of the Government to plunder the people.
> The other represents the people, contending for equal-
> ity before the law, and the rights of man. Between
> these two there is no middle ground.[1]

The portentous strength of the Populists made it impossible for the major parties to ignore the monetary
issue. The choice before them was an unhappy one,
however. They must recognize silver if they expected
to carry the West and South. They must advocate
the gold standard if they were to hold the conservatives
of both parties. The Republicans were the first to make
a decision. For some months before the national convention in St. Louis on June 16 it had been certain that
William McKinley would be the nominee. For two
years his devoted friend, Mark Hanna, an able business
man of Cleveland, Ohio, had been giving his time and
money to persuading the country that the "Major" was
the "advance agent of prosperity." As President he
would give the people a tariff bill which would undo
the mischief wrought by the monstrous Wilson-Gorman
act; he would open their factories, set men to work. Up
to the convention Hanna believed that this cry of "Bill
McKinley and the McKinley Bill" was all that would be
needed to carry the election.

For a time Hanna seems to have been able to juggle

[1] *Silver Knight and National Watchman*, Oct. 22, 1896.

A Page from "Coin's Financial School"

the gold-and-silver issue so adroitly that the East saw
under McKinley's leadership gold, the West silver. When
the convention assembled, however, the senators from
the silver states, recognizing that the gold sentiment was
going too strong for them, demanded pledges from
Hanna that silver be restored as a standard. One of the
silverites cornered him in his hotel room at breakfast,
still in his night shirt, a harassed and tormented man.
"Did the Silver Senators want to see another panic?" a
bystander later reported Hanna as saying. "Didn't they
know that, back east and as far as Chicago, able workmen were starving and shopgirls going on the streets?"
However, he promised that there should be a commission to negotiate with other nations on the subject and
also that "the major would do what he could for
Silver." [1]

The silver delegates had prior reason to trust McKinley on silver. He had voted for the Bland-Allison act
of 1878 and for the Sherman law of 1890, and they
probably saw in the approval he gave Cleveland's repeal bill in 1893 a surrender to the needs of the moment
rather than a desertion of the cause. But the plank
which the convention adopted soon after the morning
interview with Hanna was too much for their faith.
It declared opposition "to the free coinage of silver
except by international agreement with the leading commercial nations of the world, which we pledge ourselves
to promote, and until such agreement can be obtained,
the existing gold standard must be preserved." [2] Thus
it left silver to the mercies of a future problematical
international commission. When the minority tried to
substitute a plank declaring for the "use of both gold
and silver as equal standard money," the convention

[1] Thomas Beer, *Hanna* (N. Y., 1929), 145-146.
[2] T. H. McKee, ed., *The National Conventions and Platforms of All
Political Parties, 1789 to 1900* (3d edn., Balt., 1900), 301-302.

voted overwhelmingly against them. Thereupon thirty-four delegates solemnly withdrew in protest. As Hanna had foreseen, McKinley was chosen as the candidate.

On July 7 the Democrats held their convention in Chicago. A great majority came charged to vote for free silver. Their mood was belligerent, that of crusaders rather than politicians. A minority favored the single gold standard, but they knew their chance of a respectful hearing was small. Consideration of the platform caused a long and bitter debate. As finally adopted, it made the silver question the chief issue, declaring: "We are unalterably opposed to monometallism, which has locked fast the prosperity of an industrial people in the paralysis of hard times. . . . We demand the free and unlimited coinage of both silver and gold at the present legal ratio of 16 to 1 without waiting for the aid or consent of any other nation." [1]

In the speaker replying to Senator David B. Hill of New York, who stoutly defended a gold declaration, the delegates and the party found their leader: a young lawyer, well known both in his state and in Congress as a tariff reformer, William Jennings Bryan. When the thirty-six-year-old Nebraskan rose to his feet no one apparently expected anything unusual from him. Yet before he had spoken long he excited the fifteen thousand persons in the convention hall to a frenzy of enthusiasm. The fight for silver he called "a cause as holy as the cause of humanity." The speech, on which he had been working most of the previous night, voiced the incoherent but deep emotions of the plain people. Bryan said better than anybody else had said what they had been feeling for years and he said it at a moment when it struck a strongly responsive chord.

Countering the charge that bimetallism would disturb the country's business interests, he declared that

[1] McKee, *National Conventions and Platforms,* 293.

the accepted definition of a business man was too limited in its scope:

> The man who is employed for wages is as much a business man as his employer; the attorney in a country town is as much a business man as the corporation counsel in a great metropolis; . . . the farmer who goes forth in the morning and toils all day—who begins in the spring and toils all summer—and by the application of brain and muscle to the natural resources of the country creates wealth, is as much a business man as the man who goes upon the board of trade and bets upon the price of grain. . . . We come to speak for this broader class of business men.[1]

Nor was it relevant to argue that the great cities favored the gold standard. "The great cities," he thundered, "rest upon our broad and fertile prairies. Burn down your cities and leave our farms, and your cities will spring up again as if by magic; but destroy our farms, and the grass will grow in the streets of every city in the country." [2] It was in the peroration that he made his indelible impression on both the audience and the nation:

> Having behind us the producing masses of the nation and the world, supported by the commercial interests, the laboring interests, and the toilers everywhere, we will answer their demand for a gold standard by saying to them: You shall not press down upon the brow of labor this crown of thorns, you shall not crucify mankind upon a cross of gold.[3]

The convention went mad. "Bryan, Bryan, Bryan," rang the interminable cry.

[1] W. J. Bryan, *The First Battle* (Chicago, 1896), 200.
[2] Bryan, *First Battle*, 205.
[3] Bryan, *First Battle*, 206.

The head of the *Chicago Times-Herald*, H. H. Kohlsaat, has told how, as he sat in his office that day, the chief of his editorial staff burst in excitedly, declaring that he had just heard the greatest speech of his life and that he felt certain the maker of it would be nominated for the presidency. Kohlsaat, at once sending his best pen-sketch artist to make a five-column drawing of Bryan, printed the picture on the front page under a streamer caption reading: "Probable Nominee Today's Convention." About five o'clock the next morning Bryan's supporters secured five thousand copies and, pinning them on their breasts and fastening them to brooms, marched round and round the convention hall, yelling, "Bryan, Bryan, William Jennings Bryan." [1] The *Times-Herald's* prophecy was fulfilled. Bryan was nominated on the fifth ballot.

As it turned out, the Populists made a capital mistake by delaying their convention until after the gatherings of the major parties. When they met on July 22 they found themselves stripped by Bryan and his followers of their principal issue. Most of the delegates were poor men, veterans in the long struggle with adversity. Henry D. Lloyd, as he went among them, learned that not a few had walked to Chicago, others had no money for beds if they bought food, and many were hungry. Among them were railroad men, blacklisted since the Pullman strike, hopeful of swinging the convention to Debs.[2] Should the convention indorse the Democratic candidate?

Senator W. V. Allen of Nebraska, permanent chairman of the gathering, pointed out the only practical course when he told the delegates he did not want people to say that the Populists had been "advocates of

---

[1] H. H. Kohlsaat, *From McKinley to Harding* (N. Y., 1923), 49-50.
[2] Caro Lloyd, *Henry Demarest Lloyd, 1847-1903* (N. Y., 1912), I, 258-265.

reforms when they could not be accomplished, but when the first ray of light appeared . . . the party was not equal to the occasion . . . ." [1] And the convention, the wind out of its sails, accepted what the farseeing among them realized was to be their end as a militant party.[2] James B. Weaver, their candidate in 1892, nominated Bryan in a rousing speech. "This country," he said, "has recently witnessed a new Pentecost, and received another baptism of fire. . . . From the very beginning our organization has made party fealty subordinate to principle. We will not here reverse ourselves and refuse to accept victory now so easily within our reach." [3] The Republican irreconcilables, calling themselves the National Silver party, also gave Bryan their endorsement.

Although the vast majority of voters, conservative and radical, were able to justify their course in joining either the Republicans or the Democrats, a considerable group of gold Democrats found themselves homeless, unable to accept free silver and equally unable to accept tariff protection. Accordingly they held a convention in September and framed a platform pronouncing unalterably against unlimited coinage and in favor of historic Democratic principles. They nominated for President General John M. Palmer of Illinois.[4]

The Republicans began their campaign on the assumption that the tariff would be the predominant question. "In thirty days you won't hear anything about silver," McKinley is reported to have said shortly after the Republican convention, and Hanna as McKinley's manager planned his fight on that basis.[5] But he

---

[1] Bryan, *First Battle*, 270.

[2] J. D. Hicks, *The Populist Revolt* (Minneapolis, 1931), 356-367.

[3] Bryan, *First Battle*, 277-278.

[4] Edward Stanwood, *A History of the Presidency from 1788 to 1897* (Boston, 1898), 557-561.

[5] C. S. Olcott, *The Life of William McKinley* (Boston, 1916), I, 321.

was not long in seeing the futility of trying to divert the mind of the country from the issue Bryan had raised. He at first also underestimated the extent and effectiveness of the educational machinery that the Populists had built up and which the Democrats were now utilizing. They had developed an army of experienced speakers; they had an extensive literature; and they had mastered the art of wedding argument to melody.

Some of the songs sung in 1896 had done service for the Populists in the elections of 1890, 1892 and 1894. Baptized in these emotional struggles, they could easily be adapted to the moment. In every community of the South and West there were singers who made up in vigor and conviction what they may have lacked in tune and rhythm. One song to catch the popular ear was titled, "The Reps and the Demos, the Shylocks and the Pops." Its fourteen stanzas told the story of the war between the classes and the masses, and voiced the charge of the Populists or "Pops":

> They have stolen our money; have ravished our homes;
> With the plunder erected to Mammon a throne;
> They have fashioned a god, like the Hebrews of old,
> Then bid us bow down to their image of gold.

But a happy ending was in sight:

> The people are waking from dreams of the past;
> They're arousing from slumber to duty at last;
> And the sun shall not shine on a Shylock or slave,
> In the land of the free and the home of the brave.[1]

Going about among the farmers of the Northwest, James J. Hill wrote to J. P. Morgan that the free-silver epidemic raged not only among the agriculturists but also among many of the wage and salary earners of the towns. The Reverend Newell Dwight Hillis of Brook-

[1] H. F. Johnson, *Poems of Idaho* (Weiser, Idaho, 1895), 117-120.

lyn, delivering lectures in the West during the campaign, gave a graphic description of the propaganda carried on in country schoolhouses.   On a blackboard it was proved, at least to the satisfaction of the audience, that while a farmer worked eight months to produce a thirteen-cent bushel of oats, the railroad in a single day and night received seven of the thirteen cents.   Of these seven cents the first destroyed the farmer's hopes of paying the interest on his mortgage; the second deprived his wife or daughter of a new warm dress for the winter; the third kept the boy and girl out of school; the fourth took away the newspaper or a book.   After this demonstration, remarked Hillis, no amount of argument, however well founded, could convince the hearers that the single gold standard did not account for their misfortunes and that free silver was not an unfailing cure for their ills.[1]

When Hanna realized the strength of the movement, he went to work with characteristic energy to match, check and defeat it.   This could be done only by counterpropaganda.   Under his direction the Republican national committee marshaled a body of one thousand four hundred campaigners, paid their expenses and sent them wherever their services were most needed. Hand in hand with these meetings went an equally thorough circulation of campaign literature.   Over a hundred million documents were shipped from the Chicago office of the national committee; twenty million more were sent out from New York.[2]   To finance these activities Hanna collected campaign contributions of unprecedented size from business men, bankers and the big corporations.[3]

[1] N. D. Hillis, "An Outlook upon the Agrarian Propaganda in the West," *Am. Rev. of Revs.*, XIV (1896), 304-305.

[2] Herbert Croly, *Marcus Alonzo Hanna* (N. Y., 1912), 217-218.

[3] See A. M. Schlesinger, *The Rise of the City* (*A History of American Life*, X), 405-406.

The campaign was hardly under way before both sides began showing signs of hysteria. The Republicans, alarmed by the support well-known radicals like Altgeld and Debs were giving Bryan, began to cry revolution. A fairly complete vocabulary of invective might be compiled from the names applied to Altgeld alone—such appellations as "anarchist," "communist," "serpent," "hoodlum," "traitor" and "murderer." [1] Bryan came in for such epithets as "wretched, rattle-pated boy," "dishonest dodger" and "slobbering demagogue." [2] Nor was language of this kind employed only by the uneducated and irresponsible. "Messrs. Bryan, Altgeld, Tillman, Debs, Coxey and the rest," shouted Theodore Roosevelt in a speech urging the election of McKinley, "have not the power to rival the deeds of Marat, Barrère, and Robespierre, but they are strikingly like the leaders of the Terror of France in mental and moral attitude." [3] But the Popocrats, as the Populist-Democratic combination was known, were quite as inventive when it came to vituperation as well as more experienced. "Plunderers," "Shylocks," "tools of Wall Street," "asses," "liars," "plutocrats," "robbers," were among their favorite terms.

These intemperate attacks represented the surface ripples rather than the deeper currents of the campaign; and deeper currents there were on both sides. Aligned with McKinley were many liberal and high-minded men who saw in the Democratic platform a betrayal of national honor. They had no sympathy with reactionaries or with selfish economic exploitation, but they saw less danger in them than in the breakdown of controls which they believed Bryanism threatened. Nearly all the large daily papers were for "sound money" as were

[1] W. R. Browne, *Altgeld of Illinois* (N. Y., 1924), 286-288.
[2] Mark Sullivan, *The Turn of the Century, 1900-1904* (same author, *Our Times*, N. Y., 1926-1935, I), 291-293.
[3] H. F. Pringle, *Theodore Roosevelt* (N. Y., 1931), 153.

also most of the professional economists. As for Bryan, youth followed him. Owen D. Young, then a student in the Boston University Law School, asked years later why he voted Democratic in 1896, answered that it was "not because I was enthusiastic about all of the things which Bryan stood for, but because I was then opposed and am now to the things which McKinley stood for. In addition to this, . . . I would have voted for him on almost any platform because I believed in his sincerity and honesty." [1] The main body of Bryan's support, however, came from the discontented and the debtor classes. "They're hungry," a young man told G. W. Steevens, correspondent of the *London Daily Mail*:

> What's the good of talking sound finance to a man when he's hungry? Feed him first, and then he'll listen. They haven't forgotten Homestead, and they're sore. They know that they can't be worse off than they are, and so they go in for any change. If it's not free silver, it'll be something else. [2]

As the campaign drew to a close, the business and financial interests began to employ what Steevens called "political blackmail" to insure McKinley's success. Manufacturers made contracts contingent upon a Republican victory, and wage-earners were told that the factories would close should Bryan win. [3] At the same time the Republican cause was helped by an unexpected rise in the price of wheat, due to crop failures in Russia, the Argentine and elsewhere. The outcome was decisive.

[1] Ida M. Tarbell, *Owen D. Young, a New Type of Industrial Leader* (N. Y., 1932), 208.
[2] G. W. Steevens, *The Land of the Dollar* (2d edn., Edinburgh, 1897), 36-37.
[3] Steevens, *Land of the Dollar*, 168-169; Bryan, *First Battle*, 617-618; M. R. Werner, *Bryan* (N. Y., 1929), 102.

McKinley received 7,107,822 popular votes to 6,511,-073 for Bryan. His preponderance in the electoral college was far greater: 271 to 176.[1] In general, the industrial and older grain-growing states supported McKinley as against the cotton, prairie and silver-mining states.

The stability of the gold standard, however, was probably less insured by this outcome than it was by other forces working in its behalf. The world's annual production of gold, which had averaged between five and six million ounces from 1860 to 1890, reached nearly eleven and a half million in 1897, with the upward trend unchecked. This increase was due partly to the opening up of mines in South Africa, Australia and later Alaska, and partly to the new cyanide process of extracting the metal from low-content ores.[2] At the same time the volume of paper currency was enlarged through the purchase by national banks of Spanish-American War bonds and a liberalization of the old national banking act. With all reasonable fear of the scarcity of money removed, the argument for silver inflation collapsed. The farmers' condition was further alleviated by a tremendous wheat crop in 1897-1898, the greatest in years, and that at the moment when there was a wheat shortage in Europe, India, the Argentine and Australia. In July, 1896, wheat had brought but fifty-eight cents a bushel; two years later the price was nearly double, thanks to the foreign demand.[3]

When the new Republican administration entered office it gave its first attention to the tariff, not to the monetary question. Immediately after his inauguration on March 4, 1897, McKinley called an extra session of Congress for the purpose. A bill was ready. The Re-

[1] Bryan, *First Battle*, 609, 611.

[2] Sullivan, *Turn of the Century*, 296-299.

[3] For still other reasons for the decline of militant agrarianism, see Schlesinger, *Rise of the City*, 428.

publican House, elected in the fall of 1894 and first organized in December, 1895, had placed at the head of
the ways-and-means committee a serious, methodical
protectionist, Nelson Dingley of Maine, who probably
knew more about tariff schedules than any other living
man. In Congress since 1881, he had made himself
by patient toil an encyclopedia of information on the
workings of a system in which he believed as devoutly
as McKinley himself. Dingley's bill, adopted by the
House on March 31, was a moderate protectionist measure, based on the idea that the duties should be lower
than those provided by the McKinley act of 1890.[1]

The finance committee of the Senate was also agreed
that the people demanded reductions. When its chairman, Nelson W. Aldrich of Rhode Island, reported the
bill in May, he told the Senate that it was "thoroughly
understood throughout the country in the last political
campaign that if the Republican party should be again
entrusted with power, no extreme tariff legislation
would follow." He added: "Industrial conditions in
this country with a very few exceptions do not demand
a return to the rates imposed by the Act of 1890." This
was because the bitter contest "among the leading nations of the world for industrial supremacy has brought
about improvements in methods and economies in production to an extent which was not thought possible a
few years ago."[2] But Dingley and Aldrich counted
without the Industrial League, the sugar trust, the National Wool Growers' Association, the National Association of Wool Manufacturers, the Iron and Steel Association and their like. Soon Aldrich was complaining
of the trooping of the beggars of high protection

[1] Ida M. Tarbell, *The Tariff in Our Times* (N. Y., 1911), 239-244;
F. W. Taussig, *The Tariff History of the United States* (7th edn., N. Y.,
1923), 326-327.
[2] N. W. Stephenson, *Nelson W. Aldrich* (N. Y., 1930), 141-142;
Tarbell, *Tariff in Our Times*, 244.

through his committee room. When the bill became a law in July, the duties were higher than they had been under any previous tariff.[1] The new law, like its Republican predecessor of 1890, was the outcome of an aggressive protectionist spirit.

Before the economic effects of the Dingley tariff had become fully evident, the battleship *Maine* was blown up on February 15, 1898, in Havana Harbor. America's resentment at Spain's treatment of Cuba was of long standing. McKinley had inherited from the previous administration a war party which it had taken all of Cleveland's determination to hold in check. "Mr. President," McKinley had said to the outgoing President the night before his inauguration, "if I can only go out of office, at the end of my term, with the knowledge that I have done what lay in my power to avert this terrible calamity, with the success that has crowned your patience and persistence, I shall be the happiest man in the world." [2] But the destruction of the *Maine* was like the firing on Sumter, the assassination of the Archduke Franz Ferdinand at Sarajevo in 1914. It stirred a long-smoldering fire and on April 19 war was declared.[3]

The conflict that followed was no small contribution to the restoration of prosperity. Again there was work for everybody: factories busy canning foods, making uniforms, turning out guns and ammunition; a demand for civilian workers in building camps, stocking up coal for ships, and the like. The war was short, lasting in

[1] Edward Stanwood, *American Tariff Controversies in the Nineteenth Century* (Boston, 1903), II, 391; Taussig, *Tariff History*, 328-352. The new act revived the principle of reciprocity, which the Democrats had abandoned in 1894, but it did so in so complicated a form as to be virtually unworkable. Taussig, *Tariff History*, 352-354.

[2] G. F. Parker, *Recollections of Grover Cleveland* (N. Y., 1909), 249-250.

[3] For the part played by the yellow press in bringing this about, see Schlesinger, *Rise of the City*, 190-191.

all one hundred and thirteen days. It cost the United States some three hundred million dollars, including pensions and the twenty million dollars paid to Spain for giving up all claim to the Philippines, Porto Rico and Guam.[1] As a by-product of the nation's new interest in the Pacific the United States, during the course of the war, also acquired Hawaii.[2] Thus at the close of the twenty-year period the flag flew over a territorial area larger by some one hundred and twenty four thousand square miles than at its beginning. These possessions offered new markets for American goods, new concessions for American industries. The hard times of the 1890's seemed a bad dream well forgotten.

[1] See H. U. Faulkner, *The Quest for Social Justice* (*A History of American Life*, XI), 308. In addition, it eventually cost the government nearly $170,000,000 to subdue the Philippine insurgents. J. F. Rhodes, *The McKinley and Roosevelt Administrations* (N. Y., 1922), 111-112.

[2] See Schlesinger, *Rise of the City*, 419.

CHAPTER XV

AFTER TWENTY YEARS

As a matter of fact, the long depression of the nineties had not paralyzed the productive energies of the nation, however much it had temporarily weakened them. If four million men were thrown out of work, twenty million had work. Though a continuous succession of bank and industrial failures had occurred, wealth grew steadily through the decade as a whole. The total wealth of the country rose from $78,500,-000,000 in 1890 to $126,700,000,000 in 1900, up to that time the greatest gain ever made in a single decade.[1]

Moreover, the depression distributed its losses as unequally as prosperity had its gains. Many men find in hard times their chief opportunity for profit making. It is their practice to save up money in good times in order to buy cheaply what their fellows must in a depression sell at any price. Henry Clews, an acute observer of Wall Street, said that the veterans stayed at home in normal times, but when panics came could be seen "hobbling down on their canes to their brokers' offices." There they bought good stocks with the money they had been accumulating. When the emergency passed and prices went up, these wise speculators cashed in, putting their gains away for another crash.[2] The buying of stocks and bonds at the height of the Panic of 1893 enlarged more than one fortune. Besides, shrewd financiers with money on hand transacted an enormous business selling currency at a premium. Gen-

[1] R. R. Doane, *The Measurement of American Wealth* (N. Y., 1933), 11.
[2] Henry Clews, *Fifty Years in Wall Street* (N. Y., 1908), 19.

erally it was the country bank, wanting money to meet local pay rolls, that offered the best premiums; or it might be a business man who, finding himself in a particularly tight hole, willingly paid cruel rates to save himself.

Great industrial leaders, like Carnegie in steel and Rockefeller in oil, had always made it a part of their financial creed to lay aside large reserves of money for use in times of business slump. This they did partly for their own protection and partly to take advantage of the distresses of others. Both Carnegie and Rockefeller added immensely to their properties during the hard times of the nineties.

Some business men weathered the Panic because they had foreseen its coming. John H. Patterson, head of the National Cash Register Company in Dayton, Ohio, was of this type. Buying the business in 1884, he had perfected the machine, "acquired" all competitors, and consolidated his interests until the result looked so much like a monopoly that the United States began suit against him under the Sherman antitrust law. In 1880 Patterson had read a book entitled *Prophecies of Future Ups and Downs in Prices* by Samuel Benner, an Ohio farmer. The book carried a subtitle: "What years to make money on pig iron, hogs, corn, and provisions." According to the author's calculations, based on his understanding of past history, a major panic occurred every eighteen years, which made another one due in 1891. Accepting Benner as his financial prophet, Patterson would call his board of directors together whenever he believed a slump was on the way and demonstrate on a blackboard what was coming. Drawing a big "V" he would explain, "Here we have a valley of depression. Business is going to drop right down to the bottom and then come up the other side. We can drop with business or we can build a bridge and go across.

Let's build a bridge." Such a bridge they built in the crisis of the early nineties. In 1892 Patterson sold more cash registers than ever before in the company's history, and in 1893 exceeded that record by five hundred machines.[1]

Nor did the depression necessarily chill the daring of those who had ideas and no capital. *McClure's Magazine* was started in 1893 "on a shoe string" by two young editors, S. S. McClure and John S. Phillips, whose faith in ideas was always stronger than that in a bank account.[2] Not a few men discovered in the hard times a challenge to their resourcefulness. Blocked in one direction they cut out a new road. Thus Arthur J. Moxham, manufacturer of steel rails in Johnstown, Pennsylvania, found himself with many orders for which he could get no pay. While he was considering a possible shutdown, Henry George came to town and Moxham, who was a single taxer, told him his story. Whereupon George suggested that the "bonds of the street railroad companies ordering rails should be taken in payment of their orders; and that certificates to be used as money be issued against them." Calling his employees together, Moxham presented the proposal, which involved their receiving a third of their wages in cash and the rest in certificates. When they assented, the plan was explained to the storekeepers and landlords of the town who agreed to take the substitute for cash. The result was highly satisfactory. The scheme worked to the profit of both the company and the several thousand workmen.[3]

[1] Samuel Crowther, *John H. Patterson, Pioneer in Industrial Welfare* (Garden City, 1923), 77-78.

[2] See A. M. Schlesinger, *The Rise of the City* (*A History of American Life*, X), 183-184.

[3] George used this experience as an illustration of what the United States government might do if in trouble: "issue from its own treasury a paper currency, based upon its credit and interchangeable with its bonds." Henry George, jr., *The Life of Henry George* (N. Y., 1900), 557-558.

The depression failed to check the development of the two most important new industries of this generation: electric lighting and electric power.   This was amply demonstrated at the World's Columbian Exposition in 1893.[1]   The courage with which Chicago proceeded with the fair in a panic year and the exhilarating response of the people of the country to her daring presented an unusual opportunity to manufacturers of electric equipment.   The chief undertaking was the lighting of the buildings and grounds.   Only two concerns at the time were prepared to handle so large a venture: the Westinghouse and the General Electric.   Westinghouse carried off the contract, which called for the use of the alternating current.

The only efficient lamp then known, however, was entirely controlled by General Electric patents.   When Westinghouse sought to buy these lamps, the General Electric would not sell and the court refused to compel it to do so.   But he was not a man easily balked.   Already his associates had been working on the development of an incandescent bulb built around a patent which he had acquired some years before.   Now they turned full force to make practical what they had in hand.   The result was the "stopper lamp," not nearly as perfect a lamp as Edison's for it had frequently to be changed.[2]   It was with this bulb that the fair was lighted.   Taken as a whole, it was a brilliant performance, the more dazzling because unlike anything ever before seen in the country.   It marked the beginning of incandescent night illumination in the United States as well as of illuminated advertising.

Five thousand arc and one hundred and twenty thou-

---

[1] For a general account, see Schlesinger, *Rise of the City*, 283-286.
[2] F. E. Leupp, *George Westinghouse; His Life and Achievements* (Boston, 1918), chap. xii.

sand incandescent lamps made up the display, which was operated with twenty-three thousand horse power. Those who attempted to describe its magic exhausted their vocabularies in search of superlatives. Murat Halstead declared that "the earth and sky were transformed by the immeasurable wands of colossal magicians; and the superb dome of the structure, that is the central jewel of the display, is glowing as if bound with wreaths of stars." He added that the spectacle was "more resplendent than the capitals of Europe ever saw when ablaze with festivals to celebrate triumphant peace or victorious war." [1]

The success of the Westinghouse alternating current at Chicago made a deep impression on the International Niagara Commission which was engaged in advising the Cataract Construction Company as to the best means of developing power at Niagara Falls. This commission consisted of eminent engineers and scientists from various countries, headed by Sir William Thomson who was as obstinate an opponent of the alternating current as Edison himself. In the negotiations with the different power companies which sought the contract that the construction company had to award, his important influence had been in favor of the direct current. But what the Westinghouse engineers were able to show the commission in the Pittsburgh plant as well as at the Chicago Fair, combined with the company's extraordinary salesmanship, brought the contract to Westinghouse in October, 1893. A year and a half later the first of three five-thousand-horse-power dynamos was at work, and electric power was soon after on sale in Buffalo, twenty miles away. The day of long-distance transmission of power had come.

The return of normal times in the closing years of the

[1] Murat Halstead, "Electricity at the Fair," *Cosmopolitan Mag.*, XV (1893), 577-582.

twenty-year period afforded a clearer view of the laborious road which this generation had had to traverse. The most notable development had been an extraordinary unification of the nation's economic life. This had proceeded with accelerating tempo until the single year 1898 beheld the formation of twelve huge business combinations.[1] The outstanding example of the so-called franchise trust was, in 1898 as in 1878, the Western Union Telegraph Company. Its 206,202 miles of wire had grown to 874,420. Instead of carrying 24,000,000 messages, it now transmitted over 62,000,000.[2] Its only competitor, the Postal Telegraph, acted, in matters of rates and treatment of the public, as its ally. The two of them constituted a practical monopoly. As for industrial amalgamations, the Standard Oil Company, which the congressional committee had termed in 1888 "the incentive to the formation of all other trusts and combinations," was still the almost perfect monopoly. Thus the end of the period witnessed the triumph of that process of interlocking and combination which at its opening had been so generally challenged. Neither appeals to the philosophy of democracy, nor political agitation, nor restraining laws, nor even the recurring depressions which had disclosed the overexpansion and exploitation of industrial mergers, had halted their progress.

The triumph of industrial consolidation knitted the country together in ever closer bonds, increasing the feeling of nationhood. Since each aggregation strove to enlarge its market, offering more and more people something they wanted and could pay for, each worked systematically to push its organization into fresh territory. The peopling of the Great West had added a

---

[1] John Moody, *The Truth about the Trusts* (N. Y., 1904), 453-467.
[2] President of the Western Union Telegraph Company, *Annual Report for 1898*, 6.

huge new population of potential customers. From 1880 to 1900 the eleven states and territories of what the census called the Western Division had grown by nearly two and a half million. At the same time Texas had gained a million and a half; the two Dakotas nearly six hundred thousand; Nebraska and Kansas each a half million.[1] Makers of farm machinery, representatives of the telephone, salesmen for the great electric-equipment companies, the sugar trust and the oil trust penetrated to the remotest communities, weaving a network of mutual interest. Not only did they build up custom locally, but they almost invariably added a local agent to their far-flung organization.

In this immense task of building a nation-wide market it was more obvious in 1898 than it had been in 1878 that the strong man, whom Andrew Carnegie had celebrated, played a more essential part in great undertakings than did capital.[2] Still clearer was it that the leadership of strong men was the price the country was paying for its rapid development as well as for more abundant comforts and cheaper luxuries. Nowhere was this truer than in the case of the railroads. In spite of the setbacks which reckless speculation and overbuilding had forced on the railroads in 1883-1884, and again from 1893 to 1896, they had grown in mileage and had solidified the territorial divisions already well defined in 1880. There were now six recognized rail groups: the Morgan, Vanderbilt, Harriman, and Pennsylvania interests, controlling approximately 20,000 miles each, the Gould-Rockefeller group 16,000, and the Hill interests 5000.[3] The control of these giant systems did not rest on so simple a method as direct ownership. Ownership of mileage was combined with

[1] *U. S. Twelfth Census* (1900), I, xxii.
[2] See earlier, 9.
[3] See H. U. Faulkner, *The Quest for Social Justice* (*A History of American Life*, XI), 33.

leases and "community-of-interest" arrangements. In the conduct of these systems a powerful financier or speculator acting as director—a Gould, a Morgan, a Harriman—exerted more influence than a weak individual or group of individuals even though owning a bigger block of stock.

The interlocking of consolidations in different economic fields had caused grave uneasiness in 1878. By 1898 many accepted it fatalistically as inevitable. The telegraph lived off the railway; the railway could not operate without the telegraph; while the size and wealth of certain monopolistic industries made servants of them both. All these undertakings, moreover, were equally dependent on those who controlled large sums of money, whether they were bankers looking for investments or industrial magnates who, like Jay Gould or the Standard Oil group, had made greater profits than were needed for their own businesses. It was the direction which these interested groups of bankers, railway men and industrialists—these strong men—had given the country that in twenty years had so swiftly nationalized its resources and, for good or ill, had changed the whole structure of the land.

The chief complaint against this system was that its leaders had taken too big a share of the profits for themselves. The country was prone to forget the benefits it had derived. It complained of the cost of telegraphing, but failed to remember that in twenty years the number of offices had increased from eight thousand to more than twenty-two, thus giving hundreds of thousands more men and women the advantage of quick communication. Moreover, the service was cheaper, the average charge per message having fallen from 38.9 cents in 1878 to 30.1 in 1898.[1]

[1] President of the Western Union Telegraph Company, *Annual Report for 1898*, 6.

One enormous benefit, little appreciated at the time, was the example of efficient organization and operation which the big combinations were setting the country. Under the old individualistic methods of doing business each proprietor, each employee, worked along in his own way; but as undertakings enlarged and consolidated, systematized practices began to be the rule. Order, economy, stability, became the ideals of operative heads, especially those touched by Taylor's new science of management. An undertaking was analyzed as never before, and each function given proper attention. At the same time improvements in office equipment added to business efficiency. The typewriter, still regarded as a novelty early in the period, became before many years an important adjunct to the conduct of every enterprising business office. In the single year 1890 a little over $3,600,000 worth of typewriters and supplies were sold; ten years later nearly twice as much.[1] After the typewriter had come the adding machine, invented in 1886 and made practical in 1891. In 1892 the first addressograph appeared. The filing case, the card catalogue and the tabulating machine followed rapidly. Business offices were coming to have their special technology as did the farm and the factory.

The temptation to condemn industry as a whole because a few powerful men became inordinately rich not only prevented a proper weighing of the advantages the public was receiving, but it prevented cool and effective dealing with the roots of the evil. Popular attention fastened on the conspicuous or wicked individual rather than on the nature of his practices which the existing economic and political system made possible. In the twenty-year period two major attempts to correct basic wrongs had been made: the interstate-commerce act dealing with railroad abuses, and the Sherman

[1] Bureau of the Census, *Abstract of Twelfth Census,* 320.

antitrust law. Neither had proved an effective remedy. If possible, the accomplishments under the interstate-commerce act were even more discouraging than under the Sherman law. The interstate-commerce commission in its report for 1898 declared that a large part of the rail transportation of the country was still on an illegal basis.[1] Although both statutes proved unsatisfactory in operation, they at least committed the government to the principle of regulation and, as their weaknesses became clear to the public, it was certain that there would be amendments by Congress and judicial decisions which would strengthen the arm of the government.[2]

One of the chief causes of the recurrent depressions had been the wanton flooding of the land with railroad and industrial securities, issued in the name of legitimate expansion but frequently for no other purpose than sheer speculation. Apparently the country learned little from the panics of 1884 and 1893, in which gambling in unsound stocks had been a big factor—not enough at least to see to it that no security be issued without full information to the public as to what was behind it. Massachusetts attacked the evil of stock watering in the case of public-service companies, forbidding them to declare a dividend or create additional stock unless the par value was paid in cash to the treasurer.[3] James J. Hill made a suggestion which, had it been followed, would have checked if not prevented speculative orgies: a law requiring a company desiring to do business outside the state in which it was incorporated to satisfy a federal commission that its capital stock was paid in cash or in property taken at a fair valuation.[4] The

[1] U. S. Industrial Commission, *Report* (Wash., 1900-1902), XIX, 353.

[2] See Faulkner, *Quest for Social Justice*, 116-120, for later developments.

[3] U. S. Industrial Commission, *Report*, XIX, 417-418.

[4] J. J. Hill, *Highways of Progress* (N. Y., 1910), 136.

people in general preferred to take their chances. Before the end of 1898 railroads and industries were preparing to issue securities to carry on proposed expansion and consolidation such as the country had never dreamed, and, far from attempting to control these issues, a huge speculative public eagerly awaited their appearance.

The farmer, despite many ups and downs during the two decades, enjoyed a distinctly improved position in the national economy as the century drew to a close. The prices of his products had advanced. Money was easier than ever before. In ten years the per-capita circulation of the country had increased from $22.88 to $25.15; at the same time his credit facilities had improved. He had used these advantages to lift the load of mortgages, which had so shocked the country when revealed by the census report of 1890, and to better his farming methods. Labor-saving devices played an ever greater part in his operations. In 1900 he had seven hundred and fifty million dollars invested in implements and machinery.[1] From the state agricultural colleges, experiment stations and farmers' institutes he was learning more scientific methods of tilling the soil and breeding livestock and of combating plant diseases and pests.[2] Food factories were beginning to appear in his district, taking his products in bulk.[3] The handling of milk, the making of butter and cheese, the canning of fruits, the packing of apples, were being increasingly industrialized.

It was necessary that the farmer be on the alert, for he had twenty-five million more mouths to feed than in 1878. To be sure, he had placed more acres under cultivation, nearly a third more, but on this land he was

[1] Bureau of the Census, *Abstract of Twelfth Census*, 217.
[2] See Schlesinger, *Rise of the City*, 215-216, 234, 236-237.
[3] See Schlesinger, *Rise of the City*, 132-133.

asked to raise not only food for America but an increasing amount for overseas. The nation's prosperity depended, in large measure, upon the sum total he could export. By the end of the period his produce made up nearly seventy per cent of the country's total exports. That this represented a relative fall of nearly thirteen per cent in twenty years was due to the tremendous increase meantime in the output of America's factories and mines.

Not all was rosy on the farm, however. The question of uncontrolled production, of crop surpluses in the future as in the past, continued unsolved. Moreover, many farmers, preferring traditional to the new scientific methods, were storing up trouble for the years ahead. The spirit of haste, of indifference to waste, affected the agriculturists as it did every other class, causing them often to work the land to the utmost without proper provision for replenishment. At the same time they complained bitterly of the greed and wantonness of lumbermen who cut timber over wide stretches of the country, hastening soil erosion and leaving stumps and brush to feed destructive forest fires. The farseeing realized even then that such methods were preparing for one of the greatest tragedies in land history: the ravages of the wind which nothing but abundant and properly placed timber and grass could prevent.

On the whole, the conditions of the wage-earners had also greatly improved in the twenty years. After trying the "one-big-union" type of organization sponsored by the Knights of Labor, the labor movement had turned to the form of organization represented by the American Federation of Labor, one consisting of a league of nation-wide craft unions. By 1893 the Knights had dropped to less than seventy-five thousand and their activities had become political rather than economic.[1] Membership of the American Federation, on the other hand, showed a steady growth, standing at two hundred and seventy-eight thousand in 1898.[2] Under the leadership of Samuel Gompers it had become a compact, militant body, intent on spreading unionism among skilled workers and alert to encroachments on the part of the employing class.

At the beginning of the score of years most labor leaders had favored the legal incorporation of unions. This demand, for example, appeared in the original platform of the Federation of Organized Trades and Labor Unions. There were various reasons for this desire. Incorporation would protect unions against embezzlement of funds by officers, remove them from the possible operation of state conspiracy laws and, by giving the organizations greater stability, make employers more inclined to deal with them. Peter J. McGuire, secretary of the Brotherhood of Carpenters and Joiners, in urging such action on a congressional committee in 1883, pleaded that, if Congress lacked the power, "it shall assume the power; and, if necessary, amend the constitution to do it."[3] But later experience with the courts in industrial disputes convinced laborites that the disadvantages of incorporation would outweigh the advantages. By the close of the period they had completely reversed their position.

The Sherman antitrust act had an unexpected bearing on the legal status of unions. An early attempt was made to apply it to labor organizations, although the country at large undoubtedly regarded it as applying only to capitalistic combinations in restraint of trade.

[1] Leo Wolman, *The Growth of American Trade Unions, 1880-1923* (Natl. Bur. of Econ. Research, *Publs.*, no. 6), 32; J. R. Commons and others, *History of Labour in the United States* (N. Y., 1918), II, 482.

[2] L. L. Lorwin, *The American Federation of Labor* (Brookings Inst., *Publs.*, no. 50), 484.

[3] Selig Perlman, *A History of Trade Unionism in the United States* (N. Y., 1922), 152-153.

Thus, in 1893, the federal Supreme Court under the Sherman law upheld an injunction against striking draymen of New Orleans on the ground that the strikers were interfering with the transfer of goods from one state to another.   The court declared that, though the statute had evidently originated in a fear of massed capital, "when the Congress came to formulate the prohibition . . . the subject had so broadened . . . that the source of the evil was not regarded as material, and the evil in its entirety is dealt with.   They made the interdiction include combinations of labor, as well as of capital." [1] Debs's prison sentence in 1894 was based on the court's right, under the Sherman act, to issue the injunction which Debs had violated.   Other cases followed.   By 1898 judicial interpretation had made it unmistakably clear that the statute applied to combinations whether of capital or labor.[2]

Great strides had been made in state legislation protecting and improving the condition of labor.   It touched a wide range of subjects: sweatshops, laundries, mines, railways, occupational devices, the guarding of machinery, housing, free unemployment bureaus, child labor, woman's labor.[3] Some of these laws were defective in form; others were poorly enforced, or were stripped of their value by action of the courts. Nevertheless they brought the wage-earning class under the protective care of the government to a degree unknown twenty years before, and prepared the way for more effective legislation by the next generation.[4]

The American Federation of Labor credited labor's

[1] U. S. *v.* The Workingmen's Amalgamated Council of New Orleans, 54 *Federal,* 994.

[2] Felix Frankfurter and Nathan Greene, *The Labor Injunction* (N. Y., 1930), 8-9, 19.

[3] G. A. Weber, "Labor Legislation in the United States," *U. S. Dept. of Labor, Bull.,* IX, no. 54, 1421-1486.

[4] See Faulkner, *Quest for Social Justice,* 76-80.

gains to militancy. The unions had learned much from their experience in fighting organized capital—not to go into a strike without preparation, to keep within the law, to avoid violence, to educate the public as to an understanding of labor's grievances. Over 6,600,000 persons were out on strike for longer or shorter periods in the twenty years 1881-1900, at a cost to industry of about a half-billion dollars, of which two thirds was in wages. On the whole, labor issued from these conflicts more successfully than capital, primarily because what it sought was so often just. Moreover, organized labor succeeded better than unorganized. The proportion of victories, according to the labor bureau, was fifty-one per cent for labor, thirty-six for the employer and the rest undetermined.[1] Did industrial warfare pay? The answer depends on whether the real grievances could have been settled by conciliation or arbitration to the satisfaction of both sides. In a considerable number of cases undoubtedly this might have been done. The gain in developing a sound technique for threshing out common problems and adjusting them by peaceful means would have been tremendous. But neither side, unfortunately, was interested primarily in a peaceful industrial life. Both strove to achieve their immediate material ends and used those methods which promised the quickest results.

If labor and capital had changed but little in ambition and methods, the attitude of the public towards these dominant forces in the nation's economic life had changed. A continuous stream of official investigations by the state and federal governments, of private lawsuits, of reports from courts and commissions, supplied a body of data such as the people had never before known. This mass of information lay behind the legislation which increasingly manifested the government's

[1] U. S. Industrial Commission, *Report*, XIX, 864-870.

The Troubles of Labor

An unfriendly view of a walking delegate's visit to a construction job

tendency to intervene in economic concerns. An ever larger element of the public was growing to realize that the doctrine of *laissez-faire* too often cloaked the greed of the strong. "Our civilization," declared Henry Demarest Lloyd, "has followed the self-interest of the individual to learn that it was but one of the complex forces of self-interest. The true *laissez-faire* is, let the individual do what the individual can do best, and let the community do what the community can do best." [1] It was this latter principle, which Lloyd termed the "*laissez-faire* of social self-interest," that had bred such legislation as the interstate-commerce and antitrust acts.

There was, moreover, a deepening conviction that ethical and humanitarian considerations had a vital relationship to economics and that a failure to observe them constituted a continuing menace to social stability. This conviction was, in part, the intellectual contribution made by the socialists, the single taxers, the Populists and other minority groups which refused to admit that poverty was a legitimate concomitant of progress. On all sides experiments in education, technological training, economic coöperation, the shorter day, better wages, the model factory, better housing, attested the belief that life could be made more tolerable for the masses.[2] But Carnegie's strong man still occupied the saddle. He had fashioned a vast nation-wide industrial order and he had no intention of resigning the kingdom which he had so laboriously prepared.

[1] H. D. Lloyd, *Wealth against Commonwealth* (N. Y., 1894), 497.
[2] C. R. Henderson, *The Social Spirit in America* (Chicago, 1901), chap. viii.

CHAPTER XVI

CRITICAL ESSAY ON AUTHORITIES

PHYSICAL SURVIVALS

THANKS to the attention given in recent years to the preservation of the originals and models of significant inventions, permanent exhibits exist in many parts of the land which help the student to visualize the main stages of technological development in the period covered by this volume. The New York Museum of Science and Industry, established in 1924, shelters collections illustrating the progress of the food, clothing and housing industries, of all forms of transportation, and of the applications of electricity to communication, lighting and power. Among the important originals are the Hammond typewriter (1881), the Parsons steam turbine (1884), a Hoe single large-cylinder printing press (1886) and the Welsbach incandescent mantle (1886). The exhibits also include a model of the first permanent central power house in the world for the generation of electricity, the Pearl Street Station in New York City, built by Thomas A. Edison and opened on September 4, 1882.

The most complete collection delineating the history of electric illumination is to be found in the Edison Institute of Technology, established by Henry Ford at Dearborn, Michigan. In the adjoining Greenfield Village are shown the original models of Edison's mimeographing machine, his improvements on the telephone, the quadruplex telegraph, the talking machine and other inventions to which he contributed. At Schenectady, New York, the General Electric Company preserves as the heart of its great plant the original building in which Thomas Edison set up his machine shop in 1884. The Museum of Science and Industry in Chicago, founded by Julius Rosenwald in 1929 along lines similar to those of the New York Museum, is particularly note-worthy for displays of coal and metal-mining processes, including originals of early coal cutters and punchers, safety lamps and a diamond drill for sampling ore (about 1880). Like its New York counterpart, the Chicago Museum presents many of the models in motion. A fine intention of this institution is to show the effects on social and cultural life of the successive improvements in industry as well as the radical technological principles they embodied.

Most phases of American industrial evolution during the period are illuminated by exhibits in the United States National Museum in Washington. Here may be seen the experimental airplane models of Samuel Pierpont Langley, which actually flew under their own power, the first on May 6, 1896. The Langley collection embraces specimens of kites, boomerangs, airfoils, testing devices, etc., used in his aëronautical researches. Among other objects of particular interest are the man-carrying glider built and flown by Otto Lilienthal in 1894 and models of Octave Chanute's glider of 1896; the original automobiles of Duryea, Haynes, Olds and Winton; the calculating machines of Felt, Burroughs and Baldwin; Elihu Thomson's first three-phase dynamo and his first apparatus for electric welding; also a large collection of the patent-office models of important inventions, including the gasoline engine, the telephone and the typewriter. In the Franklin Institute of Philadelphia are preserved the originals of the Linotype of 1884 and the Monotype of 1890.

Certain more specialized collections help to round out the picture of technological development during the period. The Industrial Museum, maintained by the American Steel and Wire Company at Worcester, Massachusetts, contains pictures, objects and records which tell the story of wire and nails. Especially noteworthy are such exhibits as a section of the first wire rod rolled in 1888 by the Joliet Steel Company, a wire frame first installed in 1845 and used until 1910, the first wire-nail machine built in America and still in use, and specimens of barbed-wire fencing with documents illustrating the patent war which began in the 1870's and went on through the 1880's. The state of Pennsylvania in 1934 dedicated at Titusville, Pennsylvania, a museum and park in honor of the man who drilled the first oil well, E. L. Drake. This museum, located at the site of the first well, has on exhibition the drilling tools used and a replica of the well itself, also an interesting collection of lamps and of models tracing the progress in the producing and transportation of oil. The Westinghouse Electric & Manufacturing Company of East Pittsburgh, Pennsylvania, has preserved many original models of George Westinghouse's work, including the transformers (1885) which made possible the use of the alternating current, the induction motor (1888), the alternating-current meter (1888), the rotary converter (1892), and the stopper lamp which enabled him to light the Chicago World's Fair of 1893. The Westinghouse Air Brake Company of Wilmerding, Pennsylvania, maintains a museum in which may be found the originals of Westinghouse's safety inventions, including the air brake, draft gear and signaling equipment.

The celebration by corporations of milestones in the history of the industries they represent has led to several important expositions, with the result that the more significant exhibits were retained later in permanent plant museums. The most complete of such celebrations was the Centenary Exhibition and Pageant held in 1927 by the Baltimore & Ohio Railroad, which covered in detail the road's one hundred years of continuous operation. Of particular interest to the period of this volume are the engine, "Mogul 600," which took first prize at the Centennial Exhibition at Philadelphia in 1876, and the first railroad electric locomotive, put into operation by the Baltimore & Ohio in 1894. These as well as many other originals and models are on display in the railroad's Hall of Transportation on the former site of the fair in Baltimore.

For information as to other collections illustrating technological changes in industry, agriculture, transportation and communication the interested reader should consult the *Handbook of American Museums* (Wash., 1932), published by the American Association of Museums. Pictorial representations of inventions and of industrial processes and equipment may be conveniently found in R. H. Gabriel, ed., *The Pageant of America* (15 vols., New Haven, 1925-1929).

GENERAL DOCUMENTARY AND STATISTICAL SOURCES

The history of American economic development from 1878 to 1898 is most fully written in the *Report* of the United States Industrial Commission (19 vols., Wash., 1900-1902) created by Congress in 1898. This body of nineteen men over a period of two years examined more than seven hundred people, including captains of industry, business executives, public officials, leaders of organized labor and various persons concerned with the social implications of changing industrial practices. A digest of the testimony taken introduces each volume. The final volume contains the commission's findings on transportation, agriculture, manufacturing, industrial combinations, labor, immigration, irrigation and taxation. In J. D. Richardson, comp., *A Compilation of the Messages and Papers of the Presidents* (10 vols., Wash., 1896-1899), will be found official comments on social and economic conditions from the standpoint of the party in power, and also digests of importance from the departments of agriculture and the interior and the bureau (from 1888 the department) of labor. The wealth of data buried in official state publications may conveniently be consulted by using Adelaide R. Hasse, comp., *Index of Economic Material in Documents of the States of the United States* (Carnegie Inst., *Publs.*, no. 85, 1907-1922), covering thirteen states down to the year 1904.

Increasing attention was given throughout the twenty-year period to collecting and analyzing figures on transportation, farming, manufactures, merchandising, movements of population, fluctuations in wages, hours of labor and prices, and matters concerning gold and silver production and the currency. The census reports of 1880, 1890 and 1900 form the basis of all this statistical work. See A. M. Schlesinger, *The Rise of the City (A History of*

American Life, X), 441, for comment on the scope of these decennial inventories. The final volume of the *Report* of the Industrial Commission includes many tables, charts, maps and diagrams, delineating industrial and financial changes and trends. An abstract of the twelfth census issued by the bureau of the census in 1904 presents comparisons with 1880 and 1890 which are convenient. The *Statistical Record of the Progress of the United States, 1800-1906* (Wash., 1906), issued by the bureau of statistics of the department of commerce and labor, is also useful. An intelligent recent book is R. R. Doane, *The Measurement of American Wealth* (N. Y., 1933).

Excellent cartographic representations of economic phenomena are included in C. O. Paullin, *Atlas of the Historical Geography of the United States* (J. K. Wright, ed., Carnegie Inst., *Publs.*, no. 401, Wash., 1932). Sections of this work are devoted to industry, transportation, foreign commerce, agriculture and the progress of labor legislation, and bear upon developments during the period 1878-1898. Maps for the year 1880 show the distribution of national wealth in terms of value of houses and lands, taxable property and all property, and also as indicated by statistics of banks and bank capital.

PERIODICAL LITERATURE

Among daily newspapers, the best informed on economic subjects are the *New York Evening Post* (from 1801), whose financial column was particularly able; the *New York Tribune* (from 1847), which had a pronounced humanitarian bias; the *Chicago Tribune* (from 1847), a valiant fighter for tariff reform; and the *Springfield Republican* (from 1824), an exponent of free-lance liberalism. The only one of these papers which has been indexed for the period is the *Chicago Tribune* (for the years 1875-1906). *Public Opinion* (N. Y., 1886-1906) digested weekly the comment of the entire country on contemporary events, as did also the *Literary Digest* (N. Y., from 1890) with which *Public Opinion* was merged in 1906. References to general histories of American journalism and to accounts of outstanding newspapers will be found in Schlesinger, *Rise of the City* (earlier cited), 443-444.

Among the weeklies, the *Nation* (N. Y., from 1865) was the most intelligent defender of individualism and the most caustic critic of undertakings it regarded as socialistic in tendency. *Harper's Weekly* (N. Y., 1857-1916) published occasional illustrated articles on new developments in industry, immigration and transportation. Its editorials on subjects which concern this volume were well-informed and its cartoons were pointed comments on industrial and financial exploitations and fraud.

Monthly periodicals published occasional but often effective articles on economic subjects. *Harper's Magazine* (N. Y., from 1850) was inclined to descriptive articles, while the *Century Magazine* (N. Y., 1881-1930) interested itself in social reform, performing notable service in the attack on slum conditions and in the effort to arouse interest in better sanitation. The *New England Magazine* (Boston, 1884-1917), the *Arena* (Boston, 1889-1909) and the *Forum* (N. Y., from 1886) followed the struggles of labor and capital and lent a hand in stimulating social and economic reform. *McClure's Magazine* (N. Y., from 1893) gave attention to what it called "the edge of the future": scientific discoveries and inventions. It also interested itself in the problems and in the leaders of industry and finance. The *Popular Science Monthly* (N. Y., from 1872) and the *Scientific American* (N. Y., from 1859) are useful guides to scientific discoveries and technological advances; David A. Wells published many of his studies of economic phenomena in the former.

Certain periodicals devoted themselves to special phases of economic life. The *Commercial and Financial Chronicle* (N. Y., from 1865) contains as full reports as were available on the conditions of railroads and industries. It followed the stock market intelligently and its outspoken editorials against industrial malpractices are particularly informative. The *Iron Age* (Middletown, N. Y., from 1855) covering iron and steel is a first-class journal of its kind; so is the *Oil City Derrick* (Oil City, Pa., from 1871) representing the oil industry. The *Manufacturers' Record* (Balt., from 1882), the *Electrical World* (N. Y., from 1883) and the *Journal of Agriculture* (St. Louis, 1856-1921) are typical and useful organs in their particular fields. The more important weekly newspapers which sprang up to propagate the point of view of the Farmers' Alliances are conveniently listed in J. D. Hicks, *The Populist Revolt* (Minneapolis, 1931), 456-457.

Of general annual summaries the most useful is *Appletons' Annual Cyclopædia* (new ser., 1876-1895; 3d ser., 1896-1902; N. Y., 1877-1903). Its analysis of each year's work in Congress, its reviews of developments in the several states, its sketches of men who made contributions to industrial progress, its reviews of financial trends and of the doings of the stock market are of particular value. Among other annual publications are the reports of presidents of corporations to their directors, documents which give a picture of the condition and the ambition of the enterprise as its officers saw them. Those of the Western Union are notably frank. As a rule, industrial corporations made no public reports in the eighties and nineties.

PERSONAL MATERIAL

While autobiographical accounts by leaders in the economic sphere are less numerous than in the domain of political and social life, nevertheless a number of illuminating books are available, notably the *Memoirs* (2 vols., Boston, 1904) of Henry Villard; the *Autobiography* (Boston, 1920) of Andrew Carnegie; *Random Reminiscences of Men and Events* (N. Y., 1909) by John D. Rockefeller; *Memories of an Active Life* (N. Y., 1923) by Charles R. Flint; *Fifty Years in Wall Street* (N. Y., 1908) by Henry Clews; *Seventy Years of Life and Labor* (2 vols., N. Y., 1925) by Samuel Gompers; *Thirty Years of Labor* (Columbus, 1890) by Terence V. Powderly; and *From Immigrant to Inventor* (N. Y., 1923) by Michael Pupin. A neglected source of autobiographical material is the series of examinations of important industrial and financial figures conducted by governmental investigating committees in hearings preparatory to the framing of new tariff schedules, the writing of regulatory measures such as that for the establishment of the interstate-commerce commission and the making of reports such as that of the United States Industrial Commission (earlier referred to). The persons examined included key men in transportation, telegraphy, telephony, oil, electricity and iron and steel, and their testimony is usually revealing of character and personality. It also furnishes excellent material for an understanding of the problems and conduct of the enterprises.

Biographers in recent years have devoted increasing attention to inventors, business magnates and labor leaders. Such works are often "inspired" and hence must be used with appropriate caution. Among the more informative are *The Life of James J. Hill* (2 vols., Garden City, 1917) by J. G. Pyle; *The Life of Andrew Carnegie* (2 vols., Garden City, 1932) by B. J. Hendrick; *Cyrus Hall McCormick: Harvest, 1856-1884* (N. Y., 1935) by W. T. Hutchinson; *George Westinghouse; His Life and Achievements* (Boston, 1918) by F. E. Leupp, and a second and more technical study by H. G. Prout (N. Y., 1921); *Frederick W. Taylor, Father of Scientific Management* (2 vols., N. Y., 1923) by F. B. Copley; *Henry Clay Frick, the Man* (N. Y., 1928) by George Harvey; *John H. Patterson, Pioneer in Industrial Welfare* (Garden City, 1923) by Samuel Crowther; *Edison: His Life and Inventions* (2 vols., rev. edn., N. Y., 1929) by F. L. Dyer and T. C. Martin; *Alexander Graham Bell; the Man Who Contracted Space* (Boston, 1928) by Catherine Mackenzie; *The Life Story of J. Pierpont Morgan* (N. Y., 1911) by Carl Hovey; *God's Gold; the Story of Rockefeller and His Times* (N. Y., 1932) by J. T. Flynn; *Nelson W. Aldrich, a Leader in American Politics* (N. Y., 1930) by N. W. Stephenson; *Hanna* (N. Y., 1929) by Thomas Beer; *Marcus Alonzo Hanna; His Life and Work* (N. Y., 1912) by H. D. Croly; *The Portrait of a Banker: James Stillman, 1850-1918* (N. Y., 1927) by Anna R. Burr; and *E. H. Harriman, a Biography* (2 vols., N. Y., 1922) by George

Kennan. In *Poole's Index to Periodical Literature* (various comps., Boston and N. Y., 1882-1907) will be found references to voluminous biographical material in articles on the industrial and financial leaders of the time. For minor as well as major figures the *Dictionary of American Biography* (20 vols., N. Y., 1928-1936), edited by Allen Johnson and Dumas Malone, is a convenient source of information.

GENERAL TREATMENTS

The standard general histories by J. F. Rhodes and E. P. Oberholtzer touch on the economic life of the period, but are primarily concerned with politics. Much the same thing is true of A. B. Hart, ed., *The American Nation: A History* (28 vols., N. Y., 1904-1928). Certain volumes of Allen Johnson, ed., *The Chronicles of America Series* (50 vols., New Haven, 1918-1921), are devoted to narrative accounts of economic developments. Of the many recent single-volume surveys of American economic history probably the most useful for the years treated by this book are F. A. Shannon, *Economic History of the People of the United States* (N. Y., 1934); E. C. Kirkland, *A History of American Economic Life* (N. Y., 1932); and H. U. Faulkner, *American Economic History* (rev. edn., N. Y., 1931). For a particular state E. L. Bogart and C. M. Thompson, *The Industrial State, 1870-1893* (C. W. Alvord, ed., *The Centennial History of Illinois*, IV, Springfield, 1920), has great value.

Of the works written contemporaneously with the period the best general discussion is D. A. Wells, *Recent Economic Changes* (N. Y.). Although published in 1889, its analyses and judgments apply in most respects also to 1898. The comments on the effects of machinery and of the tariff are particularly illuminating. Much useful information may also be gleaned from C. M. Depew, ed., *One Hundred Years of American Commerce* (2 vols., N. Y., 1895), a composite work written by authorities in the principal fields of economic activity.

MANUFACTURING, MINING AND INVENTION

The most comprehensive single work on American manufactures is V. S. Clark, *History of Manufactures in the United States* (Carnegie Inst., *Contribs. to Am. Econ. History*; rev. edn., 3 vols., N. Y., 1929); the third volume treats the years 1860-1928. Many individual industries have received separate historical treatment. Among the more useful of these volumes are J. E. Defebaugh, *History of the Lumber Industry of America* (4 vols., Chicago, 1906-1909); F. J. Allen, *The Shoe Industry* (N. Y., 1916); M. T. Copeland, *The Cotton Manufacturing Industry of the United States* (*Harvard Econ. Studies*, VII, 1912); A. H. Cole, *The American Wool Manufacture* (2 vols., Cambridge, 1926); R. A. Clemen, *The American Livestock and Meat Industry* (N. Y., 1923); J. H. Collins, *The Story of Canned Foods* (N. Y., 1924); C. B. Kuhlman, *Development of the Flour Milling Industry in the United States* (Boston, 1929); P. L. Vogt, *The Sugar Refining Industry in the United States* (Univ. of Pa., *Series in Political Economy and Public Law*, no. 21, 1908); Meyer Jacobstein, *The Tobacco Industry in the United States* (Columbia Univ., *Studies*, XXVI, no. 3, 1907); Edward Orton, *The Progress of the Ceramic Industry* (Univ. of Wis., *Bull.*, II, no. 9, 1903); L. H. Weeks, *A History of Paper Manufacturing in the United States* (N. Y., 1916); H. N. Casson, *The Romance of Steel* (N. Y., 1907); T. A. Rickard, *A History of American Mining* (N. Y., 1932), devoted mainly to the metallic ores; and Eliot Jones, *The Anthracite Coal Combination in the United States* (*Harvard Econ. Studies*, XI, 1914).

The general works on mechanical progress include E. W. Byrn, *The Progress of Invention in the Nineteenth Century* (N. Y., 1900), still valuable though old; Waldemar Kaempffert, ed., *A Popular History of American Invention* (2 vols., N. Y., 1924), profusely illustrated; and George Iles, *Leading American Inventors* (N. Y., 1912), a biographical approach. These should be supplemented by special studies, of which the following are representative: R. H.

Thurston, *A Century's Progress of the Steam Engine* (Wash., 1899); H. N. Casson, *The History of the Telephone* (Chicago, 1910); Joseph Husband, *The Story of the Pullman Car* (Chicago, 1917); and T. C. Martin and S. L. Coles, eds., *The Story of Electricity* (2 vols., N. Y., 1919-1922).

TRUSTS, COMBINATIONS AND THE TARIFF

Federal and state investigations of industrial combinations were almost continuous throughout the twenty years. Among the more significant federal documents relating to such inquiries are *House Report*, 52 Cong., 1 sess., no. 3112, containing testimony on the whisky trust; *House Report*, 52 Cong., 2 sess., no. 2278, concerning the anthracite operators; and *House Report*, 52 Cong., 2 sess., no. 2601, dealing with the whisky trust. The United States Industrial Commission, *Report* (cited earlier), II, contains decisions of federal, state and territorial courts, together with a digest of corporation laws. The volumes of testimony, briefs of prosecution and defense and the Supreme Court decisions in the suits by the United States against the Standard Oil Company in 1906 and the United States Steel Corporation in 1909 shed much light on earlier conditions. Of the state documents the most important are those emanating from investigations by the Ohio senate in 1878 and 1898 and by the New York senate in 1888 and 1898.

The secondary literature on the growth and regulation of trusts is voluminous. Particularly useful for the period is John Moody, *The Truth about the Trusts* (N. Y., 1904), which gives a list of all trusts—industrial, franchise, transportation and miscellaneous—arranged in order of incorporation, with statistics as to the number of plants controlled and total capitalization. A full description of the make-up of each combination also appears in so far as the facts were available at the time. *Trusts, Pools and Corporations* (Boston, 1905; rev. 1916), edited by W. Z. Ripley, is a collection of scholarly papers on special combinations: salt, whisky, wire nails, tin plate, etc. The volume includes discussions of legislation and of the effects of regulation, together with a critical survey of early trust literature. Other works of interest are H. D. Lloyd, *Wealth against Commonwealth* (N. Y., 1894), concerned mainly with the Standard Oil Company; Ida M. Tarbell, *The History of the Standard Oil Company* (2 vols., N. Y., 1904); H. R. Mussey, *Combination in the Mining Industry* (Columbia Univ., *Studies,* XXIII, no. 3, 1905); R. T. Ely, *Monopolies and Trusts* (N. Y., 1900); W. M. Collier, *The Trusts* (N. Y., 1900); J. W. Jenks, *The Trust Problem* (N. Y., 1902; rev. by W. E. Clark, Garden City, 1917); and G. H. Montague, *Trusts of To-Day* (N. Y., 1904).

On the issues involved in tariff legislation salient material may be found in the *Report* of the Tariff Commission of 1882, *House Exec. Doc.,* 47 Cong., 2 sess., no. 6. For the hearings taken in 1888 by a Senate committee relevant to the Mills bill, see *Senate Report,* 50 Cong., 1 sess., no. 2332. The hearings preparatory to later tariff acts—the McKinley bill, the Wilson bill and Dingley bill—are also available in congressional documents. A pamphlet which had large influence in the eighties and nineties was Henry George, *Protection or Free Trade* (N. Y., 1886). E. L. Godkin, *Problems of Modern Democracy* (N. Y., 1896), contains a finely argued essay on "Some Political and Social Aspects of the Tariff." The course of tariff legislation during the period is treated from variant points of view in F. W. Taussig, *Tariff History of the United States* (rev. edn., N. Y., 1931); Ida M. Tarbell, *The Tariff in Our Times* (N. Y., 1911); and Edward Stanwood, *Tariff Controversies in the Nineteenth Century* (2 vols., Boston, 1903), the last revealing a protectionist bias.

RAIL TRANSPORTATION

Basic to an understanding of the railroad problems of the period is the *Report* of the so-called Cullom committee in *Senate Report,* 49 Cong., 1 sess., no. 46 (1886). This document was extremely influential in shaping the interstate-commerce act of the next year. The first *Annual Report* of the interstate-commerce commission, published in December, 1887, gives an admirable summary of the agitation that led up to the commission's establishment. In the succeeding *Annual Reports* the course of the effort to apply the law can best be traced. Of monographic studies L. H. Haney, *A Congressional History of Railways in the United States, 1850-1887* (Univ. of Wis., *Bull.*, no. 342, 1910), offers the most thorough account of the background of the act of 1887. W. Z. Ripley, ed., *Railway Problems* (Boston, 1907), discusses several decisions of the interstate-commerce commission, together with the decisions of the Supreme Court in cases of appeal. Ripley, *Railroads: Rates and Regulation* (N. Y., 1912), and his *Railroads: Finance and Organization* (N. Y., 1915), form the most important secondary material on the subject of land transportation. For individual rail lines, consult E. V. Smalley, *History of the Northern Pacific Railroad* (N. Y., 1883); Stuart Daggett, *Chapters on the History of the Southern Pacific* (N. Y., 1922); Nelson Trottman, *History of the Union Pacific* (N. Y., 1923); G. D. Bradley, *The Story of the Santa Fé* (Boston, 1920); W. H. Stennett, *History of the Chicago and Northwestern Railway System* (Chicago, 1910); Edward Hungerford, *The Story of the Baltimore and Ohio Railroad, 1827-1927* (2 vols., N. Y., 1928); and J. B. Hedges, *Henry Villard and the Railways of the Northwest* (New Haven, 1930).

LABOR AND IMMIGRATION

The most reliable official sources for a study of actual working conditions and the cost of living are the *Annual Reports* (from 1886) of the United States bureau of labor (called department of labor, 1888-1905), and the periodical reports issued by the state bureaus of labor of Massachusetts (from 1870), Pennsylvania (from 1873), Illinois (from 1883), New York (from 1884) and Wisconsin (from 1885). Very useful is the *Index of All Reports Issued by Bureaus of Labor Statistics in the United States prior to March 1, 1902* (Wash., 1902). Such documents should be supplemented by the *Annual Proceedings* of the Knights of Labor and of the American Federation of Labor, which tell the story of the ambitions and the programs of organized labor. As for the industrial outbreaks which characterized the period, there is ample official material in the investigations of the state and federal governments; the leading items have been referred to in the footnotes in the text. R. T. Ely, *The Labor Movement in America* (N. Y., 1886), published during the climax of a series of labor upheavals, gives an acute contemporary appraisal of the social forces at work. The Library of Congress in 1903 issued a *Select List of Books* (*with References to Periodicals*) *on Labor, Particularly Relating to Strikes* (Wash.).

At the head of the secondary literature useful for this period is J. R. Commons, ed., *History of Labour in the United States* (2 vols., N. Y., 1918). In the second volume (576-587) will be found a detailed bibliography of the period 1876-1897, including public documents, contemporary books, pamphlets and labor newspapers. Leo Wolman, *The Growth of American Trade Unions, 1880-1923* (N. Y., 1924), is a statistical study sponsored by the National Bureau of Economic Research (*Publs.*, no. 6). Special aspects of the labor movement can be studied in Morris Hillquit, *History of Socialism in the United States* (rev. edn., N. Y., 1910); Eunice M. Schuster, *Native American Anarchism* (Smith College, *Studies*, XVII, 1931-1932); L. L. Lorwin, *The American Federation of Labor* (Brookings Inst., *Publs.*, no. 50; Wash., 1933); N. J. Ware, *The Labor Movement in the United States, 1860-1895* (N. Y., 1929), devoted largely to the Knights of Labor; William Kirk, *National Labor Federations in the United States* (Johns Hopkins Univ., *Studies*, XXVI, 1906); W. R. Browne, *Altgeld of Illinois* (N. Y., 1924), reviewing Altgeld's relation to the pardoning of the Chicago anarchists; C. H. Wesley, *Negro Labor in the United States, 1850-1925* (N. Y., 1927); Nathan Fine, *Labor and Farmer Parties in the United States, 1828-1928* (N. Y., 1928); and Samuel Yellen, *American Labor Struggles* (N. Y., 1936).

Among the significant federal documents dealing with immigration and its effects upon labor conditions are a *Monograph on Immigration in the 19th Century* (*House Exec. Doc.*, 49 Cong., 2 sess., XXIV, no. 157); Commissioner-General of Immigration, *Report for the Year Ending June 30, 1907*, containing graphs showing immigration for eighty-eight years; and the (Dillingham) Immigration Commission, *Reports* (41 vols., Wash., 1911), which has much material on earlier conditions. The last is summarized by J. W. Jenks and W. J. Lauck, two members of the research staff of the commission, in *The Immigration Problem* (N. Y., 1911). Among other noteworthy general works on immigration, published during or shortly after the period, are Richmond Mayo-Smith, *Emigration and Immigration* (N. Y., 1890); P. F. Hall, *Immigration and Its Effects upon the United States* (R. C. Ringwalt, ed., *American Public Problems*; N. Y., 1906); and J. R. Commons, *Races and Immigrants in America* (N. Y., 1907).

There is an abundant literature on particular nationalities to which ready reference may be had in G. M. Stephenson, *A History of American Immigration* (Boston, 1926), 296-302. For the Chinese newcomers, who excited a public interest altogether disproportionate to their numbers, the student should consult R. E. Cowan and Boutwell Dunlap, comps., *Bibliography of the Chinese Question in the United States* (San Fran., 1909), which includes references to important official investigations by the state of California and by the government at Washington. Among general writings produced at the time, *Chinese Immigration in Its Social and Economical Aspects* (N. Y., 1881) by G. F. Seward is of special interest. The standard treatment is Mary R. Coolidge, *Chinese Immigration* (N. Y., 1909).

AGRICULTURE AND AGRARIANISM

A helpful guide to the extensive literature on farming and agrarian movements is E. E. Edwards, *A Bibliography of the History of Agriculture in the United States* (U. S. Dept. of Agr., *Miscel. Publ.*, no. 84, 1930). Of primary importance to an understanding of agricultural developments are two serial publications of the department of agriculture: the *Annual Reports* of the commissioner (1862-1889) and the secretary (from 1889); and the *Yearbook* (from 1894). Material on farming conditions fills two volumes (X-XI) of the United States Industrial Commission, *Report* (cited earlier).

Though this basic American industry still awaits a comprehensive history, certain aspects have received scholarly study. Among these special works are M. B. Hammond, *The Cotton Industry* (Am. Econ. Assoc., *Publs.*, I, 1897); E. E. Dale, *The Range Cattle Industry* (Norman, 1930); E. S. Osgood, *The Day of the Cattleman* (Minneapolis, 1929); B. H. Hibbard, *A History of Public Land Policies* (N. Y., 1924); F. H. Newell, *Irrigation in the United States* (rev. edn., N. Y., 1906); R. P. Teele, *Irrigation in the United States* (N. Y., 1915); and Loomis Havemeyer, ed., *The Conservation of Our Natural Resources* (N. Y., 1930). See also L. H. Bailey, ed., *Cyclopedia of American Agriculture* (4 vols., N. Y., 1907-1909), and anon., "Agricultural Progress of Fifty Years, 1850-1900," *U. S. Twelfth Census* (1900), V, xvi-xxxv.

The standard work on the farmers' political activities is J. D. Hicks, *The Populist Revolt* (Minneapolis, 1931), which contains an exhaustive bibliography, including a list of monographs dealing with the subject by states. Sidelights are thrown on the farmers' economic plight by W. C. Mitchell, *A History of the Greenbacks* (Univ. of Chicago, *Decennial Publs.*, ser. 2, IX, 1903); F. W. Taussig, *The Silver Situation in the United States* (*Questions of the Day*, no. 74; 2d edn., N. Y., 1893); and W. J. Lauck, *The Causes of the Panic of 1893* (Boston, 1907). For the social and psychological motivation of rural unrest, note the works listed in Schlesinger, *Rise of the City* (cited earlier), 446-448.

INDEX

ABBOTT, Lyman, and R. T. Ely, 125.

Adams Express Company, Carnegie invests in, 7.

Adding machine, invented, 270.

Addressograph, invented, 270.

Advertising, beginning of illuminated, 265.

Agrarianism. *See* Farmers, People's party.

Agricultural Wheel, organized, 135; merged with Farmers' Alliance, 135-136.

Agriculture, in "Hill country," 22-23; in Great West, 23-27; in Florida, 31-34; exports of, 94, 96; central position of, 127; as basis for extractive industries, 127-130; declines, 220, 227, 239-240; scientific methods of, 272; bibliography of, 292-293. *See also* Farmers, Land.

Airplane, model of, 279.

Alabama, mining in, 81.

Aldrich, N. W., and tariff, 194, 259.

Allegheny, Pa., lighting in, 58.

Allen, W. V., in Populist convention, 252-253.

Allison, W. B., and tariff, 194-195; and silver act, 244, 249.

Alternating current, developed, 56; opposition to, 56-57, 266; success of, 265-266.

Altgeld, J. P., pardons Fielden and Schwab, 165; and Pullman strike, 237; supports Bryan, 256.

Amalgamated Association of Iron, Steel and Tin Workers, opposes eight-hour day, 172; Frick and, 222, 223.

American Bell Telephone Company, Speaking Telephone Company fights, 43-44; buys Western Union telephone system, 44;

growth of, 44-45, 47; suits against, 45-47; improvements in, 47; merged with American Telephone and Telegraph Company, 48.

American Cottonseed Oil Company, formed, 89; and tariff, 194.

American Electric Company, organized, 52.

American Federation of Labor, demands regulation of telegraph, 38; contrasted with Knights of Labor, 155; objectives of, 157; agitates for shorter hours, 157-161; growth of, 166-167, 273-274; demands abolition of convict labor, 183; lauds militancy, 275-276.

American Iron and Steel Association, favors higher tariff, 188, 259.

American Pipe Manufacturing Company, and tariff, 194.

American Railway Union, organized, 233; and Pullman strike, 234, 235-236.

American Speaking Telephone Company, formed, 43; fights Bell Company, 43-44.

American Steel & Wire Company, organized, 211; museum of, 279.

American Sugar Refining Company, formed, 89; investigated, 201; incorporated, 206; controls sugar output, 206; purchases refineries, 217-218.

American Telegraph and Cable Company, Western Union leases cables from, 40.

American Telephone and Telegraph Company, organized, 47-48; takes over Bell Company, 48.

American Tin Plate Company, formed, 213.

American Union Telegraph Com-